A MIRROR TO NATURE

A MIRROR TO NATURE

TRANSFORMATIONS IN DRAMA AND AESTHETICS

1 6 6 0 – 1 7 3 2

ROSE A. ZIMBARDO

THE UNIVERSITY PRESS OF KENTUCKY

Editorial and Sales Offices: Lexington, Kentucky 40506-0024

Library of Congress Cataloging-in-Publication Data

Zimbardo, Rose A.
A mirror to nature.

Bibliography: p.
Includes index.
1. English drama—Restoration, 1660-1700—History
and criticism. 2. English drama—18th century—History
and criticism. 3. Aesthetics, Modern—17th century.
4. Aesthetics, Modern—18th century. I. Title.
PR691.Z55 1986   822'.4'09384   86-1336
ISBN 0-8131-1590-6

CONTENTS

Acknowledgments   vii

1. The Four Stages of Dramatic Imitation, 1660-1732   15

2. Imitation of Nature as Idea   36

3. Imitation of Nature as "The City Between"   76

4. The Varieties of Dramatic Satire in the 1670s   105

5. Nature as the Experiential Actual, 1680-1700   128

6. Imitation of the Inner Arena:
Sentimental, Pornographic, or Novelistic?   164

7. Emulation: The Early Eighteenth Century   204

Notes   226

Index   243

This book,
like all the works
of my hand and heart,
is for the better-than-ever
Great Zimbardos:
Adam A. Zimbardo and Paola Coda-Nunziante
and for Martin Stevens, my good old man.

ACKNOWLEDGMENTS

In 1957 Mr. Wimsatt assigned me a seminar paper on "imitation." That it has taken me almost thirty years to get the paper *right* will not surprise anybody who was a graduate student at Yale in the late 1950s. Therefore, I must first acknowledge the immense debt that I owe to the late William K. Wimsatt. I hope that he would have given my paper an Honors because I owe to that great critic and teacher almost any good thought of which I am capable.

In the intervening years I have learned so much from the work of other scholars—from my mentor, Eugene M. Waith and from Aubrey Williams, John Loftis, Earl Miner, Jean Hagstrum, Maximilliam E. Novak, Shirley Strum Kenney and Howard Weinbrot—to name just a few—that it would be impossible to acknowledge my full debt to all of them without making this section longer than the book. Nevertheless, I must make special mention of Aubrey Williams. I have learned from his scholarship, but I have also learned from his example. Mr. Williams's generosity of spirit and kindness gave me the courage to begin the project.

Among my colleagues at S.U.N.Y. Stony Brook, I am grateful to Richard Levin, Thomas Maresca, Joseph Pequigney, Homer Goldberg, and Thomas Kranidas. They keep me on my toes always, and I find that sixteen years of sparring with them has made me a reasonably good middleweight contender. Richard Levine, my former chairman and my friend, was mid-person in this delivery. I could never have written the book without his unfailing encouragement and support. I am also very grateful to the Federated Learning Communities Program at Stony Brook, to all my colleagues in FLC for allowing me to test my ideas in our special arena of discourse, and most especially to Patrick Hill, its former director, who, by Irish charm alone tricked me into the extra service that allowed me leave time enough to do the necessary scholarship for the book.

When I speculate, as we all do, on the probability of an after-life, I find that I should like to spend mine haunting the corridors of the William Andrews Clark Memorial Library. I thank the Clark Fellowship Committee for the senior research fellowship that enabled me to spend the winter quarter of 1983 in that particular paradise. Nowhere am I as warmly welcomed or as richly cosseted as at the Clark Library. I especially thank Thomas Wright, its librarian, for allowing me to return as often as I do. Everybody at the Clark, from Thomas Wright to Beverley Olney, his secretary, shares in this enterprise. They are my West Coast hearth-companions and with them I share "rings" of comitatus—and also of doughnuts.

My husband, Martin Stevens, the only living literary critic whom I happily acknowledge to be better than I am, has argued every theoretical assumption in this book with me, and "the muscular strength that it gives to [his] jaw will last [him] the rest of [his] life." But first, last and always I am grateful to my glorious son, Adam, and my beautiful daughter-to-be, Paola Coda-Nunziante. Their love, their wit, and even their teasing, sustains their Mama, and I especially thank them for the two years of relative tranquility that allowed me to think straight enough, long enough to write.

This book was begun in a time of pain and trial. For deliverance I give public thanks to God.

INTRODUCTION

It is important to realize that when it is said that the man of . . . earlier times confused the literal and symbolic approach, what is meant is that he confused, or rather combined, the two states of mind *which we today mean by those words*. Indeed the main difficulty that prevents us from breaking through the idols to the actuality of history, that is, the evolution of consciousness, lies in the fact that we go on using the same words without realizing how their meanings have shifted.

Owen Barfield, *Saving the Appearances*

We must be judged by *Nature*, say they; not at all considering that *Nature* is an equivocal Word, whose Sense is too various and extensive ever to be able to appeal to; since it leaves to the Fancy and Capacity of every one to decide what is according to *Nature* and what not.

Charles Gildon, "An Essay on the *Art, Rise, and Progress of the Stage*."

As Lovejoy showed us so long ago, "nature" is always a slippery aesthetic norm,[1] and nowhere is it more elusive than in the late seventeenth century, when our most fundamental conceptions of knowledge, reality, and epistemology were being radically transformed. The period from 1660 to 1732 in England marks a transition from the basically Medieval/Renaissance aesthetic, which understood poetry as the representation of an Ideal, or ideational, reality that is not available to ordinary perception, to the basically modern aesthetic, in which art is thought to mirror human experience—most particularly, *inner* psychological experience, the "interior space" that philosophers like Guillen and Rorty argue was *invented* in the seventeenth century.[2]

For the Middle Ages and the sixteenth century, the world was "a place of interconnected meanings, not objects."[3] Consequently, artistic representation stressed interconnectedness within a whole design, or "shape of reality,"[4] as well as continuity between the microcosm and the metaphysical harmony toward which it pointed or to which it aspired. However, as we know, in the course of the seventeenth century "phenomena lose their roles in a teleological scheme and are increasingly seen simply as phenomena. The new scientific interest in the world for itself and the stress on the doctrine of universal plenitude present a universe far more full of data, observed and inferred, than ever before. The old network of universal analogy, by which all things could figure one another . . . collapses."[5]

The seventeenth century first brought a sense of separation and locatedness in time and space to human perception and then brought the conception of an internal arena within the individual, the locus of his special "reality." Inside the human psyche we no longer find Hellmouth, as in the Middle Ages, or the "center of [a man's] sinful earth,"[6] as in the sixteenth century. Rather, we find a new frontier for exploration and, more significantly, for artistic imitation. As Montaigne, in many ways a herald of the new sensibility, said, "I turn my gaze inward, I fix it there and keep it busy . . . I look inside myself, I continually observe myself . . . I taste myself . . . I roll around in myself."[7]

For the sixteenth and early seventeenth centuries the poet, in imitation of his Maker, was a creator of worlds, a designer of that "other" Nature, the great cosmic *concordia* that lies beyond the boundaries of human sight: "But the poet makes another Nature . . . and finally in the same way makes himself another God, as it were. The other sciences are . . . users of what the Maker of them produced, but poetry, when it so splendidly gives the appearance of things that are and things that are not, seems not to narrate the events, as others, like the historians, do, but as a God to produce them."[8] At the beginning of the seventeenth century the object of poetic imitation was not the perceptible world of phenomena but the noumena, "the form toward which an object tends, the result which Nature strives to attain but never can attain."[9] But by the end of the century there were "new criteria of discovery and the types and limits of discourse which incorporate them." Poets as well as philosophers sought for ways "to reground knowledge and language in particulars gained from experience."[10] As the century drew to a close there appeared a new appreciation of fact, a new awareness of phenomena, a new valuation of experience. The artist's purpose was no longer to escape the fetters of history and experience; rather, they had become the primary objects of his attention:

History (which by expounding actions past teacheth us to regulate the future, and furnisheth us with wisdom at the cost of other Mens experience) is not unlike Painting, their scope is the same; and as in the latter it argues want of skill to look upon the whole Draught with an indifferent eye, but to select and insist upon some chief particular is proper to an Artist; so he who rests satisfied with the general relation of affairs (not fixing upon some Actor in that story) loseth his greatest benefit; since what is most particular, by its nearer affinity with us hath greatest influence upon us.[11]

In any age the drama and commentary upon it are particularly sensitive indexes of how the "nature," or reality, that art is thought to imitate is conceived, because drama, by its very nature, hovers between the realm of ideation and the realm of experience. Because the drama must always to some degree be a semblance of action and because the materials with which it renders its illusion are living human beings, it can never be entirely allegorical. A particular figure can represent "World" or "Perseverance" (or, more to the point for our discussion, "Valor" or "Heroic Greatness"), but because that figure is impersonated in a human being, we the audience are to some degree tied by it to the level of experiential perception. The very influential Abbé d'Aubignac considers the problem in terms that almost suggest actuality to be a bulky, if necessary, intrusion upon a dramatic scene: "Though this sort of Poem [drama] is but an Image, and so ought to be considered as having a representational Being; nevertheless one ought to consider that there is a reality in the very Representation, for really the Actors are seen and heard, the Verses are really pronounc'd, and one suffers really either pleasure or pain in assisting at these Representations."[12]

However, if drama cannot altogether soar into the realm of abstract Idea, neither can it, as the novel does, enable us completely to inhabit a fictional experience—in drama a character is what he does. What he "thinks" or "feels" can only be inferred from the design of his actions and the words he speaks. As concerned as he is with the "real," d'Aubignac also gives us valuable evidence of how far drama was still believed to be from imitating the actual in the 1670s. A play, says d'Aubignac, does not imitate what *is*; rather, it *pictures* an Idea. He advises the poet to think of his play as a spectacle presented to the eye of the beholder "as a Picture; that is the work of the Artist; where there are Colours, and not real things; shadows and not substances . . . in a word, appearances of things that are not really in the Picture."[13] The object of dramatic imitation, he believes, are the passions freed from experience, and the drama is the best vehicle for rendering the passions so detached, for if we "meet with them in Story, they will still be clogg'd with Circumstances [that is, experience] which will constrain the whole Design."[14]

My contention is that between 1660 and 1732 in England the conception "imitation of nature" undergoes rapid and radical change in conformity with the epistemological and aesthetic revolution of the seventeenth century. This conceptual change affects all genres of literature; indeed, it affects the very idea of literature itself, which the new way of thinking envisions to be closest among the arts to painting, rather than, as was the case earlier, to music. However, the subtle gradations of the change are most readily observable, I think, in the drama and in speculation about the drama. Finally, I believe that one major consquence of the change is that the novel replaces the drama as the primary popular mode.[15]

At the beginning of the period we shall be considering, the unquestioned aesthetic assumption is that drama imitates Idea, a *shape* of reality, an assumption that derives ultimately from the medieval understanding of Plato's *Timaeus*. This Medieval/Renaissance conception of the drama as imaging Microcosmos, or the theater of the world, persisted well into the seventeenth century and constituted the Restoration's inheritance from the "Giants before the Flood."[16] The aesthetic, in capsule, holds that "the universe . . . is a structure of relations, created by God and perceivable by man in his mind's eye. It is non-organic, quantitative, something that is made by an artificer rather than planted by a gardener. But if this is so then it is possible for the artifacts of man to be made according to the same principles, thus providing not a fragment of the visible universe, but a model or analogue of the universe itself. Because the universe is seen in terms of structures it is possible for the human craftsman to imitate the shape of reality itself."[17]

This way of conceiving of reality and artistic imitation of it determines dramatic form in the 1660s and early 1670s. Dramatic imitation can be the dialectical progression, or refinement, of Idea, which we find in its most pronounced form in the heroic drama but also find in tragedy and tragicomedy. (As we shall see in the next chapter, discrimination among the "serious" dramatic genres is not just impossible but irrelevant in the first decade of our period. The meaning of Howard's *The Vestal Virgin* [1665] is not altered a jot whether the "tragical" or "comical" ending is used.) The shape of reality can also be rendered in the parallel interplay of three structural tiers—high heroic, middle realistic, and low burlesque—that we find in comedies like Etherege's *Comicall Revenge* (1664) or Rhodes's *Flora's Vagaries* (1670) but that is also the scaffolding in tragicomedies like Behn's *The Amorous Prince* (1671) and Shadwell's *The Royal Shepherdess* (1669). Very often the two designs are used in combination, the mounting refinement of idea dominating the high plane of a three-tiered structure, as in Etherege's *Comicall Revenge*. The Dryden-Davenant adaptations of Shakespeare are evidence that playwrights not only structured the shape of reality in this way in their own plays but read "in" the structure when they "new-modelled" plays of the earlier period. The Dryden-Davenant *Macbeth* (1664) is a mounting, progressive definition of Ideas of heroic ambition and heroic love. *The Enchanted Island* (1667) multiplies figures on both the high plane and the low to strengthen and improve what the adapters read as a three-tiered microcosmic design in Shakespeare. In 1668 the effects upon an audience of these modes (the "essence" of them) is respectively: for the heroic mode (whether happy or unhappy in outcome) "admiration"; for the comic mode, "satire."[18]

It is important to realize that at the beginning of the period of transition a dramatic action clearly is *not* what happens to particular persons and how they feel about it. As Shadwell says, "I challenge the most violent and clamorous of my Enemies . . . to accuse me with truth, of representing . . . real actions. . . . if a Man should bring such a humour upon the Stage . . . as only belongs to one or two persons, it would not be understood by the Audience, but would be thought (for the singularity of it) wholly *unnatural*" (italics mine).[19] Rather, in the first decade characterization is not the portrayal of persons but the delineation of "Images of Virtue," "Shapes of Valour," "Ideas of Greatness," or "Figures of Vice and Folly."[20] Characters are "Figures of things rare . . . Well designed!"[21] Dramatic action is the juxtaposition of these figures within a moving design. Dryden says, "Every alteration or crossing of a design, every new sprung passion or turn of it, is a part of the action, and much the noblest."[22] "Of Dramatic Poesy" everywhere provides evidence that in the first decade of the Restoration period the prevalent conception of dramatic imitation is the Renaissance conception almost unaltered. For example, Lisideus's objection to the historical plays of Shakespeare makes the same conceptual point that is made in the medieval asethetic quoted above,[23] namely, that they imitate "fragments of the visible universe" rather than "the shape of reality itself":

If you consider the historical plays of Shakespeare, they are rather so many chronicles of kings, or the business many times of thirty or forty years, cramped into a representation of two hours and a half, which is not to imitate or paint nature, but to draw her in miniature, to take her in little; to look upon her through the wrong end of a perspective, and receive her images not only much less, but infinitely more imperfect than the life: this, instead of making a play delightful, renders it ridiculous. . . . For the Spirit of Man cannot be satisfied but with truth, or at least verisimility; and a poem is to contain if not ['truth'], yet ['the likeness of truth'] (Hesiod, *Theogony*).[24]

Verisimilitude here is likeness to a shape of reality, an Idea of nature as cosmic design; it is not the simulation of experience, actuality, or probability.

At the other end of our spectrum, in the 1690s and early 1700s, as John Loftis has said, plays have "a quality that may, perhaps anachronistically, be described as 'novelistic.'"[25] Just as European culture became "interiorized" during the course of the seventeenth century,[26] so too did nature or "reality" shift its locus to the inner human arena. Tracing the development from "fabulist" to "affective" drama in his pioneer study *Restoration Tragedy*, Eric Rothstein notes that a key difference between the "pathetic" play of the 1690s and the heroic play of the 1660s is that "it treats love and honor as traits of the characters, to be attained in many possible ways, while the heroic play treats characters against a fixed grid of love and honor."[27] Rothstein quotes Laura in Mrs. Trotter's *Fatal Friendship* (1698), who speaks of love and honor as "the nicest, dearest parts of me." The primacy of drama as a serious mode failed at the end of the seventeenth century, not because the audience suddenly became men and women of "feeling" and demanded a more "affective" drama, nor yet because they became more bourgeois and consequently simpleminded,[28] but because a new idiom of representation was required to express a new conception of nature—interior human nature as opposed to schematic cosmic Nature—because, in short, a new epistemology had created a new way of conceiving reality.

When we examine plays of the 1690s, such as Southerne's *The Wives Excuse* (1692) and *The Fatal Marriage* (1694) or Vanbrugh's *The Provok'd Wife* (1694), we discover how wide the shift toward imitation of experience has been. *The Provok'd Wife* is particularly interesting because on the surface it is a fairly close rendering of Etherege's *She Wou'd If She Cou'd* (1667)—Sir John Brute is Sir Oliver Cockwood; Constant and Heartfree are Courtall and Freeman; Sir John with Lord Rake is Sir Oliver with Sir Joslin Jolly; even incidents like the wife's arrival at her husband's tavern party and his mistaking her for a whore are repeated—but Vanbrugh's play penetrates the stock comic surface and makes us judge circumstances and events from the inside. The vantage reveals that the libertine is a "Brute," the Rake an antiquated grotesque, and the wronged, sexually deprived wife a sympathetic figure. Honor and virtue are neither hypocritical masks nor heroic Ideas but understandable human attributes. We are shocked by Sir John's attempt to rape his wife—as we would never have been by Sir Oliver's—because we see the incident not as surface situational confusion but as an imitation of actual experience that has an impact upon the emotional "inner" life of the characters, whom we understand as people like ourselves. Vanbrugh in 1694 revaluates conceptions of 1667 and brings a new perspective to them.

Critics have said that Southerne's plays are "psychological."[29] But Southerne is not at all unusual among playwrights of the nineties in his desire to disclose the "minds" of his characters, as widespread use of a new kind of soliloquy in this decade attests. Southerne's interest in the novel is most interesting, I think, as is his debt, never fully acknowledged, to Aphra Behn. He says he drew a "hint" for *The*

Fatal Marriage from Behn's novel *The Fair Jilt*; in fact, his entire
action is taken from it, and his play *Oroonoko* is simply a stage
adaptation of Behn's best novel. Southerne's interest in the novel is
directly related to his "psychological" exploration; it is also related to
the new ways he and his contemporaries use soliloquy. In the nineties, soliloquies are not used as they are in Tudor and Jacobean
drama, as set rhetorical pieces that exist apart from the action to
express directly to the audience a state or condition of being.[30]
Rather, soliloquy creates the illusion that naturalistically conceived
characters are thinking aloud and, often, by brokenness of expression, the style of a soliloquy suggests an inner state of feeling too
deep for words. Congreve's dedication to *The Double Dealer* (1694)
shows how uncomfortable playwrights are with soliloquy by the
nineties and how far the limits of dramatic imitation were being
strained by a new epistemological consciousness: "I grant that for a
man to talk to himself appears absurd and unnatural . . . But . . . the
poet finds it necessary to let us know the mystery of his contrivance
. . . and to that end is forced to make use of the expedience of speech,
no other better way being yet invented for the communication of
thought."[31] Words are no longer "pictures, shadows, or resemblances" of ideas, as they were thought to be in the 1660s. Language
no longer, as in Gale, shapes "a Character or Idea of the Mind."[32]
Rather, words are crude instruments, and speech a mere "expedient,"
which the poet is "forced" to employ in his attempt to plumb an
inner, psychological realm that lies beyond the reach of rhetoric:
"Soliloquies had need be few / Extremely short, and spoke in Passion
too / . . . for [Poets] must look within to find / These secret Turns of
Nature in the Mind."[33]

When we consider the plays of the last decade of the century in the
context of novels contemporaneous with them, we find an older
poetic form, the drama, straining the limits of its capacity to imitate
a conception of nature or reality inappropriate to its idiom, and a
newer poetic form, the novel, being invented to accommodate a new
understanding of nature. As its name ("what's new") implies, the
novel of the 1690s purports to imitate the actual, to be an accurate
account of real events and people.[34] Peter Motteux, editor of the
Gentleman's Journal and probable author of most of the novels that
appeared in it monthly, clearly differentiates novels from fables or

romances on the basis of their being accounts of actual events: "Now, for a Novel. I am sometimes much put to it, to discover Adventures worth relating: Take what follows for a Fable if you please; however, I am clearly informed that the Particulars are true."[35] He repeatedly asserts that the novels are accounts of recent happenings "I have here an account of a very true Adventure, happen'd, as you will see on the King's Birth-day".[36] A novel that attempts to transcend the actual or to heighten the stature of its characters is a bad novel, a "romance" (the term is pejorative): "Our Knight [a character given to lying] being Master of his own Romance, as some Writers of Novels do, with small cost could make his Hero what he pleas'd, and accordingly did not fail to give him . . . many good qualifications."[37]

Aphra Behn, in *Oroonoko*, one of the most popular novels of the time, is more vehement in protesting that her account is the actual truth—despite the fact that at one point in her narrative her hero survives being disemboweled: "I do not pretend in giving you the history of this ROYAL SLAVE, to entertain my reader with the Adventures of a feign'd Hero, whose Life and Fortunes Fancy may manage at the Poet's Pleasure; nor in relating the Truth, design to adorn it with any Accidents but such as arrived in earnest to him; And it shall come simply into the World, recommended by its own proper Merits and natural Intrigues; there being enough Reality to support it . . . without I mention I was myself an Eyewitness to a great Part of what you will find here set down."[38] We might compare this new conception of the value of the actual and particular with Lisideus's valuation of Shakespeare's history plays quoted above.

More significant, however, than the novel's ability to imitate the particularity and random movement of experience—which, after all, critics and playwrights in this decade argue that the comic drama does[39]—is its ability to imitate inner psychological experience, the new frontier in nature. The immense popularity of the novels in the *Gentleman's Journal* strongly suggests that it is not "affect" or sentimentalism for which the drama of the nineties is striving with its emotional outpourings and pensive reflections but a "way" to the inner arena, the new reality—the kind of path that the novel was opening. There is nothing "affective" or sentimental about the novels in the *Gentleman's Journal* (1691-93). Quite the contrary, the narrator almost always assumes a slightly mocking, ironic tone—

and always does so when he is fearful of being thought "romantic." For example, "At six they parted, She with a most pernicious passion for his Person and seeming piety, and he with a most unspeakable Veneration for her money."[40] In these novels we find the stock types and situations of comedy *psychologically* treated. For example, in "The Picture; or, Jealousy without a Cause" (December 1692) there is a stock jealous husband, but he is not ridiculed. Rather, the novel investigates the inner workings of jealousy, "a *Selfish Principle*, if we may call a Passion Selfish, that makes a man study how to perplex himself." Moreover, the effects of groundless jealousy upon perception and upon the reliability of the senses are explored. The jealous husband "sees" his wife in a picture, although it is apparent to everybody else that it is *not* his wife's picture. "The Witchcraft of Gaming" (May 1692) is a completely modern, unsentimental investigation of the psychology of a compulsive gambler, as sophisticated as a twentieth-century case study in its account of addictive behavior, including the addict's guilt, despair, resolutions to reform, and repeated submission to the overwhelming power of her addiction. The novels in the *Gentleman's Journal* penetrate the interior life of their characters. They investigate jealousy, gambling, romantic infatuation, "the crying modern sin of Roving"—all the stock "humours" of traditional comedy, but they differ from comedy in the depth to which they reach and, consequently, in the reality that they aim to imitate.[41]

Finally, the novel can plumb a reach of inner reality to which the drama can never go; it can imitate not just what happened but also what did *not* happen except in the fantasy daydreams of one of its characters. For instance, Mrs. Behn's Miranda, in love with a Friar who is absolutely faithful to his vows, mentally undresses him and makes him her lover in her imaginings:

She imagined, if he could inspire Love in a coarse, grey, ill-made Habit, a shorn Crown, a Hair-cord about his Waist, bare-legg'd in Sandals instead of Shoes; what must he do . . . with all that Youth and Illustrious Beauty, set off by the Advantage of Dress and Equipage? She frames an idea of him all gay and splendid, and looks on his present Habit as some Disguise proper for the Stealths of Love; some feigned put-on-Shape, with more Security to approach a Mistress and make himself happy; and that the Robe laid by, she has the Lover in his proper Beauty, the same as he would have been, if any other Habit . . . were put off: In the Bed, in the silent gloomy Night, and the soft Embraces of her Arms, he loses all the Friar, and assumes all the Prince; and that awfull Reverence due alone to his Holy Habit, he exchanges for a thousand Dalliances. . . . These, and a thousand others Self-flatteries, all vain and indiscreet, took up her waking Nights and now more retired days.[42]

We have not, I think, been sufficiently subtle and complex in thinking about the movement from "fabulist" to "affective," to "sentimental" drama. The affective drama of the 1690s is better understood when we consider what it is attempting to *imitate* (what idea of nature or reality it strives to represent) than what emotions it was designed to produce in an audience. And "sentimental" drama is best understood as a drama that draws its audience to *emulation*, which is a logically necessary next step from a drama that imitates internal, subrational human feeling. The drama of the 1690s and early 1700s attempts what the novel of the 1690s does, namely, to open a door into psychological reality. Once we enter into the "minds" of characters, who are conceived not as *figures of Ideas* but as *people like ourselves*, we are drawn to experience their experience, to share their thoughts and feelings, and, as a next step, to emulate them. It is quite logically consistent that "sentimental" drama and pornography are born at the same time, for both depend upon psychological identification. The comedies of the 1670s, which were for so many centuries thought to be immoral, are not pornographic. They cannot function as pornography does, because they *demonstrate to understanding*. But as the passage from *The Fair Jilt* above indicates, we are sailing quite close to pornography once a representational mode *invites us into* the experience of erotic imagining.

Interestingly enough, as the novel was beginning to answer the demand for artistic imitation of an internal reality, the drama and painting began to be understood as imitations of the inner arena. For example, Tate writes of Kneller's portraits of William and Mary:

> Thou, thou alone, the mystic art could find
> To paint the Monarch's Person and his Mind.
> The grosser Features common hands may strike
> A cold resemblance hit, and coursly like
> But with the Likeness, Warmth and Grace to give,

> And make the Picture seem to *think* and live,
> Are Heights reserved . . .
> For Kneller, the Apelles of our time . . .
> Behold His Royal Piece divinely wrought
> And in the Monarch's Aspect read his *Thought*.[43]
>
> [Italics mine]

If painting and drama can represent interior reality and if, by observing such a representation, the spectator can be drawn into it and made to *experience* this imitation of experience, then he must also be drawn to recreate that experience within himself, to emulate what he sees. By 1709 Addison would argue that the moral "Amendment" of an audience was "only to be made . . . by encouraging the representation of the noble characters drawn by Shakespeare and others from whence it is impossible to return without strong *impressions* of honor and humanity. . . . How forcible an effect this would have upon our minds, one needs no more than to observe how strongly we are touched by mere pictures; who can see LeBrun's Picture of The Battle of Porus, without *entering into the Character* of that fierce, gallant man, and being accordingly spurred to an *emulation* of his constancy and courage," (italics mine).[44] The theory of emulation, which was the breeding ground of the morality issue that plagued the drama of Wycherley, Etherege, and Congreve for three hundred years,[45] is directly consequent upon a changed conception of artistic imitation. When the object of imitation is no longer thought to be *Ideas* of nature but actual, phenomenal nature, then characters cease to be *figures* of Ideas or of "the Chief Complexions of our Minds"[46] and instead become likenesses of people as we observe them in life. Furthermore, when the locus of reality is the human psyche and the pleasure we derive from art is the experience of entering that inner space, then identification between our feelings and the "feelings" of characters is inevitable. The notion that we share the emotions of the characters we perceive is a penultimate step in the logical progression toward emulation; it precedes the "sentimental drama" by at least twenty years: " 'Tis the Property of Tragedy and Comedy to instruct. The characters are to be Naturall; and the Persons concerned in the Whole Action are to be such whose Vertues ought to provoke us to an Emulation, and whose Vices ought to deter us from imitating their example. The disposition of the Play is to be such that all the Characters have a proper Effect with us. Our Fear, Love and Anger are to be exerted with Justice; and we are to learn from a just Fable how to behave ourselves in earnest."[47]

Several forces converge to effect the change in artistic imitation that we have been considering. Primary, of course, is the century-long process of secularization and interiorization with which we began this discussion. Next, a new feeling about feeling arises in the latter part of the seventeenth century. Donald Greene's refutation of R. S. Crane's 1934 essay "Suggestions toward a Genealogy of 'The Man of Feeling,' "[48] while it calls Crane's conception of latitudinarianism into doubt and questions his dating for the abandonment of Augustinianism, does not, in my judgment, disprove the validity of Crane's basic assertion that, in the last two decades of the seventeenth century, there arose among Anglican divines, those most widely influential molders of opinion, a new feeling about feeling. I shall borrow just two of Crane's examples. In 1681, well within the limits of the "Restoration," or Carolean period, Samuel Parker wrote, "All men feel a natural Deliciousness consequent upon every exercise of their good-natur'd Passions; and nothing affects the mind with greater Complacency than to reflect upon its own inward Joy and Contentment."[49] This observation is significant not only in the respect that Crane finds it so—that is, as early evidence of benevolism—but also because it indicates that as early as 1681 the very process of contemplating our innermost feelings is considered to be pleasurable. In 1700 Isham calls our inclination to good-natured feeling a "Law of Nature." Indeed, he thinks that "goodness" constitutes what modern psychology would call our "hard-wiring": the "natural Motions wrought within us and moulded into our very Frame."[50]

Finally, and deeply significant, is the impact of Lockean psychology and epistemology: "[Locke's] analysis suggested that explanation and control of human behavior might be achieved by an approach that focussed attention upon directly observable stimuli and responses and that ignored the complex mental operations in which Locke himself showed continuing interest."[51] A Lockean conception of human understanding underlies Addison's "moral amendment" proposal: "If a thing painted or related can irresistibly enter our hearts, what might not be brought to pass by seeing generous things performed before our eyes."[52] The drama of the 1660s and 1670s holds designs of ideas up to intellectual understanding; it is understood to have the effect of a mind (the spectator's) contemplating the contours, or "Characters," of Mind itself. On the other hand, drama at the end of the century imitates extremes of feeling; it is understood to have the effect of drawing the spectator into the play and, by making him share the feelings of the characters he sees, to excite him to emulate their conduct. By recreating their feelings as his own he will have not only the delicious pleasure of inward good-natured passion but the additional pleasure of comparing his most interior state with the "law of nature" that a work of art demonstrates. Aesthetic pleasure, then, becomes the twofold pleasure of experiencing good-natured passions and, by the process of combining the "sensations" so experienced and "reflecting" upon them, coming to an understanding of the "law" of our nature. By operation of "association" we are then tempered to the natural goodness embodied in that law.[53]

ONE

The Four Stages
of Dramatic Imitation
1660-1732

The transition in dramatic imitation of nature from the imitation of Ideas to the imitation of interior human nature and the emulation theory consequent upon it occurs in four stages. These stages are only roughly datable, since the progression is, of course, a continuum.

Stage 1

In Stage 1 (circa 1660-70), as a derivation from earlier seventeenth-century thinking, drama imitates nature as the Ideal. It is a shape of reality seen whole, the design of a microcosmic order that may be envisioned either as the Neoplatonic scale of Caroline drama set in motion or as the old three-tiered medieval universe secularized and modified by Hobbesian thought.[1] The design may be a mounting progression toward transcendent truth that is effected by dialectical juxtaposition and refinement. These images of reality were the Restoration's inheritance from its Caroline predecessors, transmitted in large measure by Davenant, whose influence on the restored theater was profound.[2] Davenant had preserved the old conception of imitation almost intact during the Interregnum. His postscript to the 1673 edition of *Gondibert* expresses his conception of the process by which an artist imitates "reality." "I intended in this poem," he says, "to strip Nature naked and clothe her again in the Perfect Shape of Virtue."[3] In "The First Day's Entertainment at Rutland House" (1656), he applies the conception to a dramatic piece. The function of his "opera," he says, is "to advance the Characters of Virtue in the shapes of Valour and Conjugal Love."[4] The key words in this sentence are "character" and "shape." Until about 1680, "character" did not mean personage in a fiction. The word meant, as it had originally, the delineation of an Idea, or essential form. In the 1660s it was still very closely associated with the "shape of reality" that Renaissance thinkers believed to be the proper object of artistic imitation. For example, Theophilus Gale writes in 1669:

> If with attentive eye we look
>   Upon the six days of volume of the Book
>   Where *God* and mighty *Nature* doth appear,
> Writ in an *Universal Character;*
>   We still shall find in ev'ry part
>   Space and dominion left for *Art.*
> Or rather, all our *Arts* are but to know,
> How and from whence was made so great a Show.[5]

Even when the shape of reality came to be embedded in phenomenal nature as the design of Providence, the word "character" continued to denote the delineation of an idea. The Theophrastan Character itself was conceived to be the shape of an abstract essence. Characters "differ from Portracts," Flecknoe tells us, "in that they are onely Pictures of the Mind, abstracting from the Body."[6]

In his 1663 quarto dedication of *The Siege of Rhodes,* Davenant declares that his subject is "Ideas of Greatness and Vertue." He praises Corneille and says that his object, like Corneille's, is "heightening the Characters of Valour, Temperance, [and] Natural Justice."[7] The conception of imitation is Caroline English, though the method of "heightening" by dialectical juxtaposition owes a debt to French formalism and particularly to Corneille.

This foundation is the inheritance of the Restoration playwright; and it is this conception that he fosters and improves upon during the 1660s and early 1670s. "A Play," Dryden writes, "to be like Nature, is to be set above it, as Statues which are placed on high are made greater than the life, that they may descend to the sight of their just proportion." The playwright quite consciously tries to avoid portrayal of actual speech and behavior, for, as Dryden goes on to say, "If nothing were rais'd above that level, the foundation of Poetry would be destroy'd. . . . thoughts [must] be exalted and Images and Actions. . . . rais'd above the Life."[8]

We have no difficulty in accepting the validity of such a conception of dramatic imitation when it is applied to strictly defined "heroic drama," but when it comes to other dramatic genres, "we expect drama to approximate life. . . . We pronounce characters true to life, or false: hail them as interestingly independent agents or dismiss them as authorial puppets. We want drama to have ideas but we want the characters to experience those ideas, not merely to enunciate them."[9] Because he stands on this side of the great seventeenth-century divide, the twentieth-century critic cannot envision a drama that does *not* imitate experience, that purposefully does *not* attempt to approximate "real life" in its characterization. In the 1660s *all* drama—comedy as well as tragedy—imitates abstract, ideal reality. Writing of *Bartholomew Fair* in the "Defence of the Essay," Dryden says, "The Author does so raise his matter . . . as to render it delightful, which he never could have performed had he only said or done those things that are daily done or practiced in the fair. . . . the copy is of price, though the original be vile."[10] In this decade tragedy and comedy may be said to train attention upon different aspects of ideal reality, but comedy is not more "realistic" or more closely approximate to life than tragedy. The difference between the two genres, as Edward Howard argues in his preface to *The Women's Conquest*, is not in their level of abstraction but rather in the *kinds* of ideas they imitate: "whereas the business of Tragedy is in the highest nature to *dispose* and *elevate* the intrigues of passions and affections; I mean such as depend on Ambition, Revenge, Love, Honour and the like and so detect their vices accordingly, as it is the duty of Comedy to do the same in those that come nearest our Moralities."[11] (It is important to note that "intrigue" here is the movement not of persons but of "passions," a turn of idea.) Sir Samuel Tuke, whose *Adventures of Five Hours* (1663) was the longest-running comedy of the decade, says in his preface to the 1671 edition that all plays are "Moral pictures" whose "Chiefest Perfections consist in the Force and Congruity of Passions and Humours, which are the Features and Complexions of our Minds."[12] In the 1660s and early 1670s the dominant aesthetic assumption is that a play of whatever genre is "nearest nature when in certain respects it is farthest from it."[13]

Stage 2

Given the highly abstract representation that governs the designs of drama in Stage 1, Stage 2 (circa 1670-80) in the evolving conception of dramatic imitation is inevitable. In Stage 2 the drama imitates *interplay* between the ideal and the actual. The most felicitous expression of such interplay is in dramatic satire, wherein "nature" lies somewhere between the ideal vision that romantic imagination affords and the tawdry actual world that obscures and distorts it. Jean Hagstrum has said: "Caricature, both in its Italian origins and in its later English literary manifestations, was a countertendency to the dominant idealism. High culture was capable of turning itself upside down. . . . The art of distortion is to the art of idealization what bathos is to hypsos: an exact inversion, to which the same techniques apply though the direction is down and not up. The art of distortion reality is the precise reversal of *la belle nature*. It is nature consummately wrought to a lower pitch."[14] From his earliest to his latest criticism Dryden was concerned with the inextricable connection between the heroic and the burlesque, which he took to be the essence of satire. As early as the preface to *Annus Mirabilis* (1666), he locates nature between "images" of "heroic poesy," which "beget admiration," and "images of the burlesque, which . . . contrary to this, by the same reason beget laughter: for the one shows nature beautified, as in the picture of a fair woman, which we all admire; the other shows her deformed, as in that of a lazar, or of a fool with distorted face and antic gestures, at which we cannot forbear to laugh because it is a deviation from nature."[15] And late in his career, in "A Discourse concerning the Original and Progress of Satire" (1695), he declares that in "the most Noble kind of Satire . . . the Majesty of the Heroique [is] finely mix'd with the Venom of the other" and insists that "satire is undoubtedly a *species* [of] heroic poetry."[16]

The sensibility of the seventies brought the upward and downward exaggerations that Hagstrum describes into conjunction. For instance, 1675 brought to the stage at the same time the extravagances of the operatic *Tempest* and the grotesque caricature, Duffet's *Mock Tempest*. The contrasting perspectives were also brought into disjunctive unity within single satiric works, some of which are comic, like *The Country Wife* (1675); some mock-heroic, like *The*

Man of Mode (1676); and others darkly ironic, like *The Plain Dealer* (1676), *The Libertine* (1675), or *Friendship in Fashion* (1678).[17] The structure of dramatic satire derives from the high-plane heroic and low-plane mock-heroic lines of the earlier three-tiered comic model. In a satire these converge into a single line of subtle interplay. Sometimes the heroic is obviously played against, as in the broad mockery of "love and honor," "generosity," and men and ladies "of honor" in a play like *The Country Wife*. Sometimes it enters by way of quite subtle allusion, as it does in Limberham's "Tricksy hath murder'd sleep" (V, 323), or in Dorimant's recitation of lines from Waller (especially interesting, since Waller's "Instructions to a Painter" [1666] had become a persistent and well-known heroic "antithesis" in verse satires of the period).[18] However, the heroic antithesis in satire often stands as an unspoken "understood" that the playwright expects the audience to recognize—as it does in outright parodies like Duffet's *The Empress of Morocco* (1674) or *The Mock Tempest* (1675), or in forms of verse satire like the Imitation.[19] Both the formulation of the three-tiered structure itself and its relation to dramatic satire has its source in Hobbes. In his "Answer" to Davenant's "Preface to *Gondibert*" (1650), Hobbes says that philosophers divide the "Universe" into three, "Regions: *Celestiall, Aeriall,* and *Terrestrial*" and that poets, in imitating this three-planed universal design, "have lodg'd themselves in the three Regions of mankinde, *Court, City,* and *Country,* correspondent in some proportion to the three Regions of the World." Medieval heaven, hell, and middle earth have been secularized. This three-level shape of reality gives rise to the poetic genres, which Hobbes always assumes can be rendered with equal facility in narrative or dramatic modes: "From hence [the three planes of the World] have proceeded three sorts of Poesy, *Heroique, Scommatique* and *Pastorall.* Every one of these is distinguished again in the manner of Representation, which sometimes is *Narrative.* . . . *and sometimes Dramatique.* . . . the Heroique Poem narrative. . . . is called an *Epique* Poem. The Heroique Poem Dramatique is *Tragedy.* The Scommatique Narrative—*Satyre,* Dramatique is Comedy. The Pastorall narrative is called simply Pastorall . . . . the same dramatique, Pastorall Comedy."[20]

But it was Dryden who made the clearest connection between English comic structure and satire. The best satire, he says, must

have a double design: "As in a play of the *English* fashion . . . . there is
to be but one main Design: and tho' there be an Under-plot, or
Second Walk of Comical Characters and Adventures, yet they are subser-
vient to the chief Fable, carry'd along under it and helping to it. . . .
Mascardi in his Discourse of the *Doppia favola*, or Double-tale in
Plays, gives an Instance of it, in the famous Pastoral of Guarini, call'd
Il Pastor Fido; where Corisca and the *Satyre* are the under-parts."[21]
Plays like Aphra Behn's *The Amorous Prince* (1671) or Rhodes's *Flora's
Vagaries* (1670) clearly anticipate the two-faced satiric design of the
mid-seventies.

Plays like *The Virtuoso, The Country Wife,* and *The Feign'd
Courtezans* are decidedly not the "sex farces" that Hume calls them;
quite the contrary, as Earl Miner has so often and so well demonstrated, "Critics and poets during the Restoration held to a concept
of literature that was dignified, grand, and perhaps even exorbitant
in its claims for . . . satire."[22] We must remember that even *The Kind
Keeper* was recognized as satire in 1678. The charges leveled against it
were that it was too topical and that in it Dryden, like Juvenal, gave
too close attention to the vice he purports to attack, but nobody
thought it was a sex farce or any other kind of farce.

Although imitation of the dynamic interplay between the ideal
and the actual finds its best and clearest expression in dramatic satire
(which we will explore at length in chapters 3 and 4), it is also the
foundation in other dramatic forms of the mid-seventies and early
eighties. For example, we find in *Aureng-Zebe* traces of the "ladder of
love" that informs the mounting progression structure of the sixties.
Aureng-Zebe figures transcendent, prophetic passion; Arimant, heroic passion; the Emperor, passion in the world. Finally, Nourmahal
is Hobbesian passion, or power conflict. The ladder, however, is not
used as a structuring device, as it would have been in the previous
decade. The play is structured in a single linear pattern that, like a
double-backed mirror, reflects upward (the dream of heroic greatness) and downward (limiting, confining actuality) simultaneously.
Bruce King has said: "The main theme of *Aureng-Zebe* is the dis-
quieting effects of imagination. The characters are driven by their
restless minds to extremes of hope, passion and fear. The force that
drives them is the desire to fulfill impossible dreams."[23]

"Nature" in *Aureng-Zebe* is the continuous interplay between
transcendent idea and material limit. The conceptual change from a

play like *The Conquest of Granada* rests on a recognition that human mind and will are vehicles too frail for transcendence. The division between ideal and actual has become a divorce: the ideal is unreachable by spirit, however refined, and the actual is more obdurate and restrictive. In his prologue to the play, Dryden is ostensibly chafing at the restrictions imposed on him by rhyme, but I think that his lines suggest a more profound conceptual dilemma "Passion's too fierce to be in fetters bound / And Nature flies him like Enchanted Ground." Transcendent reality is no longer conceived, as in *The Indian Queen* or *Tyrannick Love*, as attainable. Nature can no longer be captured by concept; therefore, dramatic imitation requires visualization of the *lusus* between the imagined ideal and the real.

The problem set in *Aureng-Zebe* is solved in *All for Love*. As Laura Brown puts it: "*All for Love* includes a residual heroic dimension, superimposed upon a 'real' pathetic definition of the protagonists; character and plight."[24] In *All for Love* "nature" lies between a heroic understood plane that we do not see but of which we are always aware and a plane of actuality that we do see. Hovering behind the protagonists are the Antony and Cleopatra of Plutarch, Shakespeare, and Sedley. We see Dryden's figures in sharp contrast to the auras that surround them. Dryden plays upon the contrast between the heroic images the audience brings with them to the play and the figures they see on stage; indeed, that contrast constitutes the play's meaning. As he clearly indicates in the prologue, Dryden is well aware of the mock-heroic possibilities inherent in his compositional method: "His Heroe, whom you Wits his Bully call / Bates of his mettle; and scarce rants at all: / He's somewhat lewd; but a well-meaning mind; / Weeps much; fights little, but is wondrous kind."

The idealizing perspective sometimes appears in the play as it would have in a heroic play of the sixties, in rhetorical declamation, but here the rhetorical flight shapes an imagined or imaginary vision, not an image of ideal truth. For example, Antony's entrance speech is a small set piece in the pastoral style; it does not function as, let us say, Berenice's pastoral dream in *Tyrannick Love* of soul union with Porphyrius after death, that is, as a prescient glimpse of metaphysical truth. Rather, Antony's vision is conceived as the idle fancy of a paralyzed man, who, because he cannot act, is driven to daydreaming:

Give me some Musick; look that it be sad:
I'll soothe my Melancholy . . .
                                    Stay I fancy
I'm now turn'd wild, a Commoner of Nature;
Of all forsaken, and forsaking all;
Live in a shady Forrest's Sylvan Scene;
Stretch'd at my length beneath some blasted Oke;
I lean my head upon the Mossy Bank . . .
                                              [I, i]

If we compare ways that idealizing visions are used in the Amariel scene in *Tyrranick Love* or in the opening scene of *The Indian Queen*, we find that in the earlier plays the *position* of the scenes in a mounting ideational structure is paramount. (In the former, the masque of spirits delineates the boundary between sublunary and heavenly truth; in the latter, pastoral idyllic is a baseline of innocence from which we mount to ideas of heroic love and honor.) In both cases the imagination of the audience is being transported. In *All for Love* the conception of an ideal world of pastoral innocence is itself conceived as a vain imagining, a fever dream by which shackled man consoles himself in the iron world of the actual. In the 1670s and early 1680s, "the universe of mind, including all experienced qualities that are not mathematically reducible, comes to be pictured as locked up behind the confused and deceitful media of the senses, in a petty and insignificant series of locations inside of human bodies."[25] Consequently, in this decade drama shapes either satire's disjunction between the longed-for "should be" and the sourly considered "is" or the "serious" play's dichotomy between limitless imagination and the paralyzed human self. In both cases "reality" lies *somewhere between.* Earl Miner has put it most succinctly: "Between the cities of satire and those of Utopia there exists a real city; Dryden . . . [called] that reality 'nature' "[26]

Stage 3

"The clearest, best and most certain knowledg that mankinde can possibly have of things existing without him is but Experience, that is noe thing but the Exercise and observation of his senses about particular objects; and therefore Knowledg and Faith too at last resolve themselves and terminate somewhere or other in Experience either our owne or other mans."[27] So John Locke writes in his *Essay concerning Human Understanding*. Stage 3 (circa 1680-1700) in the process we are tracing moves to close the distance between ideal and experiential reality. We might think of imitation of Nature in this third stage as a closer and closer focusing upon the individual human being and his inner life. First, dramatic perspective turns away altogether from the realm of Idea toward the realm of actuality. Then the focus narrows to the behavior of *typical* men and women. Then it narrows still further to concentrate upon *particular* men and women. Finally, the beam penetrates the surface to the inner reality of particular individuals.

These changes had a profound effect upon the structure of drama. In the 1680s the primary element in a play was no longer the quintessential Idea to which it aspired but its "fable," a pattern of Providence working in experience. Later, in the 1690s, as characters came more nearly to resemble "real" people and action "real" experience, the function of plot became to exhibit character and to distinguish good-natured from ill-natured characters. Whereas in the sixties characters are figures working in the service of a design, in the nineties elaborately contrived plot exists to display the facets of character. Characterization, indeed, determines plot and language. James Drake writes in 1698: "The Fable of every Play is undoubtedly the Authors own, whencesoever he takes the Story, and he may mold it as he pleases. The Characters are not so; the Poet is obliged to take 'em from Nature, and to copy as close after her, as he is able. The same may be said for the Thoughts and Expressions, they must be suited to the Mouth and Character of the Person that speaks 'em, not the Poet's."[28]

By the late nineties characters have become those "interestingly independent agents" with whom we in the twentieth century feel comfortable.

The change, however, was gradual. In the 1680s design is still paramount, though what a design represents has changed from earlier decades because the end of drama is no longer believed to be elevation of our minds to the ideal but rather *grounding* of the Ideal to our experience. As Aubrey Williams demonstrated, "poetic justice" (which we postnaturalist critics have reduced to an absurdity) was, in fact, a profoundly important conception. Williams rightly warns that "if we are fully to apprehend the strength and import of the concept [in the late seventeenth and early eighteenth centuries] we must recapture in some sense the way it stood for the mirroring of God's justice in a literary form."[29] The new emphasis on "poetic justice" in the eighties is best understood in the light of the epistemological changes we have noticed. As Locke said in 1695, "No man inspired by God can by any revelation communicate any new simple ideas which they had not before by sensation or reflection."[30] We cannot *know* the metaphysical order except through experience, sensation, and reflection. Poets cannot imitate ideal, transcendent truth because they cannot envision it. Moreover, even if, like St. Paul, they could be rapt to the third heaven and see the cosmological shape of reality itself, they could not communicate their vision "by words or any other signs."[31] Consequently, the poet and the philosopher must look to experience, must search the physical world for signs of the metaphysical imprint. Poetic justice mirrors metaphysical truth as it is grounded in experience, or Providence. The conception of dramatic imitation that gives rise to poetic justice assumes a providential design *embedded in* perceptible reality, which is the only reality we can know. Imitation of that design is a solution to the problem that was set in Stage 2 by the divorce between the ideal and the actual, between free mind and bound senses.

Rhymer, an archempiricist, is convinced that God's perfect order is the truth poetry shapes; he trusts to the poet's powers of sensation, observation, and reflection to find and disclose it. A poet's job, he thinks, is "observing that constant order, that harmony and beauty of Providence, that necessary relation and chain, whereby the causes and the effects, the vertues and rewards, the vices and their punishments are proportion'd and link'd together; how deep and dark soever are laid the Springs, and however intricate and involv'd are their operations."[32] Notice that the proportions, links, and chains, which less than a hundred years earlier had held together the great *discordia concors* of Universal Nature, are now conceived as cause/effect connections in the history of human experience. The shape of truth is still the poet's subject, but he does not look for it among the fixed stars. The medium through which it is translated and in which it is known is matter. In 1679 Dryden no longer believes that "A Play to be like Nature, is to be set above it," as he did only nineteen years earlier. Instead of lifting us above nature, a play brings truth to ground. "Fable" is the paramount compositional element in drama: "'Tis the moral that directs the whole action of the play to one centre; and the action or fable is *the example built upon the moral, which confirms the truth of it to our experience;* when the fable is designed then and not before, the persons are to be introduced with their manners, characters, and passions" (italics mine).[33] It is true that in 1680 character is still subordinate to design, but design is wrought out of human actions, which alone can confirm its truth to our knowledge and experience.

In adapting Shakespeare (*The Ingratitude of a Commonwealth* and *King Lear*, 1681), Tate has a very different aim from that which Dryden and Davenant had had in 1664. He is not concerned to create the balances and symmetries for which the earlier adapters had striven; rather, his aim is to strengthen Shakespeare's fable. Despite his reverence for Shakespeare, Tate finds the plays deficient as imitations of Providence and probability. *King Lear,* he says, is "a heap of Jewels unstrung and unpolisht," but, fortunately, he finds among the ruins "such Conceptions" as justify the "Probability," or fidelity to human experience, that his adaptation will supply: "'Twas my good Fortune to light on one Expedient to rectifie what was wanting in the *Regularity* and *Probability* of the Tale, which was to run through the whole, a Love betwixt Edgar and Cordelia, that never chang'd a word with each other in the Original. This renders Cordelia's indifference and her Father's Passion in the first scene probable. It likewise gives Countenance to Edgar's Disguise making that a generous Design that was before a poor Shift to save his life . . . . This Method necessarily threw me on making the Tale conclude in a success to the innocent distrest Persons."[34]

Tate's expedient not only makes the events in *King Lear* more probable by the standards of dramatic probability of 1681, but it develops a Fable, present only in embryo as "Conceptions" in the original, that illuminates the working of a just Providence. Like Davenant and Dryden before him, Tate "reads into" Shakespeare and builds into his adaptation images of reality that are appropriate to the time in which he writes. Perhaps the most interesting feature of Tate's dramaturgic method is that his persons, or, more specifically,

their fate in the hands of a benign Providence, dictate his design. This
change represents a quite radical turn from the Dryden-Davenant
Macbeth or *Tempest*, wherein design dictates the figuration and placement of characters. In the descent to experience, character moves to
the foreground of perspective. Dryden's departure from the position
he held in "Of Dramatic Poesy" illustrates the same radical change in
sensibility that has occurred in twenty years. In "On the Grounds of
Criticism" he begins to exhibit a new conception of character. Character is not, as it had been earlier, the figurative shape of Idea; it is a
complex of attitudinal postures, "that which distinguishes one man
from another." Character is still typologically conceived, but a
character no longer figures one Idea. A character, Dryden now
argues, "cannot be supposed to consist of one particular virtue, or
vice, or passion only but 'tis a composition of qualities not contrary
to one another in the same person . . . . Falstaff is a liar, and a
coward, and a glutton because these qualities may agree in the same
man."[35]

We are still about a decade away from seeing characters as persons
like ourselves. In the 1680s verisimilitude in characterization is consistency to type. Dryden says that "when a poet has given the dignity
of a king to one of his persons, in all his actions and speeches that
person must discover majesty, magnanimity and jealousy of power,
because these are suitable to the manners of a king."[36] However,
characters have broken loose from the gridwork of ideational design.
Indeed, it is their "experience," as Providence directs them, that
determines the contours of a dramatic composition. For instance,
Cordelia's and Edgar's "distrest innocence" must be relieved, or
Cressida's falsity justified, in order that the presence of a just Providence working in human affairs may be disclosed. However, character has not yet become what it will be in the nineties, the portraiture
of particular men and women, as distinct from each other as they are
in life. Probability is to type; it has not yet become linked with
particularity. Rhymer's criticism of Shakespeare is more intelligible
when we understand it in light of what dramatic imitation of nature
meant when he wrote. He chides Shakespeare because he finds him
deliberately perverse. Rhymer thinks Shakespeare unfaithful to
"reality" because he conceives fidelity to nature to be truth to a
typology determined by convention: "Shakespeare knew his Char-

acter of Iago was inconsistent. In this very play he pronounces, 'If thou dost deliver more or less than Truth / Thou art no Souldier.' This he knew; but to entertain the Audience with something new and surprising, against Common Sense and *Nature*, he would pass upon us a close, dissembling, false, insinuating rascal instead of an open-hearted, frank, plain-speaking Souldier, a character constantly worn by them for some thousands of years in the World."[37] It might be well to note here that "character" still means the delineation of an essence. Rhymer does not say "his character Iago," making person and character equivalent. Character is still an idea, but it is the idea of a type. We might say that we are midway between character as an idea of a passion or "Complexion of our Minds" and character as a believable, particular individual.

However, types were not always determined by some thousands of years of literary convention; in the eighties they were sometimes contemporary, most often political, stereotypes. In the list of dramatis personae to *The City Heiress* (1682), Behn describes one of her characters simply as "a Tory," which for her betokens a whole complex of known, admirable qualities. More and more frequently as the eighties progressed, more value is given to the particular and experiential. Rather than protesting, as he certainly would have in the seventies, that his characters had no reference to particular people, the playwright of the eighties more often than not tells his audience that they are watching themselves. And the audience appears to have been delighted by the prospect:

In Comedy your little selves you meet,
'Tis Covent Garden drawn in Bridges-street,
Smile on our Author then, if he has shown
A jolly Nut-Brown Bastard of your own.
Ah! Happy you, with Ease and with Delight,
Who act those Follies Poets toil to Write![38]

Certainly new ideas about biography confirm a continuously growing interest in the particular for its own sake. In *The Life of Plutarch* (1683) Dryden tells us that a biographer must train his attention upon the "minute circumstances and trivial passages of life." Like the novelist, by the very requirements of his genre, the biographer must draw his reader *into* his subject: "You are led into the private

Lodgings of the Heroe; you see him in his undress, and are made
Familiar with his most private actions and conversations. You may
behold a Scipio and a Lelius gathering Cockle-Shells on the shore,
Augustus playing at bounding-stones with Boyes. . . . The Pageantry of Life is taken away; you see the poor reasonable Animal, as
naked as ever nature made him; and are made acquainted with his
passions and foibles, and find the Demi-God, a Man."[39]
In the 1690s attention to the particular and idiosyncratic grows.
Characters are no longer the instruments through which providential design is expressed. Rather, a complete reversal occurs, and
Providence becomes a backdrop to which our attention is called from
time to time, but always to highlight some admirable or despicable
personality trait of the characters, who are very much in the forefront of our attention. Characterization dominates and determines
dramatic representation, and plot exists to exhibit the facets of
character. A design, indeed, may carry very little or no meaning in
itself but may seem rather to meander randomly, as in *Sir Anthony
Love*, for example. Moral is no longer to be found in "Fable" but, as
Vanbrugh says, is to be found "much more in the Characters and
Dialogue than in the Business and Event."[40] Characters are representations of particular individuals like ourselves. In his dedication to
Love Triumphant (1694), we find that Dryden has taken another long
jump toward the "perceptible" real in conceiving of the nature drama
seeks to represent: "I dare affirm that the several manners I have
given the persons of this drama are truly drawn from nature, *all
perfectly distinguished from each other*; that the fable is not injudiciously
contrived; that the turns of fortune are not managed inartfully; and
that the last revolution is happily enough invented" (italics mine).[41]
    The priority of elements in composition has been reordered.
Characters, their manners, and—most important—their sentiments
are now primary and constitute the wellspring from which action
and design flow. A playwright is valued for his ability to imitate
"things . . known and familiar to every Bodies Notice . . and
consequently delightful to the times, as *Pictures* of *Faces* well known
and remarkable."[42] Writers openly acknowledge that they take the
likenesses and conversation of real people as their materials, and
critics understand plays of their own and earlier times as imitations of
the actual. Praise or condemnation is accorded on the basis of that
fundamental aesthetic assumption. The author of *A Comparison*

between the Two Stages, for example, praises Southerne both for the accuracy with which he draws "real life" and also for being acquainted with people who are worthy to be drawn:

R. I have a particular regard for Mr. Southerne's Stile and agreeable Manner; there's a Spirit of Conversation in every thing that he writes.
S. I think very few exceed him in Dialogue; his Gallantry is natural, and after the real manner of the Town; his acquaintance with the best Company entered him into the secrets of their Intrigues, and no man knew better the Way and Disposition of Mankind.[43]

If we simply compare the style and conversational tone that is used in this criticism with the structure of dialectical argument that shapes "Of Dramatic Poesy," we can see the striking changes that have occurred in ways of *seeing, understanding, and talking about* drama. Clearly a whole new perceptual set had developed in thirty-odd years. *A Comparison* disapproves of Dryden. While the speakers acknowledge that Dryden often "hits the sublime," they think that he fails as a dramatist because he does not touch upon the *inner feelings* of his characters "above twice or thrice in all, and then *not very naturally neither.*"[44] Critics of the nineties are distressed by Dryden's plays of the sixties and seventies because the primacy of design in them acts as a barrier to spectator identification with the characters: "His *Rival Ladies* is a confusion of Intrigues and Incidents, so generally obscure that there's no possibility of keeping the *Ladies* company with our understanding: I like the Story better (I must needs say) in the *Novel* from whence he took it."[45] Precisely this conceptual set, as I have argued above, caused the novel to replace the drama in popularity. The most appealing of Congreve's plays to the author of *A Comparison* was *The Double Dealer* (which, later in the century, Walpole was to consider a melodrama).[46] But in general, they find fault with Congreve because they "don't take his Characters to be always natural . . . some are out of probability, one in his *Old Batchelour* and several in *Love for Love* obsolete."[47] The aesthetic assumption upon which these judgments and most critical judgments at the turn of the century are made is that a play must be "founded in Truth, or Some story very near to it; aut Veram aut Verisimilem; I would have every Scene made probable."[48] The test of truth is probability.

Once dramatic representation is thought to imitate actuality, the line of demarcation between the play and the spectator blurs. First, the audience is drawn into the scene. Dennis tells us that "Comedy is as it ought to be, when an Audience is apt to imagine, that instead of being in the Pit and Boxes, they are in some Assembly of the Neighborhood."[49] Steele calls for a tragedy wrought out of "such adventures as befall persons not exalted above the common level" because "nothing can relate to the [spectators] . . . that does not happen to such as live and look like themselves."[50] The *Gentleman's Journal* accepts as commonplace that "Dramatic Poesy . . . aims at a Just Representation, and that which deviates least from *our common apprehensions of Nature's force*."[51] Second, the audience, once having entered the scene, is drawn still further inward to the interior life of the characters. A dramatic poet, it is thought, cannot *describe* the passions because the passions, our interior and truest reality, cannot be captured in words. He must "go to the very bottom of the heart, or it is all mere language; and the writer . . . is no more a poet, than a man is a physician for knowing the names of distempers without knowing the causes of them."[52] By the turn of the eighteenth century drama has become—insofar as is possible—imitation of the human inner arena. Its object is not to design ideas but to penetrate emotional and psychological states: "The Poet must not be content to look into his Mind to see what he should *think* on such an occasion, but he must put himself into the Passion, Quality, and Temper of the Character he is to draw; that is, he must assume the Manner he gives his Dramatic Person, and then see what Sentiments or Thoughts such an Occasion or Passion, or the like will pro-duce."[53]

The effects of the conception that drama imitates actuality, born in the 1680s and extended in its range to a new frontier of representa-tion in the 1690s, are several. Emphasis shifts from formal balancing of attitudes or positions to the attempt to stimulate behavior. Dra-matic tension comes to rest in the contrast between good and bad temperaments and in the disclosure of deep psychological experi-ence. Plot becomes more and more elaborate but more loosely contrived to display the myriad facets of character, as in *Sir Anthony Love* (1691), or to provide the opportunity for characters to display their inner emotional or mental states, as in *The Wives Excuse*. We are invited to *share* the inner thoughts of wicked characters as they plot, as in *The Double Dealer*, or the process of emotional change that misguided good-hearts undergo as they are brought back to the path of natural virtue by their exemplars, as Hilaria is in *Love's Last Shift* or Constant is in *The Provok'd Wife*.

We have too often been misled by inaccurate labels like "sentimental" in our efforts to understand what is in fact a narrowing of imitative focus to the particular and a penetration below the surface into interior human experience. Starting in the eighties, the individual and his inner life compose the nature that art must imitate if it would please and instruct. As early as 1683 Dryden said, "As the sunbeams, uniting in a burning-glass to a point, have a greater force than when they are darted from a plain superficies, so the virtues and actions of one man, drawn together . . . strike upon our minds a stronger and more lively impression than the scattered relations of many men, and many actions; and by the same means that they give us pleasure, they afford us profit too."⁵⁴ This conception is opposite to both his theory and his practice of the sixties and seventies.

Shirley Strum Kenney provides insight into the social consequences of the shift in focus from ideas to feelings, from public to private in dramatic imitation:

The plays [of Etherege and Wycherley] focus on the public rather than the private aspect of people's lives . . . even the infamous china scene in *The Country Wife* is intellectual—there is nothing pornographic about it. In the period . . . [1690-1720], the focus begins to turn toward the private rather than the public aspect of life. . . . It is at the moment the focus begins to change that the theatre edges toward pornography—seductions begin to occur on stage to truly virtuous and occasionally tempted women. . . . Suddenly the game is no longer a game; the stakes are very high. . . . Obviously the change in the author's vision of the social scene created a vastly different kind of comedy. Characterization, dialogue, plot all change when comedy turned into a mode somewhat akin to the problem play.⁵⁵

The problem play is the very child of naturalism. Its end, as G.B. Shaw conceived the matter, was to use the theater as a social science laboratory and as an instrument of social reform and revitalization. Of those uses critics and playwrights two hundred years before Shaw were quite well aware. Once drama imitates the interior human condition and once its effect upon spectators is thought to be entrance into and participation in the hidden life of characters, the inevitable next step has to be an attempt to condition the social behavior of spectators.

Stage 4

In Stage 4 (circa 1700–1732) of the four-phase progress we have been tracing, the playwright's primary aim is not to imitate nature but to draw nature to imitate art. In 1694 James Wright says that the end of tragedy is "the Reformation of Manners," and in a little over a decade, Steele is arguing that his own benevolence has been more powerfully implanted in him by drama than by his experience: "I am convinced that the impulses I have received from theatrical representations have had a greater effect than otherwise would have been wrought in me by the little occasions of my private life . . . and made me *insensibly* more courteous and humane to my friends and acquaintances. It is not the business of a good play to make every man a hero, but it certainly gives him a livelier sense of virtue and merit than he had when he entered the theatre."[56]

The key word in this passage, I think, is "insensibly." Drama's effect on us is now thought to be insensible. Its appeal is not to our understanding; it does not seek to elevate our minds to Idea. Rather, as we explore the interior lives of the characters on stage, subtle changes are wrought in the secret recesses of our own interior lives. As early as 1687, Aphra Behn had said that plays are "secret Instructions to the People, in things that 'tis impossible to insinuate into them any other way."[57] At the beginning of the so-called Age of Reason the most profound effects of dramatic art were considered to be subrational. The paradox, however, is that from the inner depth upon which the drama operates springs the behavior that shapes our most public life. The purpose of tragedy, says Addison, is to "soften Insolence, sooth Affliction and subdue the Mind to the Dispensations of Providence," but, those effects obtained, the theater must go on to promote in the hearts of the audience "the Religion, the Government, and the Public Worship of its Country."[58]

Curiously enough, the progress we have been following has described a circle from imitation of an ideal to imitation of an ideal. We have traced the movement of dramatic representation as it went from the transcendent ideal to the actual. Within imitation of the actual, we have watched it move step by step from public to private, from typical to particular, and over the threshold to inner space. Now suddenly we find ourselves moving outward, albeit with a new aesthetic, to the public arena again. Like Alice, we have gone through the looking glass. The function of drama in the early eighteenth century is to move inward in order to modify our public behavior: "To wake the soul by tender strokes of art, / To raise the Genius and to mend the heart. / To make mankind in conscious virtue bold, / Live o'er each scene and *be* what they behold."[59] A.S. Bear has convincingly demonstrated that the Collier controversy was no controversy at all.[60] Both the attack and the defenses it provoked were based upon the same assumptions. Neither side ever questioned the validity of the idea that what we see in a play is what we see in the world, nor that audiences emulate or are led not to emulate characters in whom they "believe." Attacks upon the immorality of the drama in the late nineties vary only in the degree to which they hold playwrights responsible for the harmful effects of their plays. Blackmore, for instance, suspects the playwrights of willful perversity: "Our poets seem engag'd in a general Confederacy to ruin the end of their own Art, to expose Religion and Virtue and bring Vice and Corruption of Manners into Esteem and Reputation . . . . The Man of Sense, and the Fine Gentleman in the Comedy, *who is the Chiefest Person propos'd to the Esteem and Imitation of the Audience* . . . . will appear a Finished Libertine . . . . whence the Youth of the Nation have apparently receiv'd very bad impressions."[61] Steele leans more to the opinion that the playwrights simply are not good enough psychologists to understand the effects that plays have upon impressionable youth: "It is not every Youth that can behold the fine Gentleman of the Comedy represented with a Good Grace, leading a loose and profligate Life, and condemning Virtuous Affection as insipid, and not be secretly Emulous of what appears so amiable to a whole Audience."[62] Because the assumption is that neither reason nor judgment is involved in our response to the drama but, rather, that we are receptors of "impressions" that insensibly insinuate behavioral models into our hearts, the spectator, especially if he is young and particularly impressionable, must be protected against the drama. These propositions once admitted, it is only a very short time until they are extended. By 1732 the spectator is to be protected not only from subtly seductive plays but from actors and playwrights themselves:

'Tis plain . . . the Management of the Stage is by no Means fit for the Players, and consequently 'tis necessary to chuse some other. . . . Our Design . . . [is] to build a *new Theatre* . . . with a quite different view. . . . calculated for the Good of the Publick, for the Encouragement of Learning, the Improvement of Politeness, and the Honour of the Age . . . . But the question is who shall put it into Execution? We have already determin'd Players to be incapable, and all the World will be convinc'd that Authors are so too . . . . Both these therefore must be set aside in Favour of disinterested, impartial Reasons; such are Men of Quality, and Figure, Taste, and Fortune; such only are fit to be at the Head of the Stage, and dictate to the Pleasures of an elegant and understanding People.[63]

This position is, of course, the extreme at which emulation theory becomes the instrument of political behavior modification. But even this extreme begins with the same aesthetic, with the same conception of dramatic imitation that forms the ground upon which attacks and defenses of the theater alike are built. For example, Steele attacks *The Man of Mode* as true enough to nature, to "real" behavior, but argues that "it is nature in its utmost corruption and degeneracy" and that, however true to life it admittedly is, it is nevertheless harmful as a "contradiction to good manners, good sense, and common honesty."[64] Dennis defends *The Man of Mode* on the same grounds. The "proper Business" of a comedy, he argues, is to "expose Persons to our View, whose View we may shun, and whose Follies we may despise; and by shewing us what is done upon the Comick Stage, shew us what ought never to be done upon the Stage of the World."[65] Both critics assume that drama imitates real people and that audiences imitate characters with whom plays ask them to identify and shun characters whom plays direct them to dismiss.

The last step of emulation theory is to recommend the good behavioral models drama holds up for us, even if they are not realistic. The *St. James's Journal* recognizes that *The Conscious Lovers* is not a faithful imitation of ordinary reality, but it recommends the play's extraordinary principals because they make virtue appear graceful and attractive and draw us to imitate them. "As for the

Characters and Manners, if there are not many such in real Life (I mean of the principal ones) 'tis pity. They appear at least very gracefully, I believe, in the opinion of the most Profligate. That there are some such Characters in the World, is very certain. I think that the plot has shown that the Splendour and Shine of high Life is not at all eclips'd by the Honour and Innocence of it."[66]

We in the twentieth century carry these assumptions as part of our aesthetic luggage. Consider, for instance, the widely held belief that watching Tom and Jerry cartoons makes children violent or breeds in them a contempt for life. There is no question that the animated drawings of a heroic mouse and a prodigious cat do not imitate experience, but so strong is our conviction (1) that the spectator identifies with the character on stage and (2) that the "inner" emotions of the characters insinuate themselves into the inner lives of the audience that we accept the proposition without question. Moreover, the conception that we become what we see on the stage extends in reference far beyond the impressionable young. Women Against Pornography makes the case that watching pornographic movies makes men abusers of women. The National Organization of Women argues that television commercials depicting women as household slaves thereby turn them into slaves. Prison officials in Ohio and California do not allow inmates to watch "Kojak" or "Mission Impossible." The list is almost endless. For our purpose, however, it is significant that few literary critics and fewer psychologists seem to be aware that the fundamental assumptions upon which our beliefs about drama rest were not handed down on Mt. Sinai but were invented in the last decades of the seventeenth century as part of a new epistemology and a new model of mind.

> Minds from each other's motions take their bent;
> In Love, Joy, Rage, and even in Hate consent,
> The Angry urge us, and the Fearful fright,
> The Sad disturb us, and the Gay delight.
> The Proud and Scornful our aversion prove,
> As all the Tender our Affections move.[67]

I have, of course, been drastically schematic in this chapter and have used only those examples that would clearly illustrate my point. I do so because the chapter is intended as a blueprint or an outline guide to the full argumentation and proofs of succeeding chapters.

TWO

Imitation of Nature as Idea

Ideas have their causal being in God, their formal in the first Mind, their participated in the rational Soul. In God they are not, but produced by him in the *Angelick* nature, through this communicated to the Soul, by whom illuminated, when she reflects in her intellectual parts, she receives the true forms of things, *Ideas*. . . . Those employed in corporeal office [human beings] are depriv'd of Contemplation borrowing science from sense, to this wholly enclin'd, full of errors: Their only means of release from this bondage, is the amatory life; which by sensible beauties, exciting in the Soul a remembrance of the Intellectual, raiseth her from this terrene of life to the eternal; by flame of love refined into an Angel.

Thomas Stanley, "The Doctrine of Plato Delivered by Alcinuous"

The World is a *universal Temple*, wherein man may contemplate natural *images* and pictures of Divine *Wisdome* and *Goodnesse*. The Sun, Moon, and Stars, yea this dul element of the Earth furnisheth us with *Divine Characters, Ideas,* and *representations* of eternal Wisdome. . . . But now man by reason of his fal being greatly wounded in his *Intellectuals* [is] thereby disenabled to contemplate that Natural Wisdome. . . . God sends forth a book of Grace whence all Arts and Sciences are sprung.

. . . for the moving the Affections, especially *Admiration, Love, Joy,* or *Sorrow* there this Poetic vein is most *pregnant* and *ripe.* For as speech was given for the communicating his *conceptions* or mind unto others; so *Poesie* (which is the most witty and affectionate speech) for the more lively representation of our choicer Apprehensions and Affections.

Theophilus Gale, *The Court of the Gentiles*

In the first stage of the progression we are following, the function of drama is to lift the minds of its audience to a truth that is not discernible in experience. The design of a play does not consist in its events or rest upon the actions of its personae. Whether we are dealing with what Robert Hume calls the "chilly, super-subtle ethical calculus" of an Orrery tragedy[1] or the "Moral Characters" and "preacepts" of a comedy by Tuke or Edward Howard, the end is the same: to elevate the understanding to an apprehension of Ideas of truth. Love and honor are the chosen vehicles of imaginative transcendence because, as in the epigraph above, love excites "in the Soul a remembrance of the Intellectual, [and] raiseth her from this terrene of life to the eternal," while honor, or heroic virtue, is "a habit of Mind . . . inspir'd from above" that elevates a man "above mankind, and as much as human nature could bear, it render[s] him like a Deity."[2] In the drama of the 1660s, love and honor are channels through which the way to transcendence flows.

Dryden, after denying that we can compare "the use of Dramatic Poesie with that of Divinity," considers that the primary function of poetry is not instruction in ethics or morality but the revelation of metaphysical truth, of eternal Ideas or "images of piety." He describes the process by which dramatic representations elevate the mind and indicates the end toward which "admiration," the essence of serious drama, moves: "By the Harmony of words we elevate the mind to a sense of Devotion, as our solemn Musick, which is inarticulate Poesie, does in Churches; and by the lively *images of piety*, adorned by action, through the Senses allure the Soul; which while it is charmed in a silent joy of what it sees and hears, is struck at the same time with a secret veneration of things Celestial."[3]

One interesting clue to the conception of imitation at work here is the comparison of dramatic poetry with music, the most abstract of the arts; later, as experience becomes the focus of dramatic imitation, the parallel will more often be made with painting, the plastic art. In this early stage a play focuses upon the ideal; it renders *images* of piety, love, heroic virtue. Action is ancillary to idea; it is an ornament. Admiration, or imaginative elevation, is achieved by the harmony and/or the dialectic of language, for the philosophic assumption still at work is that *word* comes closest to Idea. Action, because of necessity it is encumbered by matter, is clumsily inaccurate. Theophilus Gale expresses the notion this way: "*There are in speech certain Symbols or notices of the Souls passions.* . . . Look as in the *mind* there is a certain *Character* or *Idea* of things; so likewise in oration or speech there is a *Character* or *Idea of the Mind.*"[4]

Dramatic composition in the 1660s consists in arrangement of rhetorical, dialectic "positions," which imitate "the movements and affections of the mind, either combating between two contrary passions or extremely discompos'd by one."[5] I have called this arrangement the heroic, mounting progression structure. However, even in the three-tiered design that we find in most comedy in this decade, the middle plane of action is clearly an inferior realm. In the descent from high-plane debate or encomium exchange to middle-plane action, ideas lose their stability and purity. Let me provide a very brief example from *The Enchanted Island*. On the high plane, Prospero and Hippolito debate the issue of Fate and Free Will:

> **Prosp.** O gentle youth Fate waits for thee abroad,
>   A black star threatens thee, and death unseen
>   Stands ready to devour thee.
> **Hip.**   You taught me.
>   Not to fear him in any of his shapes:
>   Let me meet death rather than be a prisoner.
>   [II, ii]

On the plane of action, governed "from Sense . . . and ful of errors," Idea is translated by ignorance, appetite, and misdirected will into confusion—to mock-heroic effect:

> **Trin.** I say this Island shall be under Trinculo or it shall be a Commonwealth, and so my Bottle is my Buckler, and so I draw my Sword. [II, i]

The high plane of a three-tiered structure achieves its effects in the same way as the "serious" drama does, in the arrangement of concepts or ideas, "according to the rule, *contraria juxta se apposita magis elucescunt*."[6] The middle plane, on the other hand, images the grossly imperfect world, and the low plane constitutes a further exaggeration downward to parody. As George R. Guffey's research on adaptations of *The Tempest* shows, when the Dryden-Davenant adaptation is exploring ideas that have immediate political relevance—like the civil strife that follows upon factionalism or the effect of Continental power struggles upon English foreign policy—they are played on the middle plane as delusion and on the low plane as slapstick.[7]

As it had been since the Middle Ages, the world of experience in the 1660s is figured as a vastly imperfect realm under constant threat of darkness and confusion. The important point for us to recognize is that in the comic drama of the sixties the plane of action constitutes a *part* within the dramatic design. It is not the central focus. The whole design carefully avoids too close an imitation of experiential reality, for, as Dryden argues in "A Defence," "there may be too great a likeness" to the phenomenal world; "as the most skillful painters affirm, that there may be too near a resemblance in a picture; to take every lineament and feature is not to make an excellent piece, but to take so much only as will make a beautiful resemblance of the whole."[8] Whether, then, we are dealing with a structure that shapes the design of mounting progression from the world to the realm of pure Idea or with a three-tiered structure (heroic, actual, and mock-heroic), the level of experience is an inferior domain: a baseline *from* which heroic aspiration rises or *to* which pure Idea descends.

Aubrey Williams has said, "There are doubtless those who will wish to confine Dryden's 'patterns of piety' and his 'lively images of piety' rather strictly to such patently religous plays as *Tyrannick Love, The Virgin Martyr,* or *The Mourning Bride* . . . I would . . . argue that such patterns and images are commonly adjusted and reconciled to a large assortment of plays heroical, tragical, and tragicomical. Such patterns and images, along with a variety of emblematic situations . . . [are of] great importance in finding audience response and discerning authorial content and dramatic meaning."[9] I am in complete agreement with Williams; an understanding of the pattern of ideal truth and its representation is essential to any study of Restoration drama. The concept, as well as the changes that occur in ways of envisioning and picturing it, is centrally important to the understanding of what dramatic imitation of nature means and how it is variously conceived during this period. I also agree with Williams that—at least for the drama of the 1660s and 1670s—the patterns are transgeneric, and I shall deal in this chapter with samples from comic plays as well as from heroic and tragic plays. Because the pattern that I have called the design of mounting progression is so strongly etched in *Tyrannick Love* (1669), however, I should like to examine the structural design of this play in some detail in an effort to establish precisely the means by which Dryden attempted in "the Harmony of words . . . to elevate the mind" of his audience to a contemplation of things "celestiall." Such an analysis should reveal the compositional method in abstract; we can then use it as a prototype in looking at other plays of any genre. In his commentary on *Tyrannick Love* Maximillian E. Novak said: "Catherine does not react to Maximin's love; she plays out her life on the same stage but in a different spiritual dimension from Maximin."[10] The idea of material and spiritual dimensions is important in the play, and to some extent we can indeed think of the figures of Maximin and St. Catherine as poles between which the current of the play moves from the plane of the world to the metaphysical plane. These poles, however, are not fixed. As we shall see, within the progression the play designs, each of these figures mounts higher than its initial position. Maximin, "vastus corpore [et] animo ferus,"[11] is the sign of power in the world; St. Catherine is the opposing spiritual sign. Although there are gradations between them, those gradations are not marked as static points—that is, the design of the play is not the fixed NeoPlatonic scale that we find in Caroline drama. Rather, the scale itself is in motion, and movement upward is effected rhetorically. Our understanding mounts, by the medium of dialectic, from plateau to plateau of ever more refined argumentation and definition to an overarching and embracing conception of the ideal.

The play begins with Maximin in complete ascendence in the world. The "Martial monarch" has by strength of arms conquered as far as his desire has reached. He images egoistic heroic power—the strength, rage, and personal valor that is the sign of the "Herculean hero."[12] We begin with this sign in ascendence; Maximin's powers "have with success been crown'd; / And found no stop, or vanquish'd what they found" (I, i, 1-2). In the course of the play this heroic sign is not brought down, though Maximin is brought down from it; he loses his sign, so to speak. Rather, the idea of the heroic is enlarged. We move upward by degrees from the baseline of world-conquering, egoistic heroic greatness to the pinnacle of world-conquering, spiritual heroic greatness in the triumph and martyrdom of St. Catherine. The ground upon which we begin is an idea of personal greatness figured in an "irregular hero" who recognizes no power but his own and no strength but force: "That Senate's but a name; / Or they are Pageant Princes which they make" (I, i, 35-36).

Charinus, a fledgling Maximin, figures the Herculean hero in little. When he comes to the throne, Charinus says, he will "chuse to dye, or reign alone" (line 46). His fate sets the limit against which egoistic heroic greatness must break: death.

When the play begins, everything that can be controlled by egoistic heroic power is under Maximin's control. He cannot, however, control fate (Charinus dies), and he cannot control love (Porphyrius's for Berenice). Even the degree of control that he exercises over love's free expression is granted to him by the heroic codes of the lovers, not forced by the exercise of his own will. Those powers, love and death, are the ideas with which the conception of heroic honor that Maximin figures will contend throughout the play. The contention will modify, elevate, enlarge, and redefine greatness.

The very short act 1 sets the baseline from which we rise to contemplate celestial things, and it also sets the terms of the first dialectic. Act 2 begins to widen the definition of heroic greatness in the love debate between Porphyrius and Berenice. Porphyrius is caught in the conventional conflict between love for Berenice and duty to his king. On the platform of personal heroic honor the familiar Y scaffold is built, which branches duty to an evil king who will destroy the beloved from duty to liberate the beloved. The dilemma has no importance in itself; it is a structuring device to move us from the baseline definition of personal courage to the first plateau: heroic love and honor. Not the scene itself but its position within the whole design is important.[13] Porphyrius's personal courage urges him to destroy the obstacle to his desire, which is, of course, the Maximin method of egoistic valor "that found no stop, or vanquish'd what [it] found." However, Berenice's code, as well as Porphyrius's own obligation as a subject, modify Porphyrius's high courage. Berenice's method is to refer personal honor to a higher level of definition:

> Por. Heav'n as its instrument, my courage sends.
> Ber. Heav'n ne'er sent to those who fight for private ends.
>
> [II, i, 46-47]

The structure of this small scene encapsulates the method that obtains within each segment of the whole play: (1) it *begins with* Porphyrius's daring the anger of Maximin for love of Berenice; (2) it *consists in* a debate that elevates the conceptions of both love and honor to a higher plane of definition—"Hope in Heav'n, not in me" (69); and (3) it *ends by* pointing beyond itself to the next dialectical debate. At the end of the encounter Berenice has kept her code of honor and, by means of it, has purified Porphyrius's love, but she laments, "How hard the Praecepts of my Vertue grow!" (92). The next contention, between St. Catherine and Apollonius, will enlarge the "praecepts" of virtue. The scene between Porphyrius and Berenice, then, is a step in motion; it is a step up from the wild, animal spirit of Maximin, but it is also a process of ascent to the next level of debate. At the end of the scene Porphyrius has been given leave to love by Berenice and has been made heir to the throne by Maximin. The scope of those concepts which were in conflict at the beginning of the scene, personal love and honor, has been enlarged to the public sphere, and their conflict has been resolved in a new compound, heroic love.

St. Catherine enters the play at this level, the first plateau to which our upward progress has lifted us. From the first she is the image of heroic majesty, which is the highest reach of worldly honor: "See whence she comes with that high air and mean / Which makes, in bonds, the greatness of a Queen" (II, i, 159-60). With her entrance a new baseline is established—the highest plane that is possible in *this* world—and from that plane another dialectic progression is launched. The debate between Apollonius and St. Catherine is a contention between two powerful ideas of good: the highest moral ideal possible without redemptive grace and the redeemed truth, that is, the highest moral ideal *in* the world versus the highest metaphysical ideal.

The debate is sparked by Maximin, who is himself the emblem of a power great on earth but inadequate to confine the soul. Apollonius is Maximin's spokesman. Though his spiritual reach is much above the animal soul of Maximin, it is inadequate to the truths that are available to St. Catherine. Apollonius begins as a figure of the rational soul. By his own admission his religion is merely a "pleasing Fable," the sugar coating of an ethics. The highest good to which it can reach are "praecepts of morality" (184). These *are* good, but they are not strong enough to be vehicles of transcendence. St. Catherine defeats Apollonius's argument and saves his soul by demonstrating that his precepts are not sufficient to the mounting motion of the human spirit:

> **S. Cath.** . . . love of Vertue is but barren praise,
> Airy as fame; nor strong enough to raise
> The actions of the Soul above the sence.
>
> [II, ii, 193-5]

Apollonius's religion is effective only in the realm of action, the arena in which Maximin reigns supreme. The virtues it teaches are good, indeed are the same ethical ideals that Christianity holds, but human mind and spirit aspire above sense and experience:

> **S. Cath.** 'Tis true, your virtues are the same we teach;
> But in our practice they much higher reach. . . .
> So much your Vertues are in ours refin'd.
> That yours but reach the actions, ours the mind.
>
> [II, i, 212-13; 220-21]

At this point in the dialectic Apollonius has reached as far as his religion can take him. Acknowledging that St. Catherine's rises higher, he embraces it, and with the conversion of Apollonius the whole design of the play attains still another plateau. If we look back from this new level of elevation to the plateau that preceded it (Porphyrius's "conversion" to heroic love), we discover that we have climbed from a peak of earthly love to a higher peak of heavenly love. The two ideals, moreover, are conceived much as they were a hundred years earlier in Spenser's *Four Hymns*. Heroic earthly love is a good; heavenly love is a higher good. We pass through the former to reach the latter.

Structurally the martyrdom of Apollonius provides passage from the physical to the metaphysical planes of idea. Maximin vows to punish Apollonius for embracing a religion different from that of the highest worldly authority, himself. Apollonius replies, "My martyrdom I to thy Crown prefer; / Truth is a Cause for a Philosopher" (II, i, 237-38). Apollonius crosses the barrier to eternal life, sent by St. Catherine to prepare her way and sent in triumph. Her words "Give to him [Maximin] your blood, but give him not a tear" (240) are not just a "render unto Caesar" maxim; they are also the playwright's way of setting a line of demarcation between the worldly and heavenly orders by differentiating the debt we owe to the world (our lives) from the debt we owe to heaven (our hearts and spirits). The line stands as a kind of roadmark on the way to spiritual transcendence, which the whole design of the play delineates.

Act 3 presents us with a triple configuration of heroic love that is played out between earth and heaven: heroic love as fierce desire and rage in Maximin, heroic love as self-denial and sacrifice in Placidus, and heroic love of God—which is both fierce and self-sacrificial—in St. Catherine. All three varieties of love *elevate*. Even the beast-souled Maximin is lifted out of himself by his love for St. Catherine. We must recognize that though he is egoistic, from the beginning Maximin is a heroic figure, and quite in keeping with conventional wisdom and tradition, the heroic temper is necessarily drawn above itself and refined when it is in the presence of ideal beauty and majesty.

Since we are here considering compositional method, it might be well to point out that in this kind of dramatic imitation (that is, the imitation of Idea), it matters not a bean *who* speaks a key passage (here it is a relatively minor figure), nor does it matter whether or not what is spoken is appropriate to the speaker's "character." Rather, it is vitally important *where in the design* the speech occurs. Placidus sets the terms of the configuration:

> Love various minds does variously inspire:
> He stirs in gentle Natures, gentle fire;
> Like that of Incense on the Altars laid:
> But raging flames tempestuous Souls invade.
> A fire which every windy passion blows;
> With pride it mounts, and with revenge it glows.
> [III, i, 293-98]

We are now at the border between earth and heaven, and the vehicle for mounting into the air that separates them is love. The two kinds of love, one driven by pride and rage and one by self-sacrifice, are first in antithetic juxtaposition, but as they rise, they converge. For example, Maximin is lifted by his love out of the egoism that limits him and is moved to heroic generosity. He first offers St. Catherine the crown of Egypt. The terms in which the offer is made make it clear that the beauty toward which Maximin's heroic love aspires is ideal, spiritual beauty. The terms in which St. Catherine's refusal is couched demonstrate the process whereby an earthly heroic goal, the crown of empire, is translated out of the world to become a higher heroic goal:

> **Placid.** Madam I from the emperour am come
> T'applaude your Vertue, and reverse your doom.
> He thinks whatever your Religion be,
> This Palm is owing to your constancy.
> **S. Cath.** My constancy from him seeks no renown
> Heav'n that propos'd the course, will give the Crown.
> **Plac.** But Monarchs are the Gods Viceregents here,
> Heav'n gives rewards; but what it gives, they bear. . . .
> **S. Cath.** The Deity I serve, had he thought fit,
> Could have preserv'd my Crown unconquer'd yet:
> But when his secret Providence design'd
> To level that, he levell'd too my mind:
> Which, by contracting its desires, is taught
> The humble quiet of possessing nought.
> [III, i, 26-33; 36-41]

St. Catherine's heroic love of God combines self-sacrificial love ("like Incense on an Altar") and aspiring heroic love that strives for glory. Maximin's heroic love aspires to capture the ideal virtue and constancy he sees in St. Catherine, but St. Catherine's greater-souled love aims to catch a "Heav'nly Diadem." St. Catherine has attained a level of spiritual greatness that the world can neither increase nor diminish. She is above the world, but she is not proudly above it. For instance, she scorns Placidus's assertion that heroic greatness has no need of the "little business of the world" as an Epicurean error. Heroic Christian love celebrates everything in the world that proclaims God's presence: its "workmanship so rare" and the watchful Providence that "propos'd the course" and that alone can "give the Crown." However, while it values signs in the world of the eternal presence, Christian heroic greatness also reaches upward beyond the limits of the world.

To appreciate the intricacy of Dryden's design we must realize the subtlety with which this triangular configuration functions here. On the one hand, it enlarges the idea of heroic love—out of the opposition of two antithetical ideas of love, a larger and more embracing conception emerges. On the other hand, the configuration moves all the figures upward in a progressive elevation toward the Ideal. Maximin's love *does* elevate him. When finally it is great enough to drive him to offer the Roman crown to St. Catherine, Maximin is transformed from a heavy-souled beast to a towering eagle that follows St. Catherine's soaring flight: "We look like eagles, tow'ring in the sky / While her high flight still raises mine more high" (III, i, 110-11).

The Placidus/St. Catherine/Maximin configuration is reenacted in Valeria/Berenice/Porphyrius. Porphyrius is torn between empire and love, the Maximin position: "Here Empire stands, if I could love displace; / There, helpless Love, with more Imperial Grace" (III, i, 227-28). Valeria's gentle, self-sacrificial love stands in the Placidus position. She vows to be more worthy than her unknown rival by being more constant. Berenice and Porphyrius engage in debate, and as each offers greater and greater evidence of willing self-sacrifice, both become more heroic. Berenice adopts the St. Catherine position when she caps the exchange by professing a love strong enough and constant enough to break through the barrier between earth and heaven:

> My earthly part—
> Which is my Tyrant's right, death will remove,
> I'le come all Soul and Spirit to your Love.
> With silent steps I'le follow you all day:
> Or else before you in the Sun-beams play.
> . . . .
> And when at last, in pity, you will dye,
> I'le watch your Birth of Immortality;
> Then, Turtle-like, I'le to my Mate repair;
> And teach you your first flight in open Air.
>   [III, i, 312-16; 325-28]

Her metaphor of the spirit's flight echoes Maximin's soaring eagles image but, significantly, translates it to a new dimension. First, Berenice's imagined flight with Porphyrius will occur beyond that airy sphere that is the upper limit of Maximin's imaginative scope. Second, the union crowns a gentle turtle-love, the very antithesis of Maximin's striving, heroic eagle-love.

Act 4 sets a new baseline. All the truths derived from act 3 converge and are figured emblematically in the confrontation between Damilcar and Nakar, "Daemons of Air" and sublunary powers of love, and Amariel, who is St. Catherine's guardian An gelick Spirit, the agent of a power superior to and in charge of the daemons in Nature. The masquelike operatic debate of the spirits lifts us to a new apprehension of truth. It transforms what we have seen figured on the plane of moral action (Porphyrius, Berenice, Placidus, and Maximin) and on the plane of philosophic debate (St. Catherine and Apollonius; St. Catherine and Maximin's spokesman, Placidus) into an imaginative vision, or purely poetic metaphor. Earthly good, "dreams of sweet delight," are hymned by the earthly powers in pastoral style—in visions of "purling streams" and "flowery Meads"—and celebrated in softly sensuous dance. But the goods of the world, good though they are, are not high enough or full enough to satisfy the human soul.

Introducing a heroic strain, Amariel comes to check and rebuke the pastoral spirits. The "Daemons of Air" (which, we might recall, is the eagle's medium) are sublunary powers. They have their place and function, but they cannot stand before the clarity of "Heav'ns high noon." As soon as Amariel reminds them of their place, they instantly recognize and acknowledge his superiority to them and the justice of his right to govern them:

> **Dam.** Thou, Prince of day, from Elements are free,
> And I all body when compar'd to thee,
> Thou tread'st the Abyss of light!
> And where it streams with open eyes canst go:
> We wander in the Fields of Air below;
> Changlings and Fools of Heav'n.
>
> . . . .
>
> Gross-heavy-fed, next man in ignorance and sin.
> [IV, i, 173-80]

When the masque has ended a new platform has been built from which the dialectic of acts 4 and 5 will arise. The question that sets the new dialectic into operation is this: Having seen and recognized heavenly truth expressed in a revelation, how does a man achieve it? The play answers: by espousing it whatever the cost. St. Catherine,

"Heav'n's Embassadour," brings the same truth to each of the characters in a formula appropriate to the spiritual condition he or she figures: we must look beyond the goods of this world, and without rejecting this life, we must understand and govern it by reference to a higher, metaphysical order. Once again, the progressive definition mounts by degrees. Maximin, the ferocious monarch of the world is admonished to fix his course by the steady light of eternal truth:

> **S. Cath.** But, when you place your joy on things above,
> You fix the wand'ring planet of your Love.
>
> . . . .
>
> Poor humane kind all daz'd in open day,
> Erre after bliss and blindly miss their way
> The greatest happiness a Prince can know—
> Is to love Heav'n above, do good below.
>   [IV, i, 407-8; 410-13]

Berenice, a finer soul than Maximin's, finds the means to cross the barrier between worldly and eternal life that she had willed to break in act 3. She converts to that "Faith which . . . / Is Nobler than Purple Pageantry;" "which still with Nature is at strife, / And looks beyond it to a future life" (IV, i, 423; 426-28). Berenice's willingness to leave the world is a step up from Maximin's immersion in it. St. Catherine's is a step further upward still. She does not reject the world. Rather, the formula she offers is that honor is high, but faith is higher; life is good, but heaven is better:

> **S. Cath.**   I do not life despise;
> But as the greatest gift of Nature prize
>
> . . . .
>
> Were there no sting in death, for me to dye
> Would not be conquest, but stupidity.
> But if vain Honour can confirm the Soul
> And sense of shame the fear of death controul,
> How much more then should Faith uphold the Mind,
> Which, showing death, shows future life behind?
>   [IV, i, 519-20; 523-28]

St. Catherine directly expresses here an ethics redeemed, which she had espoused in her act 2 debate with Apollonius. Act 4 presents each of the characters with this choice between lesser and greater goods. One by one succeeding characters choose, and with each choice the concept is amplified and elevated. When Porphyrius rejects Maximin's offer of the succession, he rejects empire in the world and is freed from his bond of loyalty to Maximin. When Placidus allows Porphyrius to escape, he risks his own life and the life of his most treasured good, Valeria, and he thereby achieves the ideal of perfect generosity. Berenice chooses to lose her own life and the life of Porphyrius, her greatest good, to save the life of the tyrant she hates, and thereby achieves the ideal of Christian love. St. Catherine's choice is, of course, the hardest. She must choose between the purest of earthly loves, love for a mother who has given her life and has preserved her, and loyalty to the fate heaven has decreed for her.

> **S. Cath.** Thus my last duty to you let me pay. [*Kissing her*]
> Yet Tyrant I to thee will never pray.
> Though hers to save I my own life would give,
> Yet by my sin, my Mother shall not live.
> [V, i, 280-84]

Once again, the formula figured by St. Catherine grants that the best good in this life is good and demands a due regard, but that the good of heaven is better. St. Catherine does not reject the claims of her mother's love; rather, she becomes the means by which the idea of death is transformed so that her mother can accept it. After the revelatory miracle, Felicia acknowledges the claim of a truth above life. St. Catherine will not even permit anger or hatred of Maximin to soil her royal entry into heaven: "No streak of blood (the reliques of the Earth) / Shall stain my Soul in her immortal birth; / But she shall mount all pure, a white, and Virgin mind; / And full of all that peace, which there she goes to find" (V, i, 347-50). The angel's descent to destroy the torture wheel, like the masque of Amariel, renders a metaphysical truth emblematically. It asserts the idea that though the human body cannot escape its final fate, the soul that has chosen and fixed its sight upon transcendent good is permitted by the intercession of divine grace to enter heaven in its own resplendently heroic way.

After St. Catherine's death Maximin descends lower and lower. From a figure of irregular but heroic greatness, he becomes a ludicrous figure of evil, a medieval Herod. For example, when Berenice from the scaffold forgives him, he jeers, "How much to piety she is inclin'd / Behead her while she's in so good a mind" (V, i, 429-30). To Valeria's goodness his response is even more preposterous, the satirically exaggerated, topsy-turvy attitude of an Addams family father: "Away thou shame and slander of my blood / Who taught you to be pitiful or good" (V, i, 518-19). At Valeria's suicide he becomes the open foe of the gods, but his challenge to them is rendered in mock-heroic style. "Did I molest your Heav'n?" he asks, and he accuses them of greedily lapping up his incense offerings without suitable payment. Finally, he not only kills Placidus but, like a recalcitrant tantrum child, insists upon sitting on the corpse. That Maximin should fall from heroic, if limited, power to grotesque, mock-heroic self-parody is completely consistent within the ideological structure of the play. In killing St. Catherine he has murdered the only idea of transcendent beauty that his matter-bound spirit was capable of receiving, and once a soul has lost *all* contact with the ideal, it is condemned beyond even the darkness and confusion of this world to a hell of spiritual deformity and burlesque.

As I hope that this examination of the play has shown, the movement of *Tyrannick Love* does not depend upon what its dramatis personae do—indeed, they *do* almost nothing. It is an error to think of them as "characters" in the twentieth-century sense of the term. They are, rather, constantly changing, grouping and regrouping *positions* in a continuous dialectic; as Anne Barbeau Gardiner observed, they are "simply the best or most efficient means of expressing certain concepts."[14] Character figures concept, and as *characterization* it is not complex. As concept, however, it is quite complex, and the conceptual design is as full of subtle nuance and delicate ambiguity as the heart of a critic could wish. When we erroneously think that this play or any play of the 1660s is an imitation of experiential reality, however heightened, we make nonsense of it. When we expect of it a mode of characterization it never intended (thinking, for example, as one critic does, that "So long as the heroic play insisted on creating archetypal figures of will, there could be little in the way of memorable characterization")[15] we miss the point. For instance, if we do not understand the confrontation between Amariel and the Daemons of Air as an emblematic expression and an important conceptual crux in a pattern of ideational definition, then the scene must appear to us to be pseudo-epic fluff, an ornamental excrescence. Or if we think of Maximin as a character in the modern sense and try to investigate his "motivations," we can make sense neither of his ascent to the borderlands of heaven on the wings of heroic love nor of his fall into mock-heroic self-parody. And surely, if we do not recognize that St. Catherine is an *Idea* of the redeemed human spirit, a concept that moves within a gridwork of concepts, we must find her altogether unacceptable. In "real life," as well as in the dramatic imitation of it, one who buys classy martyrdom at the expense of watching her mother torn to gobbets by an infernal machine is not a saint but a monster, and only the most tinpot of little Godots would send an angel to melt a torture wheel merely to prevent the exposure of a maidenly bosom.

Not only are there no "characters" in *Tyrannick Love*, there is also no heroine. When we think of St. Catherine as the heroine and Maximin as the villain, we reduce a quite complex conceptual design to a simplistic, melodramatic absurdity. Moreover, Berenice, Porphyrius, Apollonius, Placidus—even Charinus—are as important within this conceptual design as St. Catherine and Maximin are. They are not extras; they are equally central to the meaning of the play because meaning here rests in ideational structure. We can think of *Tyrannick Love* as a dramatic imitation of exaggeratedly heightened "real life" only if we are willing to think of the greatest critic of the age (in some areas, of any age) as a moral idiot or a lunatic. Geoffrey Marshall is quite right, I think, in arguing that the difficulty faced by modern criticism in its approach to Restoration drama is that we have lost the key to perception. Because our consciousness really *is* different from the consciousness of 1660 or 1670, in reading the plays we accept the "sign for the substance."[16] For the drama of the 1660s I would agree with Marshall's notion that a play was designed upon "divisions and dichotomies of an abstract kind" and that "these divisions, contrasts and pairs are signs and not things signified."[17]

My interpretation differs from Marshall's in three respects. First, I do not believe that this level of abstraction in imitation extends beyond the 1670s, and even in the seventies abstraction is put to a quite different, new use. Second, I do not believe, as Marshall does, that sign in this drama signifies *emotions within* characters. Rather, as I have argued, characters are themselves signs of abstract qualities. Finally, I do not believe that dramatic imitation of Idea is limited to the serious drama (a term I am not sure is useful for plays written before 1680). In the preface to *Tyrannick Love* Dryden tells us that his aim is to elevate our minds by "the Harmony of words." He said elsewhere that this was Shakespeare's intention as well: "the raising of Shakespeare's passions are from the excellency of his words and thoughts."[18] We ought to accept him at his word. If, rather than demanding of the drama of this time a conception of imitation incongruent with its intention, we are receptive to it on its own terms, we can recapture the key to perception that we have lost. The reward, as John Loftis has shown us, is that we gain better access not only to the works of art themselves but to the aesthetic and epistemological consciousness of the age in which they were written: "If we conceive of history as a dialogue, as the meeting place between a modern intelligence and a body of material surviving from an earlier time, the plays assume importance because they are, unlike such forms of evidence as vital statistics and tax reports, not merely the raw material for historical judgment, but are, within the changing conventions of drama, themselves judgments."[19]

The controversy between Dryden and Robert Howard on the suitability of rhyme in drama has led many critics to assume that by rejecting rhyme Howard was advocating a closer imitation of actuality. Thus Pendlebury concludes: "This [Howard's position] is the argument of the so-called realist, which is based on the delusion that art is the attempt to imitate life by faithfully copying its superficial aspect in detail."[20] But Howard was by no means a realist. He rejects rhyme not because it makes speech improbable but because, used throughout a play, it can restrict or inhibit the very elevation to Idea that we have been discussing. Howard's rejection of the rules is precisely an attack upon probabilism. Among the rules advocates, he says, "that is concluded most natural which is most probable." This view is in error, he argues, "for all being impossible, they are none of them nearest the truth . . . for Impossibilities are all equal and admit of no degrees."[21]

In Howard's view dramatic imitation is not to copy the random variety and vagary of the phenomenal world but to design a coherent image of abstract truth, the form of an idea of greatness: "I dispute not but the Variety of the World may afford pursuing Accidents of . . . different Natures; but yet though possible in themselves to be, they may not be so proper to be Presented; an entire Connexion being the natural Beauty of all Plays; and Language the Ornament to dress them in, which in serious Subjects ought to be great and easie, like a high-born Person that expresses Greatness without pride or affectation."[22] Howard scornfully rejects accidents of fortune or the probabilities of life as the stuff of novels; he dismisses Spanish plays on the grounds that, like novels, they are inclined to imitate actuality. "The Spanish Plays . . . indeed are not much, being nothing but so many Novels put into Acts and Scenes, without the least attempt or design of making the Reader more concerned than a well-told Tale might do; whereas *a Poet that endeavors not to heighten the Accidents which Fortune seems to scatter in a well-knit Design,* had better have told his tale by a Fire-side, than presented it on a Stage" (italics mine).[23] For Howard, to imitate nature is to imitate a coherent design of ideas in a mounting progression of definition that achieves in its conclusion the Idea of Glory. Love and honor are the channels through which this ideational design flows. Rhyme is *used* when it facilitates, and is *abandoned* when it impedes, the upward movement of progressive definition.

Moreover, Howard employs this dramatic method in all his plays, making no distinction between comedy and tragedy. *The Duke of Lerma,* for instance, is called a tragedy, but it has no deaths and has a "happy ending." *The Indian Queen* (which bears so close a resemblance in design to Howard's other plays and is yet so typical of Dryden's practice in the sixties that it seems irrelevant to our discussion to whose canon we assign it) is called a tragedy on the title page.

The Surprisal provides an interesting example of the uncertainty of generic categorization in the sixties. It is called a comedy on its title page, but the typical sixties' comic structure, the three-tiered division into high-middle-low, is very faint in it, indeed is not much stronger than the faint shadow of demarcation that we find even in a "serious" play like *Tyrannick Love.* Low figures are not mock-heroic parodies but "naturals," too weighed down by matter to bear the impress of love or honor:

Bran. Only the obeying part of Man
    Observe the rules of Honour in their Friendship
                                        [I, i]
    Would any woman be so simple to refuse me?
                                        [I, i]

On the high plane, which comprises much the dominant part of the
design, heroic debate on the nicer points of friendship, love, and
honor are conducted with the same exquisite refinement that we find
in *The Indian Queen*. This example substantiates the point that
generic category is not an essential determinant of meaning in plays
of the sixties, because whether they are tragedy, comedy, tragicomedy, or declared heroic drama, the object of dramatic composition in them is equally the imitation of *a design of ideas*, an abstract,
ideational conception of reality, or "nature."

I chose Sir Robert Howard for illustration because he has so often
been thought a "realist" and because he himself makes the point most
forcefully in his criticism and, in one particularly interesting instance, in his practice.

In his prefatory epistle to *The Duke of Lerma* (1668), Howard says,
"In difference of *Tragedy* and *Comedy*, and of *Farce* itself, there can be
no determination but by Taste; nor in the manner of their Composure."[24] This radical statement places the burden of the play's
meaning on the understanding of its audience. And as we have seen
above, according to Howard, it is by means of a "well-knit Design"
that the playwright lifts his audience's understanding to an apprehension of "Greatness." It follows that this playwright, whom we
have been led by the rhyme controversy to consider a realist and the
theoretical adversary of Dryden, has as his object in dramatic imitation precisely the same aim that we have seen realized in *Tyrannick
Love*. Howard's compositional method, too, is the same. Nowhere is
this more evident than in *The Vestal Virgin* (1665), a play that to my
mind offers strong evidence that the imitation of Idea is transgeneric
in the sixties. Alternate tragic and comic endings were written for
the play, and, interestingly enough, either ending completes its
conceptual design and meaning with equal facility.

The Vestal Virgin is structured, as a Caroline love and honor play
is, around pairs of lovers who figure various aspects of love and
honor; for example, Hersilia and Tiridates are images of fixed, or

stable, reason-ruled love and honor, while Sertorius and Messalina are love and honor in a more passion-driven guise, and Vergenis and Artibaces are figures of purity and innocence. However, the Caroline evaluative gradation of love is absent here. The figures are only vestigally higher and lower kinds of love. Their primary function is to serve as counters within a variety of love and honor debates. Processes of definition rather than a scaled degree among characters distinguish among and evaluate the various kinds of love presented. And here, as in *Tyrannick Love*, the debates taken together comprise a larger dialectic that constitutes the movement of the play. Each debate is a segment that sets, challenges, and redefines an idea, or a step, within the greater design of progressive definition. For example, Sertorius's passion is challenged by Sulpitius's reason. The nature and operation of that passion is declared, and then a point of honor—obedience to the will of the beloved—is set in antagonistic relation to it, which modifies and redirects the passion:

> **Sulp.** These starts are the Convulsions of weak Reason
> When fits of passion grow too strong upon you.
> We have all our haggard Passions, but none so wild
> Or so unman'd as yours—
> **Sert.** Without your Similie I will endeavor to endure it,— But—
> **Sulp.** But what?
> **Sert.** I find a mutiny in all my Faculties,
> That will not yield to this cessation:
> My tongue seems to consent without Commission;
> But I'll go wrangle with myself,
> And will obey her—if I can—
>   [I, i]

Or Sulpitius sets his too narrowly defined (and therefore false) standard of an honor dictated by love as the *ground* upon which a debate between Tiridates and Sertorius springs up that enlarges upon and elevates the original conception:

> **Sulp.** That mighty rate which nicely you assign
> Your love and honor, I have fixed on mine.
>   [I, i]

In arguing about who shall accept Sulpitius's challenge and duel with him for love of Hersilia, Sertorius and Tiridates conduct a debate that

brings their antithetic dialectical positions together and, by redefin-
ing the relation of love to honor, enlarges and elevates the Sulpitius
conception to a more refined idea of heroic love:

> **Sert.** [*to Tirid.*] Brave Prince, with your fair temper I am brought
> To reason, by a Rival's Friendship taught;
> Had you or I sunk under t'others hate,
> The living would have pittied his hard fate.
> Though love condemns, our grief may be the same
> For death's all one brought by a Sword or Flame;
> T'were mean if love had not the pow'r to shew
> That gen'rous grief which honour can bestow.
> Why shoul'd the steps rais'd by our honour prove
> Too hard to be ascended by our love?
>
> [I, i]

Reason and heroic friendship modify passionate courage and love
(the Sulpitius position) and, in doing so, redefine heroic love. Hon-
or, the gift to aspiring minds from above, makes love a vehicle to
glory. By this compositional method the movement of the play
proceeds, in an always ascending progression, within the framework
of rhetorical debate. Rhyme is used, not when it is appropriate to the
person who speaks, but when it is appropriate to the conception that
is delineated in his speech. For example, the first of Sertorius's
speeches quoted above ("Without your similie, I will endeavor . . .")
is not in rhyme because the passion delineated is rebellious against
honor, while the second ("Brave Prince . . .") is in rhyme because
heroic love must be regulated and tempered by honor. Characters are
constantly regrouping positions within one or another rhetorical
movement that contributes to the pattern of meaning. Sulpitius is
not a villain; that is, he is not an evil "man." Rather, he is the figure of
a false conception of love, false because it is untempered by right
honor. Messalina describes Sulpitius's false honor as the cause and
condition of his false, earth-bound love: "In such mean paths as
cous'ning Statesmen move / To walk in greatness, others tread to
love; / Both creep upon the strength of fawning lyes, / And on Men's
blasted fames attempt to rise" (I, i).
    A "tragic" ending does not in any way impede the mounting
progression of ideas that dictates the structure and meaning of the
play, for "Death reconciles the World's and Nature's Strife, / And is a

part of Order and of Life" (II, i). In the tragic ending Messalina and
Sertorius die united and therefore triumphant. As in *Tyrannick Love*
death is conceived as a threshold and not an end. The alternative
ending—as "it was Acted the Comical Way: the Alteration beginning
in Act IV toward the latter end after the words, / And injur'd Love"
(p. 194)—merely extends the debate and brings a greater number of
figures across the threshold by the only other method of crossing:
conversion to a higher ideal. Sertorius vows to love Messalina in an
encomium exchange on constancy and love. Corbulo is so impressed
by the increasingly extravagant love vows of Vergenia and Artibaces
that he turns back from blinding Artibaces and joins forces with him.
Sulpitius once again falsely defines the relation between love and
honor—that is, he fights Tiridates to show Hersilia that he deserves
her: "Love's Thrones by Conquest are made good, / Like Empire
where there is no claim in Blood" (IV, i). When Tiridates, having
conquered Sulpitius, spares him because Sulpitius was once his
friend, the right relation of honor to love is restored and Sulpitius is
converted. Tiridates demonstrates that the refusal to fight, when it is
demanded by honor, is a truer sign of love than mere courage is.
Honor corrects love, and conversely a form of love, friendship, is the
right guide of honor. Honor, now rightly defined and powerful, kills
Sulpitius's love for Hersilia: "That Life thou giv'st is Death unto my
Love."

In the sixties, then, the difference between "tragical" and
"comical" seems to rest in whether death or ideological conversion is
the occasion of transition to a metaphysical realm. Either does
equally well, for the transcendence is not of characters but of ideas,
and the vehicle is not action but language. As Margaret Cavendish
observed: "The true Comedy is pure Love and Humours. . . . And
right Tragi-comedies are the descriptions of the Passions which are
created in the Soul; And a right Tragedy is intermixt with the
Passions, Appetites and Humours of men, with the influence of
outward actions, accidents and misfortunes."[25] Ideas of the passions
are the subject, focus, and vehicle of all plays. Kinds of ideas will
dominate in one or another genre, but actions or events are at best an
occasion for, or a momentary obstacle to, the movement of ideas.

Margaret Cavendish might well have been expected to be a proba-
bilist, since she was a luminary in the Newcastle group of intellec-

tuals who were largely responsible for bringing Epicurean and
Gassendist ideas into English intellectual life in the sixties. If any
playwright or critic of the decade ought to have advocated imitation
of the actual in drama, it is she. Therefore, when we find her
describing dramatic writing as the imitation of ideas, we must
assume that such an understanding of the nature of drama was deeply
ingrained and almost unconsciously held. In the epilogue "Letter to
Readers," which Cavendish appends to her volume of plays, she
says, "Writing is a pencilling of thoughts, and I take as much delight
as Painters, which draw men, and other creatures; so I too draw my
fancies opinions and conceptions upon white Paper, with Pen and
Ink, words being the figures of thoughts . . . writing is but figuring
of the figure, and Writers are but Copiers."[26]

As a playwright Cavendish is a strong contender for worst in the
tradition; her plays, quite justly, were never performed. But she is a
thinker of some stature, and even her mockery of the popular
practice of her time is enlightening. It provides us with a valuable
insight into the way that dramatic imitation of nature was conceived
in the sixties: "I expect my Playes will be found fault with, by reason
I have not drawn the several persons presented in a Circular line, or a
Triangular point, making all the Actors to meet at the latter end upon
the Stage in a flock together."[27]

Whatever their faults, her plays do not fail because they are not
sufficiently abstract. Bad as they are, we can learn from them—in
fact, bad plays, because they are so obviously constructed, are often
quite good guides to the method of composition that obtains in
good, more subtly complex plays. If we need confirmation that in
the 1660s character is concept, structure is dialectical debate moving
in ascending progression to ideal truth, and dramatic imitation of
ideas is transgeneric, we need only to examine Cavendish's *Youth's
Glory and Death's Banquet* (1662). Characters are crude personifica-
tions of ideas: Lord de L'amour, Sir Thomas Father Love, The Lady
Incontinent, Lady Contemplation, and Lady Sanspareille. The action, or, in Dryden's more precise term, the occasion, that sets the
long series of debates that comprises the structure of the play is Lady
Sanspareille's decision not to marry but to pursue glory through
study and contemplation. She is supported by her father, Sir Thomas
Father Love, while her mother, Lady Mother Love, attempts to

thwart her out of envy of her learning. Cavendish had no regard
whatever for conventional dramatic structure. She scorns to be
bound to the limits of five acts, even as she scorns the triangles and
circles of formal structure that she says are demanded by the pedantic
critics. Act and scene divisions are purely arbitrary and in this play
she stacks acts of different length upon one another to a total of about
ten. Most significant here, however, is that this maverick playwright, who defies all convention and is led only by the "pleasure"
her "mind takes in creating of Fancies, as Nature to create and
dissolve and create creatures anew,"[28] builds into her play the heroic
mounting progression of ideas and the three-tiered comic structures
that are typical in dramatic imitation and composition in the sixties.
For example, on the high plane Lady Sanspareille pursues heroic
glory: "My dear Father, know it is fame I covet, for which were the
ambitions of Alexander the Great and Caesar joyned [*sic*] into one
mind, mine doth exceed them, as far as theirs exceeded humble
spirits" (I, p. 130). She mounts to glory in a series of lectures and
debates before ever more elevated audiences on ever more exalted
subjects. Her subjects are, indeed, rungs on a ladder of progressive
definition, rising from nature, to the passions, to the arts of oratory
and poetry, to war and heroic exploit. Lady Sanspareille achieves
glory when she addresses the Queen (Majesty) on the subject of
justice, after which she dies. On the middle plane Lady Incontinent
has left her husband, "who was rich and used [her] well. All for love
of [Lord de L'amour] and with him live[s] as a Wanton." Interestingly, the low plane encounters between Sir Golden Riches and
Moll Meanbred, his country wench paramour, exactly parody in
mock-heroic style the high plane *literary* imaginings of Lady Contemplation: a host of ideal, heroic lovers engaged in continuous
romantic debate that flood her "Fancy."

What does the appearance of these structures indicate? I maintain
that, when a playwright as firmly in revolt against the standard
conventions and practices of her day as Cavendish was, nevertheless
produces dramatic imitations of ideas arranged in prototypical designs, we must conclude that the notion that drama imitates the
shape of ideal reality was a deeply held aesthetic assumption at the
time. Furthermore, when an average member of the audience reports seeing this same imitation of ideas in plays, we have further

evidence that in the 1660s a perceptual set existed that was radically different from our own. Whereas in *The Conquest of Granada* we see persons like ourselves who are motivated by feelings somewhat exotic and extravagant but recognizably similar to our own inner emotions and who are awkwardly speaking a lot of fustian in verse, we must believe that a Mrs. Evelyn saw what she says she saw in this play: "I have seen 'The Seige of Grenada,' a play so *full* of ideas that the most refined romance I ever read is not to compare with it; *love* is made so *pure* and *valour* so *nice*, that one would imagine it *designed for an Utopia* rather than our stage. I do not quarrel with the poet, but admire one born in the decline of morality should be able to *feign such exact virtue.*"[29] Mrs. Evelyn saw exactly what bad playwrights (like Cavendish) and good playwrights (like Dryden) expected her to see: images of love, valor, and virtue that could transport her to Utopia. We must accept that audiences really perceived exhilarating "Images of virtue," "Characters of Love and Friendship," and "Figures of [the] Minde"[30] in plays that bore us to distraction, like those of William Killigrew; the weight of evidence will not permit us to believe otherwise.

C.S. Lewis once said,

Lovers, unless their love is very short-lived, again and again feel an element not only of comedy, not only of play, but even of buffoonery, in the body's expression of Eros. And the body would frustrate us if this were not so. It would be too clumsy an instrument to render love's music unless its very clumsiness could be felt as adding to the total experience its own grotesque charm—a sub-plot or antimasque miming with its own rough-and-tumble what the soul enacts in statelier fashion. . . . The highest does not stand without the lowest. There is indeed at certain moments a high poetry in the flesh itself; but also, by your leave, an irreducible element of obstinate and ludicrous unpoetry.[31]

Lewis's vision of love—the body miming what the soul enacts in stately fashion, its very clumsiness adding a grotesque charm to the total experience—perfectly captures comic form as it was conceived in the 1660s. The distress of critics like Hume who find the structure "hip-hop" and "schizophrenic" arises largely from their misapprehension of it. Modern critics are pleased by what they mistake for an imitation of familiar experience in the plays—the middle plane of action and confusion—and they take that plane, which is a necessary part but, nonetheless, only a part, to be the center of meaning. Consequently, they are led to think that the rarefied love-and-honor debates of the high plane are either vestigial Caroline baggage that the playwright was not clever enough to discard or evidence of poetic schizophrenia. If the body and the world are there, what need, they think, for the stately, old-fashioned postures of the spirit? But in the comedy of the 1660s, and even in the satire of the seventies that derives from it, the rarefied realm of the spirit is essential. As much as tragedy or heroic drama, comedy imitates Idea. It designs a shape of reality whole; it does not copy fragments of the phenomenal world. "The language [of comedy at this time] does not characteristically seem to express movement or change. The components of experience seem fixed and discrete. The sense of experience expressed by the language appears to be more a matter of 'being' than 'becoming.' . . . it is not a sensuous language. It is only sporadically interested in projecting the immediate and concrete surfaces of experience. As a rule it deliberately abstracts that level of experience into generalized classes and categories."[32]

Comic design figures a three-tiered microcosmic structure that brings high and low expressions of ideas of love into concordance. We find in comic designs the same planes of matter and spirit that we found in *Tyrannick Love*, but in comedy they are not set in antithetic relation as they are in the heroic structure, nor are they conceived as upward and downward distortions of the norms of nature in art's looking glass, as they will be in the satiric plays of the seventies. Rather, high, middle, and low are different keys in which love's melody is played to the creation of a cosmic *concordia*, an aesthetic conception that is not too far distant from the ways it was visualized in Renaissance imitation.[33]

A.C. Spearing, discussing parodic miming and linkage between Chaucer's high romance *Knight's Tale* and the low Miller's fabliau that is its structural rejoinder, makes some interesting points about contrasts that are essential in comedy.[34] In the romance, he says, we never *see things*. Palemon and Arcite fight, of course, but they are emblematic knights on a tournament field set in no space. We do not even know what the beauty they fight to win looks like; all that is said of Emilie is that she is slim and has yellow hair. Moreover, we watch these figures forming their triad somewhere off in the middle distance, from a detached vantage, like Theseus. On the other hand, the Miller's Alisoun, the carpenter's wife and ladylove of hendy Nicholas and not so hendy Absalon, is described piece by piece. Not only do we know what her eyes, lips, hair, and rosy cheeks look like, but every item of her dress and the material of which it is made is described for us as if by a fourteenth-century *Vogue*. The carpenter's house is full of things. We know its buckets, basins, stools, and lavours. We have measured it in inches from crossbeams to infamous windowsill. This twinning of sheer spirit and its necessary counterpart, the clattering, cluttering world of things, is the master stroke of a comic poet. A complex comic design sweeps body and soul, mind and matter, tinted-wash landscapes and attics full of stuff into one generous embrace. It celebrates high and low, and mocks each by reference to the other without denying the validity or the charm of either.

Etherege's *The Comicall Revenge: or, Love in a Tub* is such a design.[35] The prologue, like countless other prologues, prefaces, and commendatory verses of the decade, acknowledges as the play's predecessors "Fletcher's Nature" and "The Art of Ben." We might think of these as the keys in which the melody is played. On the high plane "Fletcher's Nature" prevails. In the middle distance, in a pastoral atmosphere like that of *The Faithful Shepherdess*, the stately motions of the soul are executed in figures of valor, courage, and constancy. Characters speak exclusively in verse. The formal patterns of their rhetoric are the focus of our interest and the medium by which movement is effected. Action is a meek handmaiden to rhetoric, and scene is all but effaced. We could as well be in Arcadia as in London, and, in fact, a "bower" is handily ready for purposes of retreat and solo love-lament. Formulae are paired and repaired, aligned and realigned: constancy and courage, passion and duty, love and honor. The familiar ascending pattern of definition in debate is argued until the figures who have been tangled in improper relation—Aurelia in love with Bruce in love with Gratiana in love with Beaufort, and so forth—are sorted out and have achieved positions in the dialectic worthy the crown of heroic love. The most tumultuous passions are declared in the most restrained couplets: "My Passions grow unruly, and I find / Too soon they'll raise a tempest in my Mind" (III, iv).

The whole upper tier of this wedding cake could be detached and inserted into *The Vestal Virgin, The Siege of Urbin,* or *Juliana* without the slightest emendation were it not for the intricacy with which it is fitted to Ethrege's embracing comic design. Played by themselves the movements of the high plane are indistinguishable from heroic tragedy or tragicomedy. When these same ideas are replayed on the middle plane (in Sir Frederick Frolick's bizarre push-me-pull-you pursuit of the Widow Rich) and on the low plane (in the grotesque high jinks of a man and a maid and a mercury tub), the ideas of love and honor are not canceled out. They are enriched in texture and made more complex as well as funny.

Bruce, a Herculean hero, has just returned from a war so remote that it could as well be the Trojan as the Dutch, where he has done deeds of astonishing valor and greatness. In his absence Aurelia, who loves him, has been his advocate in wooing her sister, Graciana, whom he loves but who does not love him. In vain has she suppressed her own passion and pleaded his cause as the rightful claim of heroic valor upon beauty with her sister. In her bower retreat Aurelia argues with herself the warring claims of passion, will, and constancy in high romantic strain:

> **Aur.** With curious diligence I still have strove
> During your absence, Bruce, to breath your love
> Into my Sister's bosom; but the fire
> Wants force: Fate does against my breath conspire:
> I have obey'd, though I cannot fulfill
> Against my self the dictates of your will.
> My love to yours does yield; since you enjoin'd,
> I hourly court my rival to be kind.
>
> [I, iv]

Heroic love and valor appear quite differently on the middle plane. Here we are *located* in present time and familiar space—in the dear, damned, distracting Town. Sir Frederick, suffering not the pangs of unrequited passion but the mundane discomfort of a crashing hangover, acknowledges to his own maid, Betty, the justice of the anger aimed at him by his beloved's maid, Jenny. (There are, of course, no maids on the high plane. In its passage through the Caroline period the Fletcherian love scale acquired class stratification.)

Sir Fred. In a word, rambling last Night, we knock'd at her Mistress's
Lodging; They denid us entrance, whereupon a harsh Word or two flew
out, "Whore," I think, or Something to the purpose.
Maid. These were not all your Heroick actions. Pray tell the Consequence,
how you march'd Bravely at the rere of an Army of Link-boys; Upon the
sudden, how you gave Defiance, and then wag'd a bloody war with the
Constable; and having vanquish'd that Dreadful enemy, how you com-
mitted a general Massacre on the glass windows: Are not these Most
honorable achievements, such as will be Register'd to your eternal Fame
by the most Learn'd Historians of Hicks's-Hall. [I, ii]

This mock-heroic banter underscores the relation of high to low
planes. In the descent from the plane of spirit to the plane of the
world, Idea cannot maintain stability or clarity. Besieged towns
become ladies' lodgings, heroic challenges turn into Billingsgate, the
hero of irregular greatness gets lost in his irregularity and follows the
light of his linkboys instead of glory's flame, and if he is deprived of
his lady, he makes do with her maid. There is no fiercer opponent
than the Constable, and the hero breaks through no more formidable
barriers than glass windows. The topsy-turvydom is wonderfully
funny, but it is also serious in the manner of comic seriousness. Man
is a fierce spirit yearning for transcendence; but man is also an ass
yoked to the bewildering mill of the world, a place full of things that
clutter his way and deflect and confuse the direction of his energies.

One step down, on the low plane, the yoke is a mercury tub, and
the poor ass is a diseased, ignorant alien, so far stuck in the mud of
unpoetry that he cannot pronounce a proper English sentence, the
butt of even Betty the maid. I am not suggesting that the valet in the
mercury tub or the gull, Sir Nicholas Cully, are to be pitied. God
forbid! Pity in comedy is one of the more regrettable aberrations in
taste that resulted from inner space exploration at the *end* of the
century. Comic design in the sixties joyfully celebrates man the ass,
man the fool, and man the heroic aspirant to greatness. I cannot agree
with John Barnard that Etherege's purpose is to mock a dying
aristocratic idealism. "The divorce between the actual and the myth-
ic" that Barnard finds is, in my judgment, a requirement in satire, the
dominant mode of the seventies, but even in seventies' satire the
divorce is a necessity of the specific generic form, satire.[36] It is never
the statement of a personal, political, or sociological position. Car-

icature and parody depend upon idealism. *La bête nature* reflects
downward in the same mirror that holds the contrastive image of *la
belle nature*; otherwise, a comic or satiric work of art would not be
funny, indeed, would not have meaning.

However, comedy weds where satire divorces. In *Love in a Tub* the
low plane does not undercut the high. On the contrary, the two plots
are barely related: Sir Frederick is the friend and cousin of Beaufort.
In the dueling scene, the one place where they do touch, the high-
plane figures, by the same exquisite ethical calculus that dominates
in Orrery's *The General*, for instance, realize that they cannot fight,
because each must give due honor to the heroic nature of his rival; the
low-plane characters also cannot fight because Sir Nicholas Cully's
cowardice will not let him. Low plane does not undercut high but
replays it. And the same pattern holds throughout the play. The very
same conceptions—love, honor, boundary-breaking spirit, and
so on—are played in three different modes: straight, upside-down,
and inside-out; or ideal, real, and mock-heroic; or Arcadia, Upstairs,
and Downstairs.

I have chosen *Love in a Tub* to illustrate the three-tiered dramatic
design for the same reason that I chose *Tyrannick Love* to illustrate the
design of mounting progression, because it etches a prototype so
strongly that we cannot fail to see its contours. Both patterns are
deeply embedded in the consciousness of playwrights and audiences
of the sixties. We find them everywhere in the plays, sometimes
lightly sketched and at other times more obviously present. We find
them as the deep structure in plays we have been led to think are
different in kind from one another, like Tuke's *Adventures*, Howard's
The Women's Conquest, Behn's *The Amorous Prince*, and Rhodes's
Flora's Vagaries. Moreover, the mounting progression design and the
three-tiered design are not mutually exclusive, nor is their use confined to one or another genre. Howard's *The Women's Conquest*, for
instance, is indistinguishable from *Tyrannick Love* in method, style,
and structure. Usually the patterns appear in combination. In Tuke's
Adventures, for example, the heroic design is overwhelmingly pre-
dominant, but the two lower planes—located in time and space,
wherein heroic ideals are distorted or used to antiheroic ends—form
equally necessary parts of the whole ideational structure.

The Adventures of Five Hours (1663) was recognized by contemporary audiences as a dramatic imitation of Idea. In one of the four commendatory poems that preface the second edition of the play, John Long says that Tuke "With Fletcher's Nature, Learned Jonson's Art / Of others to the more Transcendent part" has "new Perfections into Praecept brought."[37] He exclaims in admiration, "What Figures of things rare! how well design'd!" Evelyn understands the play as a soaring flight beyond the limits of the world that not only imitates heroic transcendence but is itself a heroic act of imagination:

> The Fates do limits to each thing dispense,
> To Poets rage, to Arms, to Eloquence!
> Thus Learn'd Greece, and the more Polish'd Rome,
> Had bounds like Seas; Hitherto shall ye come,
> And hitherto our Stage; Olympus top
> Who has once gain'd (which does the Heavens prop)
> Can soar no Higher! Your head has brush'd the Sphears.[38]

Just as the heroic conceptual progression to metaphysical truth was immediately apparent to contemporary audiences, so also was the wedding of high and low planes. The Jonson key was as audible to them as the Fletcher, and the whole was recognizable as a microcosmic shape of reality:

> . . . as from th' Elements contrariety
> Almighty Nature forms a harmony;
> So by the Magick of your Artful Muse,
> You from your Rivals discords do produce
> . . . delightful concord.[39]

Furthermore, those audiences that kept the play running for so long knew that the medium by which they were transported to such heights, to the apprehension of "Figures of things rare" and microcosmic shapes of reality, was language: "Language, [that] with her powerfull'st influence / Instills herself into the ravish'd sense."[40]

On the high plane the *Adventures*, like *Love in a Tub*, refines upon the nicer points of love and honor by the usual dialectic juxtaposition. Restraining himself from killing Octavio, Antonio declares for honor: "Passion [ne'er] could deter Antonio / From the strict rules of Honour" (V, i). But then, executing the kind of delicately balanced turn demanded by high-plane linguistic ballet, he immediately prepares to kill Octavio for love's sake: "my Love now / Requires its Dues, as Honour has had his." Characters are counters used to discriminate between rightly and wrongly defined conceptions. Don Henrique figures wrongly defined heroic honor—cruelty and rage "Which he to palliate Vice with Virtue's name / Does Sense of Honour call" (I, i)—while his opposite, Don Carlos, figures true heroic generosity of spirit.

On the middle plane, the servants of Don Henrique and Don Antonio, closer to actuality by class and language, argue contemporary politics. The function of their topical, mildly satiric debates is to mock the Dutch, but it also clearly marks off an arena in which man is a poor creature, made up of "turf and butter," whose gross appetites and unreliable senses pervert his ideals:

Sylv. But, pr'ythee, Brother, instruct me a little.
Tell me, what kind of Country is this *Holland*
That's so much talk'd of, and so much fought for.
Ern. Why, Friend, 'tis a huge Ship at Anchor fraught.
With a sort of Creatures, made up of Turf and Butter.
Ped. I pray, Sir, what do they drink in that Country?

. . . .

Ger. A Nation sure of Walking Tuns; the World Has not the like.
Ger. [*sic*] What a God's name could come into the Heads of this People, to make them Rebell?
Ern. Why Religion, that come into their Heads A God's name.
Ger. But what a Devil made the Noble-men Rebel?
Ern. Why that which made the Devil himself Rebel, Ambition.   [I, i]

The style itself, especially in the comic reversals of the last seven lines above, delineates the reversal of ideals and values that governs in the middle-plane world of action.

The low plane stands in typical parodic relation to the high, though *The Adventures* does not exaggerate downward either as far or as obviously as *Love in a Tub* or *Youth's Glory and Death's Banquet* do. Diego and Flora translate high-plane self-sacrifice and heroic courage to self-love and mean self-interest, to mock-heroic effect.

Diego. . . . . there lives not in the world
A more valiant Man, than I, whilst Danger

Does keep its distance; but when sawcily
It presses on, then (I confess) 'tis true,
I have a certain Tenderness for Life
That checks my Ardor, and enclines my Prudence
Timely to withdraw.

[II, i]

Richard Rhodes's *Flora's Vagaries* (1670) is interesting for the
varieties it plays on the three-tiered structure that anticipate the
bilevel interplay of the seventies.[41] A three-tiered conceptual structure still informs the meaning of the play, but the planes are distinguished stylistically, as voices, rather than structurally as distinct
spheres. The figures are still scaled positions. Otrante figures love in
the high-plane style, and Lodovico, a Caroline soldier-who-has-
never-loved, figures harsh honor that must be transformed into
heroic honor by love. One level below them are Flora, the female
wit, and Alberto, the deep-drinking chaser of whores, who loves
Flora for her wit. At the nadir is the antilove, antihonor Sullen
Shepherd figure, Francisco, who hires bravos to ambush a rival
rather than fighting himself and who attempts to carry Otrante off
against her will. The positions are still distinct. The unusual feature
is that they operate on the same structural plane and even as opposing
voices within a single scene. For example, in act 1, scene 1, Otrante
laments her plight in typical high-plane romantic style, while Flora
sounds a middle-plane counterpoint:

Otr. Did'st thou but feel the burden of my woes, or could'st derive them
from the same Spring-head, thou would'st not laugh at, but assist my
Griefs, and help me raise them to a pitch of Wonder, so thou and I like two
forsaken Turtles, would sit enduring one another's sorrows.
Flo. . . . . Does not the old man plague me, and Ferret me about as much as
you? Yet I have no mind to be a Turtle, you had better be a Magpie and
chatter at him as I do.
Otr. O but he is not thy Father; mine he is, and piety forbids the breach of
duty: sure Justice has laid by her equal scales, to blend misfortunes thus
with Innocence, were but my Father's passions just, his anger I could
bear, like thee, and smile at, but to be guiltless and used thus, who can but
grieve? [I, i]

Interestingly, when Otrante falls in love and descends into the
world of action, her transition is marked stylistically:

Flo. Your Father stamps and stares and calls for you.
Otr. Why let him call on, and fume on, there's no great heed to be taken on't,
  do I speak right, *Flora?*
Flo. Most excellent. Where got you this spirit?
Otr. No matter, thou see'st I have it . . . I am like to prove a great Politician, I
  have designs afoot. [II, i]

The heroic/active/mock-heroic conceptual levels are still present
and still govern meaning. The centrally important matter is not what
Otrante does but the fact that she acts. The idea of a realm of action is
important, that is to say, but the nature of the actions performed or
the "motivation" of the characters who perform them is not.

In this play the mock-heroic level is also rendered in opposing
voices rather than on opposing structural planes. However, structural contrasts underline and reinforce what is rendered stylistically.
For example, act 2, scene 1, replays the act 1, scene 1, counterpoint of
Otrante and Flora in a lower register in the exchanges of the thieves:

Pes. . . . I that have been a Souldier,
Pie. And twice strappadod for running from your Colours
Pes. Would be ashamed.
Pie. To look the Enemie in the face.
Pes. To think of these poor trifles [which they are about to steal]. I do aim at
  something higher.
Pie. The Gallows, and may come to it.
Pes. For when I consider
Pie. How you will deserve it.
Pes. That men are born,
Pie. Sometimes to be hang'd
Pes. Mistake me not, to be Commanders of the World and Fortune too, I
  scorn to think of hunger, I trample upon cold.
Pie. That is you walk barefoot in the streets. [II, i]

As in act 1, scene 1, juxtaposition of high and low takes place within
the dialogue, but the structural juxtaposition of act 2 with act 1 also
contributes to a larger heroic/mock-heroic structural opposition.

Figures also move upward or downward from Idea to action. For
example, though Otrante moves from remote Arcadian lament,
drawn into action for love of Lodovico, this movement is a preparation for her reascent, which raises Lodovico's conception of honor to
a higher level. Because Lodovico has been a courageous soldier,

Otrante, with typical high-plane logic, expects him to be a heroic lover and assumes that the only reason he has not attained heroic love is that he has never seen ideal virtue.

> **Otr.** I thought you had been noble minded and not to have been won from the strict humour [refusal to love] but by the pitch of Vertue, which perhaps you thought none of us ever arrived at, and I resolv'd to show you I was Mistress of. (V, i)

He is, of course, converted by her speech. He sees her virtue (because she has declared it) and instantly loves. However (anticipating the seventies), as soon as the high lovers, each of whom has been drawn to love by the other's honor, have been united, the drunken Alberto stumbles on the scene singing, "He took her about the middle so small / And threw her on the ground."

Perhaps the most fertile ground for exploring and determining the nature of "nature" in dramatic imitation is the adaptation. A book like George R. Guffey's *After the Tempest* is invaluable not only for the information it provides but for the questions it raises for criticism, such questions as: Why is Prospero a weaker figure in the Dryden-Davenant adaptation than he is in the original? Why is Sebastian taken out of the play and Antonio changed? Why is the place from which Alonzo and Antonio are returning no longer a distant wedding but a famous heroic combat against the Moors in defense of Christianity? Tracing the play, as Guffey does,[42] enables us to see what adapters saw in it from decade to decade and by that means to catch perceptual set as it flies, so to speak. Such careful tracking raises the question of why the Dryden-Davenant adaptation, which was so successful in the sixties, was not presented unchanged in the seventies? What in the temper of the seventies caused the divorce in sensibility that produced in the very same year (1675) on the one hand the extravagant Operatic *Tempest*, and, on the other, Duffet's *Mock-Tempest*?

The Dryden-Davenant adaptations *Macbeth* and *The Enchanted Island* are particularly enlightening for a number of reasons.[43] First, both Davenant and Dryden were practical men of the theater and also sensitive critics and important theorists of drama. In part because we have lost the key to understanding seventeenth-century drama, we do not take seriously enough Davenant's theoretical speculations about what he was trying to do in his plays. We should remember that Hobbes, one of the most influential thinkers of the age, did do so. Secondly, what Davenant and Dryden saw in, or read into, Shakespeare is an even better indicator of their perceptual set than their own compositional methods or theoretical pronouncements are because it can reveal hidden aesthetic assumptions and prejudices that the two Restoration playwrights might not even have been aware of having.

The adapters of the sixties saw in the two plays the typical patterns we have been discussing, the heroic, mounting progression pattern and the three-tiered comic pattern that dominate drama in this decade. The emendations they made in Shakespeare's plays attempted to reveal these patterns more sharply. The Davenant-Dryden *Macbeth* shapes the heroic progression form, while *The Enchanted Island* is built upon a triple-planed structure.

Macbeth rises by careful dialectic juxtaposition to a full definition of heroic ambition, or glory. The adapters drastically reduce the cast to those figures who in themselves and in their placement with relation to each other represent the usual play upon ideas of love and valor: love that fosters honor in opposition to love that undermines honor; noble ambition against ignoble striving, and so forth. Five major passages are added: three new scenes of dialogue between the Macduffs, to balance against Shakespeare's dialogues between the Macbeths, and a passage between Lady Macbeth and Lady Macduff just before Lady Macbeth receives Macbeth's letter in act 1, which contrasts a self-effacing love that draws ambition to glory with a self-aggrandizing love that leads heroic aspiration to ruin. The dialogues between Macduff and his lady are the same kind of ethical debates we have observed in Tuke, Howard, and Dryden; their function is to refine upon ideas and to move the design upward on a conceptual scale:

> **Lady Macduff.** You, by your Pitty, which for us you plead
> Weave but Ambition of a finer thread [than Macbeth's]
> **Macduff.** Ambition do's the height of power affect
> My aim is not to Govern but Protect.
> [III, ii]

Because the adapters understand the function of Hecate and the witches to be the arousal of "wonder" in the minds of the audience, the better to prepare them to receive "ideas of greatness," these figures sound very much as though they might appear with equal facility in *The Enchanted Island*. They closely resemble the Daemons of Air in *Tyrannick Love*; like them, they are emblematic figures who inhabit a realm between earth and heaven, and their strain is pastoral:

> O What a dainty pleasure's this:
> To sail 'i th' Air while the Moon shines fair;
> To sing, to Toy, to Dance and kiss,
> Over Woods, high Rocks and Mountains
> Over hills and misty Fountains.
>   [III, viii]

As ludicrous as this seems to us, it did not seem so to the audience of 1666. Pepys writes of *Macbeth* that it is "a most excellent play in all respects, but especially in *divertissement*, though it be a deep tragedy, which is a strange perfection in a tragedy, it being most proper here, and suitable" (January 7, 1666-67).[44] Furthermore, Pepys admires in *The Enchanted Island* (which he saw three times in as many months in 1666-67) *precisely* what he admires in *Macbeth*: that it is "full of so good variety" (November 13, 1667).[45] In the Shakespearean adaptation Pepys, an intelligent spectator, saw design embracing and ordering a variety of interacting concepts—exactly what the adapters saw and tried to show by their "improvements." Dryden says of *The Enchanted Island*: "It was originally Shakespear's . . . our excellent Fletcher had so great a value for it that he thought fit to make use of the same Design, not much varied. . . . But Sir William Davenant . . . soon found that somewhat might be added to the design . . . and therefore . . . he design'd a Counterpart to Shakespeare's Plot, namely that of a man who had never seen a woman; that by this means those two *Characters of Innocence and Love* might the more illustrate and commend each other" (italics mine).[46]

The Tempest was assigned to Davenant's company as early as 1660, but it was never acted before it was revised by Davenant and Dryden.[47] Since less than a third of the original was used in the adaptation, it is relatively easy for us to determine the intention of the adapters and what emendations they considered essential to fit the play to the understanding of their audience. All of the changes have

as their end the sharpening and highlighting of conceptual design
and the fitting of the events of the original to the contours of a three-
tiered comic structure. For example, Prospero is a much weaker
figure in the adaptation than he is in the original because in the
adaptation no single character is central in the design. None of the
figures is more important than the concept or various aspects of the
concept he or she represents, and all the figures are subordinate to the
planes on which they move.

On the high plane, as in Etherege or Tuke, "Characters" of "Love
and Innocence," ambition, valor, and honor dance their stately,
ideational dance. The two couples, Dorinda and Hippolito, Miranda
and Ferdinand, figure faces of love that are played upon and glanced
off one another, while points of honor and heroic ambition are
debated by Alonzo, Antonio, and Gonzalo. Sebastian is removed
from the play altogether, so that rebellion, confusion, and selfish
greed can be confined to the lower planes. Alonzo and Antonio have
not only repented of their crime against Prospero but have chosen
heroic combat as their means of repentance:

> **Gonz.** . . . . Both of you have made amends to Heav'n
> By your late Voyage into *Portugal*.
> Where in defence of *Christianity*.
> Your valour has repuls'd the *Moors* of *Spain*.
>
> [II, 1]

The masque of the devils is emblematic and functions in just the
same way as the Amariel masque functions in *Tyrannick Love* or the
Hecate masque in *Macbeth*—to arouse wonder and also to give
heavier weight and clarity to high-plane concepts of heroic valor and
ambition:

1 D. Where does proud Ambition dwell?
2 D. In the lowest Rooms of Hell.
3 D. Of the damn'd who leads the Host?
4 D. He who does oppress the most.

On the middle plane, ideas of ambition and heroic greatness are
played in another key. In the world, Idea becomes muddled by sense
and appetite, and all direction is lost. Stephano, Mustacho, and
Ventoso figure the woeful inadequacy of clownish man to govern

himself or the state. Quite often the middle plane parodies the high,
sometimes by allusion. For example, Mustacho's "Know then to
prevent the further shedding of Christian blood, we are content
Ventoso shall be Vice-Roy" directly alludes to the heroic holy war in
which Alonso and Antonio have so valiantly fought.

Usually, however, parody is affected structurally. For instance,
Ferdinand, hearing Ariel's "come unto these yellow sands," follows
him in pure pity for his father's death: "The mournful Ditty men-
tions my drown'd Father, / This is no mortal business, nor a sound
which the / Earth owns: I hear it now before me, / However I will on
and follow it" (II, i). His exit on the trail of Ariel's song is immediately followed by the entrance of Stephano, Mustacho, and Ventoso, Ventoso lamenting the demise of the brandy: "The Runlet of
Brandy was a loving Runlet / and floated after us out of pure Pity."
On the lowest plane, of course, burlesque becomes quite literally
monstrous. Monster political ambition and monster love are the
furthest downward distortion of heroic valor and love:

> **Trinc.** Here's two subjects got already, the Monster
> And his Sister
>
> . . . .
>
> From this worshipful Monster, and Mistress,
> Monster his Sister,
> I'll lay claim to this Island by Alliance.
> Monster, I say thy Sister shall be my Spouse.

On the lowest plane, as at the peak of the highest, action is emblematic.

The movement of the play (what Dryden calls its "turns") is
completely structural and rhetorical. The high plane mounts in a
progressive refinement of conception from the baseline of perfect
beauty and innocence to an almost metaphysical, heroic, self-sacrificial love. Conversely, the low plane descends from clownish man
playing at kingship, to civil war, to gross distortion and immersion
in matter. Characters can descend from the high to the middle
planes, but their descent is metaphoric. (Hippolito, for instance,
mistaking sexual appetite for love, wants all the women in the world;
consequently, he falls into matter and finally to death.) Movement is

not achieved by means of action but by figuration and refiguration, alignment and realignment of ideas. For example, Dryden and Davenant balance high-plane figures of untempered nature, "Innocence and Love" (Hippolito and Dorinda), against low-plane untempered nature, conceived as ignorance and lust (Trinculo and Sycorax). Most interesting, the adapters give the impresario of the high plane, Prospero, a low-plane counterpart in Caliban. Caliban does not bear the relation to Prospero that he bears in the original; he is, rather, a director in the realm of matter.

When we consider the play in terms of the 1660s, as a complex ideational design, it is quite interesting and, as Pepys said, is full of good variety. Only when we force post-seventeenth-century aesthetic criteria upon it does the play appear to be repetitious and confused.

In 1632 I. M. S. understood Shakespeare "to give a Stage / (Ample and true with life) voyce, action, age, / As *Plato's* yeare and new *Scene of the World*."[48] Thirty-four years later, Dryden's conception of Shakespeare as a microcosmic architect was not very different from I. M. S.'s:

> *Shakespear*, who (taught by none) did first impart
> To Fletcher *Wit*, to labouring Jonson art
> He Monarch-like gave those his subjects law,
> And is that Nature which they paint and draw.
> Fletcher reach'd that which on his heights did grow,
> Whilst Jonson crept and gather'd all below.
> This did his Love, and this his Mirth digest;
> One imitates him most, the other best
>
> . . . .
>
> That innocence and beauty which did smile
> In Fletcher, grew on this Enchanted Isle.[49]

THREE

Imitation of Nature as "The City Between"

Is there not an Architecture of Vaults and Cellars, as well as of lofty Domes and Pyramids?

Peri Bathos; or, The Art of Sinking Poetry

Although perspective theory did not undermine epistemological confidence, it did shift the grounds of certainty. The introduction of the idea of distance into painting required the corollary development of an individual viewpoint. Such a viewpoint could adequately claim accuracy but never absoluteness. . . . Divine and metaphysical sanctions yield to the particular terms of perception; fact resolves itself into the truth of human vision. This alteration in the basis of authority is important not only in itself, but also as a clue to understanding the translation of perspective theory into other artistic mediums.

David W. Tarbet, "Reason Dazzled"

As we have seen, the shape of microcosmic reality in the 1660s drew disparate images of nature or ways of envisioning nature into concord. Man the hero, man the clown, and man the grotesque sounded, each on his own ground, a single strain of the great *discordia concors*. The theme, played in three different keys, comprised a whole greater than the sum of its parts, an Idea of comic/cosmic truth. In Stage 2 of the evolution we are charting, truth and reality become a matter of perspective. Ways of envisioning are brought together to express not union but divorce, not harmony but dissonance. This method of dramatic imitation is best caught in the conception of a double-faced mirror that reflects simultaneously upward and downward: at the same time heightening to heroic proportions and ideal truths and diminishing to base, anti-heroic dimensions and stubborn, experiential "facts." The effect of the new double focus upon dramatic composition is that the highest and lowest planes of the earlier three-tiered structure are absorbed into the middle plane and are realized in a single, linear design. However, as they are absorbed they do not come into conjunction. Quite the contrary, their radical disjunction and continuous opposition form the reality, or "nature," that is the very object of dramatic imitation.

Recognition of the opposing strains in Restoration thought is not new. In our own time Dale Underwood has described the conflict as a philosophical opposition: "In the pervasive opposition between two broadly opposing sets of thought concerning nature and man— Hobbes, Machiavelli, the libertine, versus Christian and classical, the courtly and the traditional honest man— one may see the age's consciousness of an increasing conflict between an older orthodoxy, and an emerging individualism which looks to our age."[1] Even if we restrict ourselves to a consideration of the history of philosophy, however, the idea of opposition or conflict is by itself too simple. This is borne out by Tillotson's recognition that the moral perspective of his greatest adversary was inextricably connected with his own: "I remember it as the saying of one, who hath done more by his writings to debauch the age with atheistical principles than any man that lives in it [Hobbes] that 'when reason is against a man, then a man will be against reason.' "[2] While Hobbists argued that man's immurement in his material nature established the necessity for vice and Christian theologians argued that man's imprisonment in matter established the necessity for transcendence, neither side denied that man's nature was a field upon which the great divorce between mind and matter, refining imagination and confining appetite, was played out. Poets accommodated their designs to the demands of the conflict with greater and greater dexterity as it grew more intense, with the consequence that the decade 1670 to 1680 gave birth to some of the most brilliant achievements in dramatic satire in English.

Earl Miner was the first modern critic to consider the drama of the Restoration period in terms that could relate it to contemporary theoretical speculations on the relation of panegyric to burlesque. In *Restoration Dramatists* he says, "The heroic play is related to comedy in . . . [a] major respect growing from the rhetorical conception of poetry. Both are distortions in the artist's mirror of the norm of nature, the comic in the lower direction of satire, the heroic in the higher of panegyric and heroic. No doubt the departure seems greater for the heroic drama, but it is nevertheless a departure from the same normative standard."[3]

Here Miner discriminates between separate genres, the heroic play and the comedy, as he does not in his criticism of verse satire. There he makes it quite clear that in a single work the opposing distortions in the artist's mirror take place in a single double-faced glass. H.T. Swedenberg caught the process neatly in discussing *Macflecknoe:* "Here is the coronation poem (a genre of praise), here is the panegyric in reverse, here is satire in the heroic mode."[4] The Abbé d'Aubignac considers "pastoral" (a term he uses alternately with "heroic") and "satyr" to be the same genre, and he finds precedent among the Ancients for a mixed heroic-satiric dramatic mode: *"Pastoral* or *Satyr* had a mixture of serious and pleasant: *Heroes* and *Satyrs* were its Actors; and this sort of poem ought to be consider'd two ways; at first it was but a little poem call'd *Idylium* or *Eclogue,* sung or recited by one man alone, and seldom by two or more. . . . The other sort was a Drammatick Poem, carry'd on according to the Rules of the Stage, where *Hero's* and Satyrs were mingled together, representing both grave and pleasant, ridiculous things; and for that reason this poem had the name of *Satyrical Tragedy."*[5]

While most Restoration critics—Dryden especially—consider satire in and of itself a subgenre of epic, few make the connection that d'Aubignac does with tragedy. Rather, for the most part, they unconsciously follow Hobbes, and relate satire to comedy. Shadwell's *The Humorists* (1671) is called a comedy on the title page, but in the epistle dedicatory to "Margaret [Cavendish], Dutchess of Newcastle," Shadwell makes three definitive points about the play. First, he plainly states that "the Play was intended as a Satyr against Vice and Folly." Second, he establishes that satire is a reverse form of panegyric—"to whom is it more properly presented than your Grace / who are above all your Sex, so eminent in Wit and Virtue" (satire's *ideal antitheses* of "vice" and "folly"). Finally, he acknowledges that the model he follows is Juvenal, "the best Satyrist and Wittiest Man of all the Latin Writers."[6]

I shall examine two works that exemplify the beginnings of the disjunctive unity that dominates the drama in Stage 2: Shadwell's *The Humorists* for theory and Dryden's *Marriage à la Mode* for the direct effects of the new double perspective upon composition. In his preface to *The Humorists* Shadwell takes pains to assure us that he is imitating Idea: "Characters in plays being representations of the Virtues or Vices, Passions or Affectations of Mankind, the Ideas of these."[7] Imitation of the actual, he says, is an error at all costs to be avoided. The poet's aim in instructing is to transmit to his audience images of Ideas, for virtue and vice are conceived by Shadwell not as composites of particular kinds of behavior but rather as Ideas or features of the mind: "I confess a Poet ought to do all he can, decently to please, that so he may instruct. *To adorn his Images of Virtue so delightfully* to affect people with a secret veneration of it in others, and an ambition to practice it in themselves: And to render *Figures of Vice and Folly* so ugly and detestable, to make people hate and despise them, not only in others, but (if it be possible) in their dear selves."[8] (italics mine)

As we can see, virtue and vice are essential qualities, almost detachable from human beings. They are not traits manifested in the various actions of characters who are representations of actual people; rather, they are "characters in the mind," and Shadwell protests the judgment of those who would accuse him of imitating the actual behavior of particular individuals: "But I challenge the most violent and clamorous of my Enemies . . . to accuse me with truth, of representing the real actions, or using the peculiar, affected phrases of any one Particular Man, or Woman living."[9] For Shadwell, as for Lisideus in *"Of Dramatic Poesy,"* to imitate particulars is to imitate fragments of reality and not the shape or truth of reality itself. A poet's imitating the particular, Shadwell argues, would present an obstacle to understanding and would be perceived by the audience as "unnatural." "If a Man should bring such a humour upon the Stage . . . as onely belongs to one or two people, it would not be understood by the Audience, but would be thought (by the singularity of it) wholly unnatural."[10]

The "wit," or special imagination, of the poet is a mediator between the realm of idea and the realm of experience. "Humour" is the *idea* of folly. This idea can, of course, be realized in various ways in the actual behavior of real people, but it exists *in poetry* as a pure

form. The very aim of the poet is to extract and abstract it from the
real and familiar and to render it conceptually. Perception of folly in
experience is a dull exercise; perception of ideas of folly is both
delightful and instructive and, indeed, constitutes one manner of
aesthetic perception:

> If this argument (that the enemies of humour use) . . . that a Poet, in the
> writing of a Fool's Character needs but to have a man set to him, and have his
> words and actions taken; in this case there is no need of wit. But 'tis most
> certain, that if we should do so, no one fool (though the best about the Town)
> could appear pleasantly upon the Stage, he would be there too dull a Fool,
> and must be helped out by a great deal of wit in the Author. . . . wit in the
> Writer . . . may be said to be the invention of *remote and pleasant thoughts* of
> what kind so ever; and there is as much occasion for *such imaginations in the
> writing of a Curious Coxcomb's part, as in the writing the greatest Hero's;* and that
> which may be folly in the Speaker, may be so remote and pleasant, to require
> a great deal of wit in the Writer. " (italics mine)[11]

The focus of dramatic imitation for Shadwell, then, as for dramatists in the 1660s, is upon the "remote and pleasant" realm of ideas.
Poet and audience meet in a conceptual design that weds phenomenal reality to ideational reality and holds Idea up to understanding. A play is the realization of that design; it is not a doorway to
vicarious experience. "Creditur, ex medio quares accessit, habere /
Sudoris minimum, sed habet comeodia tanto / Plus oneris, quanto
venie minus" That which (besides judging truly of Mankind) makes
Comedy more difficult, is that the faults are naked and bare to most
people, but the Wit of it understood, but by a few."[12]
Mediating wit in *The Humorists* brings the high heroic and low
anti-heroic planes of earlier comedy into disjunctive unity on a
middle plane of action. The play opens with Raymond's visit to
Crazy, who suffers from syphilis in its bone-rotting stage and who
appears in conversation with his haberdasher and his bawd, Mrs.
Errant. In Crazy the heroic and anti-heroic strains converge in a
single emblematic figure:

> **Raym.** [to Crazy] I'll swear all Women ought be believe thou lov'st 'em, for
> thou hast suffer'd more for them than all Knight Errants in Romance ever
> did. I'll say that for thee, and thou hast as much Passive-Valour as to Pill
> and Bolus, as any man in Christendom.

Errant. It shows him to be a person of much generosity and honour.
Craz. Perhaps there is not a truer Lover of the Sex than my self among
  Mankind . . . [ellipsis his] Oh, my Shoulders!
Raym. . . . well certainly so much Love and Pox never met together in one
  Man since the Creation. Nor 'faith do I know which is the more tolerable
  Desease of the two. [I, i]

Crazy is middan-geard man, monarch of the city between. Heroic
imagination drives him to extremes of daring self-sacrifice for love
and valor, but the effects of that daring flight are ludicrously regis-
tered on his poor, diseased, and appetite-driven body:

Craz. . . . Beauty, Heav'ns brightest Image, the thing which all the World
  desires and fights for; the Spur to Honour and all glorious Actions,
  without which no Dominion would have been priz'd or Hero heard of,
  the most gentle, sweet, delicate, soft thing—
Errant. Oh dear Mr. Crazy! . . . thou art a sweet man. (*She claps Crazy on
  the shoulders*
Craz. Oh death! what have you done? You have murder'd me; oh you have
  struck me just upon a Callous Node, do you think I have a body of Iron.
  [I, i]

The objects of Crazy's heroic devotion are the whore/cits, Friske
and Striker. Their quarrel over who is more worthy of Crazy's
admiration parodies heroic love and honor debate; each attempts to
prove herself more worthy than her rival by references to minuscule
differences in rank that govern among the cits—Friske accuses
Striker of unworthiness because she is a haberdasher's wife, while
Striker disdains Friske as the daughter of a journeyman tailor. Raymond's comment directs us to understand the mock-heroic intention
of the debate: "I see there are Punctilos of Honour among Whores as
well as Bullies" (I, i). The mounting refinement of definition that
forms the structure of heroic dialectic has been embedded in matter,
stood on its head, and stuck in the mud, so to speak.

In act 1 Crazy and company function emblematically, as an enlarged image of the human arena as the city between. The emblem
encapsulates the central meaning of the play. Just as Crazy's language
and circumstances reflect upward and downward at the same time,

so, too, does the mock-heroic debate of his ladies. Heroic and mock-heroic are not set apart on separate planes as they would have been in the sixties, nor is high dialectic set apart from the plane of action. Crazy is emblematic man (indeed, his figure alone is to a great extent a capsule statement of theme), but the figure is not static; he moves in the action as one of the suitors for Theodosia's hand. Friske and Striker parody heroic debate, but they, too, move in the action; they are the inevitable masked whores at hand to marry up the heiress's rejected suitors in the end scene.

Comic action is formulaic, conventional, and slight because its only function is to frame, or provide occasion for, the display of satiric interplay that constitutes the central conceptual meaning of the play. Lady Loveyouth loves Raymond, who loves her niece, Theodosia. She attempts to keep Raymond from marrying her niece, of whose hand she has sole disposal, by providing three suitors who are three classical types in satiric portraiture: Crazy, the pox-ridden, mock-heroic lover; Brisk, the fop; and Drybob (Dryden), the poetaster. By endless stratagems the fools attempt to reach assignations with Theodosia and, of course, fail. Raymond and Theodosia marry; Lady Loveyouth's husband, presumed dead, returns; and, with a maid's usual ingenuity, Bridget pairs off the couples by trickery. The conceptual design of the play, the true focus of our interest, is the thesis/antithesis structure of satire, not comic action. Very often, indeed, action stops to allow for rhetorical set pieces rendered in the stylistic mode of formal verse satire, which are aimed directly at the audience.

It might be useful here to recall the binary structure of satire, since much of this chapter will refer to it.[13] The conceptual design of satire consists in a *thesis,* a downwardly exaggerated vision of fallen, ridiculous man, which composes the disproportionately larger portion of a work, and an *antithesis,* an upwardly deflected ideal, "right way," or standard, from which the defective "world as it is" of the thesis deviates. Antithesis forms the much smaller portion of the work, sometimes consisting in scattered single lines or allusions that merely hint at an ideal. The "background" of satire is a cluttered scene of bustling but directionless activity that is peopled by fops, fools, and knaves. This scene is surveyed by the satiric spokesman and his interlocutor, or "adversarius." As I have demonstrated elsewhere,[14] when satire is rendered in the dramatic mode, "background" becomes the foreground scene of dramatic action, and the role of the satiric spokesman is diminished but not dropped; traditional spokesmen, like the satyr-satirist, became dramatic types. The audience is directed to see "folly as it flies" without the intervention of the observer/narrator required by verse, but the observer/narrator is most often retained as a dramatis persona, either a "man of sense," a social critic, or an exploiter of the vices and follies he sees, a parasite. The satiric spokesman makes logical connections between the dramatic scene we watch and the world as we, who are presumably sophisticated social observers, know it to be.

This satiric binary opposition, rendered in the dramatic mode, is the shape of reality as it is conceived in *The Humorists*. Act 1 encapsulates satiric truth and functions as a prologue to the whole, which, as Shadwell plainly tells us, is "a Satyr on Vice and Folly." Man is a Crazy whose romantic, outsized, yearning will is misdirected by his folly into vice. Double perspective reflects upward to the heroic, in romantically overblown rhetoric of knight-errantry and courtly service, and downward to the stubborn facts of sexual appetite and the confining, corrupted body. Imagination soars, but gross matter drags poor Crazy down. The rest of the play is an amplification of this initial dichotomy, much in the manner of a Juvenalian satire.

Sometimes satiric thesis appears in set rhetorical pieces that resemble verse satire in tone and direction. Consider, for example, Theodosia's commentary in act 2. Ostensibly she is simply rejecting Crazy, Drybob, and Brisk as suitors, but her speeches are really a vehicle for Shadwell's social satire on the denizens of "satire's falling city."[15] In this exchange Theodosia takes the role of the satiric spokesman, the honest woman of sense observing the follies of her times, and Lady Loveyouth takes the role of the hostile adversarius:

Theo. They Husbands, why a Nunnery were more tolerable, to be mew'd up with none but musty old Women, or your melancholy Eaters of Chalk. I had rather be kept waking at a Conventicle than hear the name of them.
La. Lovey. You are a foolish Girle! I protest they are Gallants and Wits of the Town.
Theo. Gallants and Wits! Buffoons and Jack-puddens! rather condemn me to a little City-Shop-Keeper, with whom I may never have a new Gown

and Handkercher, but half a year behind the Fashion; where I may be bred to rail against the Ladies of the Court, among my publick She-Neighbours, and to mince and simper at an Up-sitting or Christning.

La. Lovey. Ay, ay, go on, go on.

Theo. To live the Week in a melancholy Back-room, and on Sunday go to Church with my Husband in a Broad hat strutting before me, and the Foreman of the Shop having me in one hand, and a huge Bos'd Bible, as big as I am, in the other.

La. Lovey. Good Mrs Dis-dain, make much of them, for I'll assure you, you are like to have no other; . . .

Theo. No other! Why I had rather marry a Countrey Justice, that lives in a Hall-place, two mile from a Town, that's too covetous to keep a Coach, and too jealous to suffer me to come to *London*; . . . and to receive Geese and Capons as bribes to his Worship for Justice.

La. Lovey. How your tongue runs? . . . Good Mrs Nimble Chops they are fit for your betters.

Theo. Yes, for your Ladyship, why don't you chuse one of them?

La. Lovey. So I would, Mrs Malapert, had I not vow'd to live a Widdow.

Theo. A Widdow, that keeps a Vow against Marriage, were a more monstruous Creature than the Fish taken at *Greenwich*. [II, i]

Shadwell is not a Wycherley; his talent is not really adequate to his model, Juvenal. Even so, it is plain that this passage is not intended as dramatic comic interchange. Theodosia and Lady Loveyouth are not the center of attention, nor is the encounter between them the focus of our interest. Rather, we are directed to consider the little scenelets invoked in Theodosia's speeches—scenes of upstart Puritan shopkeepers, city wives, corrupt country justices, and hypocritical widows such as we would encounter in the "background" of verse satire.

The kind of caricature sketch that we encounter in verse satire is also enacted in set piece scenes, like that between Brisk, the fop, and Drybob, the poetaster.

Brisk. Here's a Periwig, no flax in the world can be whiter; how delicately it appears by this Colour'd Hanging, and let me advise you ever while you live, if you have a fair Peruke, get by a Green or some Dark colour'd Hanging . . . Oh, it sets off admirably.

Dryb. A very Metaphysical Notion.

Brisk. And be sure if your Eye-brows be not black, to black 'em soundly;

ah, your only Eye-brow is your fashionable Eye-brow. I hate rogues that
wear Eye-brows that are out of Fashion.
Dryb. By the soul of *Gresham* a most Philosophical Invention. [II, i]

The point is that *The Humorists* answers the generic demands of
satire. It is not comic imitation of the actual. In the rhetorical style of
set speeches, in the exchanges between caricature types drawn from
classical satire, even in the finished satiric portrait of Dryden, the
conventions that dominate Shadwell's composition are verse satire
conventions, not dramatic conventions. If we mistake the play for
simple comedy, it is because its satiric thesis pictures "satire's falling
city" in the lighter tones that dominate expression at the end of the
satiric spectrum that lies closest to comedy, as opposed to the dark
tones that dominate expression at the end that lies adjacent to black
irony (for example, in plays like *The Plain Dealer* and *The Libertine;* I
shall explore this gradation in the next chapter).

Antithesis appears in the play in a single exchange between Theodosia and Raymond, which takes place in act 5, after they are
married:

Theo. I can sooner distrust my self than your honour, and cannot but be
very easie to believe what I like so well; though my own want of merit
would persuade me to the contrary.
Raym. I find the wisest have still less knowledge of themselves than of
others, or you would value more what all men do; your Beauty, Wit and
Virtue are so admirable that Nature could have added nothing to you, nor
is there one Charm in all the rest of your Sex, that can one moment divide
my thoughts from you.
Theo. I have so great belief in your constancy and truth, your words can
ne'er confirm me more. [V, i]

The ideal, as is usually the case in satire, is to be found in old-
fashioned virtues: married love, honesty, chastity, and constancy.

In sum, then, in the second stage of the evolution we are tracing,
the shape of nature or reality is still ideationally conceived. Ideas are
drawn downward into the dimensions of experience, but *within* the
boundaries of that plane of envisagement the audience's eye is drawn
upward toward ideality and downward toward caricature to effect a
double perspective upon the human condition.

Although in writing *Marriage a la Mode* (1673) Dryden abjures the
company of "stabbing Wits to bloody Satyr bent," the play was

understood as satire by his contemporaries. Neatly catching the panegyric/burlesque paradox I have discussed, the writer of *Marriage Asserted: In Answer to a Book Entitled Conjugium Conjurgium* (1674) argues that Dryden *"celebrated, Love* and Marriage" in this "gentile Satyre": [italics mine] "What is either wicked or silly in modish colours he has so well painted, as would divert any person that is owner of the least ingenuity, from both; more particularly this shunning of Marriage, and being entred perfidiously to break a vow so easy to be kept, in his Play of *Marriage à La Mode:* a more gentile Satyre against this sort of folly, no Pen can write, where he brings the very assignations that are commonly used about the Town upon the Stage."[16]

In their commentary the most recent editors of the play, John Loftis and David Stuart Rodes, have finally put to rest Langbaine's 1688 misreading, which had asserted that the "two Stories" that comprise its structure were irresponsibly "tack't together" to the confusion of any aesthetic or moral coherence in the whole. As Loftis and Rodes observe, much of nineteenth- and twentieth-century criticism of the play has centered upon defense or denial of a connection between the two plots.[17] They, on the other hand, see the double plot as a "particularly appropriate vehicle" for bringing "disparate ideas and ways of confronting experience into a generously unified whole": "While the 'pattern of highest human virtue' represented by Palmyra and Leonidas appears unrelated to the libertinism of the comic characters, the two are in fact distant (but not polar) marks on an ethical scale whose mean is a balance of respect and sexual gaiety, . . . Of course, the opposition is exaggerated for artistic effect, and both the comic and the heroic are distortions of a practical mean or of any Restoration reality."[18]

I would extend upon this crucial critical insight. Both upward and downward exaggerations in *Marriage á la Mode* are those "distortions in the artist's mirror of the norm of nature" that Miner calls hallmarks of the conceptual mode in satire. Their opposition is aimed not at achieving balance but at expressing the perspectival ambivalence or disjunctive unity that dominates dramatic imitation in the 1670s. Like *The Humorists, Marriage à la Mode* (probably composed in 1671) is an early expression of the interplay between ideal and actual that reaches fullest refinement in mid-decade in the finished perfection of plays like *The Country Wife* (1675), *The Virtuoso* (1676), and *The Man of Mode* (1676) and that falls into decay at the end of the decade, when satiric form becomes extraneous to yet another conceptual focus.

Structurally, *Marriage à la Mode* presents a continuous vacillation between the stable realm of ideational truth and the constantly shifting realm of confusion and change in which we are caught, the world of experience. Marriage is a perfect metaphor for the uneasy union in disparity that our human condition is, because it is at once a sacramental sign of the union between two spirits and a galling yoke that confines our animal appetites to the necessities of civilization. As we saw in chapter 2, the amatory life is our vehicle for transcendence to the glittering ideal; it is also, however, the surest evidence of how tightly shackled we are to that grotesque and clumsy-footed ass, the body. By Dryden's play we are made to assume a running alternation of perspectives upon this central paradox: "The two worlds . . . alternate with precise regularity between comic and heroic, each comic scene followed by a heroic scene of about equal length, until the fifth act, where the comic overbalances the heroic taking over twice the number of lines to bring the play to its general comic conclusion."[19] Each scene has a twin opposing scene. Each pair of opposites illuminates a contradiction: idea and matter; constancy and change; spacious time in the world of pastoral innocence and frenzied, fractured time in the courts of men; free-flying imagination and imagination trammeled in the coils of hypocrisy and deceit; love as mingling of "our most spiritous parts" and love as feeding "on a dish" or refusing to feed because the appetite is cloyed; heroic singularity, alone as "was the Godhead when he made the world," and the common bestiality of "poor Animal" man; language as the perfect union of word and will expressed in verse and language as a compulsive appetite for novelty expressed in rag-tag prose; the world as a "maze of Fate" and the world as a masquerade wherein "we move and talk just like so many overgown Puppets." We jump back and forth across a dividing line, our angle of envisagement shifting from one extreme to the other in continuous alternation. However, neither perspective cancels the other; each is a terminal equally necessary to the electric interplay that constitutes the "nature" that is the object of dramatic imitation here. It is interesting, I think, that in 1707, when the revolution we are charting was finally completed, Colley Cibber, in his adaptation *The Comicall Lovers; or, Marriage a la Mode,* erased the heroic plane and emphasized Melantha's role to make her the central character in his shortened version. Once actuality had become the object of dramatic imitation, the plane of Idea was an intolerable intrusion, and individual character and manners became the center of interest.

Loftis and Rodes argue that a major improvement Dryden made upon the source of his high plot (Scudéry's "Sesostris and Timareta" story in *The Grand Cyrus)* was to effect union between action and character: "To modern taste, the loss of integrity in Scudéry's tale comes in the separation between action and character. Plot seems to have no fundamental effect on character, but simply demonstrates stability rather than testing or provoking growth or degeneration. Plot offers a series of discrete, variously decorated display boxes to show off virtue."[20]

To my mind this perfectly describes the high plot of Dryden's play. Palmyra and Leonidas are figures of heroic love and honor; their action exists *precisely* to demonstrate stability, the stability of pure forms in the realm of Idea. The scenes in which they appear are indeed a series of discrete display boxes to show off ideas of virtue. Moreover, as is so often the case in formal verse satire, the ideal is quite glaringly, intentionally literary. Dryden's plot does not distract us from, but deliberately points us toward, its source. Leonidas and Palymra come trailing clouds of Scuderyan glory for the same reason that Fidelia recalls the green world of *Twelfth Night,* or that Dorimant recites lines from Waller's odes, or that Juvenal's spokesman in *Satire IX* mockingly breathes a soft line from Virgil's *Eclogues* at the corrupt Naevolus. The conceptual mode of satire centers on a conflict between ways of envisioning truth, and the conflict is often pictured, as it is in this play, in a contrast between the pure, somewhat remote realm of literary imagination and the dear, distracting present of experience.

The worlds of the play meet and comment upon one another not in action but in conceptual opposition. For example, let us consider how transitions among this series of discrete display boxes is effected. Act 1 ends with an exchange between Palmyra and Leonidas that is quite clearly set in the atmosphere of French ro-

mance. The lovers are to be separated from their timeless pastoral
world and from each other by the intrusion of the king and his court.
Leonidas has not time nor scope to speak his love, but he hangs back
from the departing courtiers to reassure Palmyra of his constancy:

Leon. I dare not speak to her; for if I should I must weep too.
Poly. Come my *Leonidas* let's thank the Gods;
    Thou for a Father, I for such a Son. [Exeunt all but Leonidas and Palmyra
Leon. My dear Palmyra, many eyes observe me,
    And I have thoughts so tender, that I cannot
    In Publick speak 'em to you; some hours hence
    I shall shake off these crowds of fawning Courtiers,
    And then—[Exit Leonidas
Palm. Fly swift, you hours, you measure time for me in vain,
    Till you bring back Leonidas again.
    Be shorter now; and to redeem the wrong,
    When he and I are met be twice as long.   [I, i]

Upon this quiet and graceful French romantic atmosphere, act 2,
scene 1, explodes like a bombshell in the fractured, giddy language
of the pseudoromantic Francophile, Melantha:

Phil. Count *Rhodophil's* a fine gentleman indeed, Madam; and I think
    deserves your affection.
Mel. Let me die, but he's a fine man; he sings and dances *en François, and
    writes Billet doux* to a miracle.
Phil. And these are no small tallents, to a Lady that understands and values
    the *French* ayr, as your Ladyship does.
Mel. How charming is the *French* ayr! and what an *étourdy bête* is one of our
    untravel'd Islanders! When he would make court to me, let me die, but he
    is an *Aesop's Ass* that would imitate the courtly French in his addresses;
    but in stead of those comes pawing upon me, and doing all things so *mal a
    droitly*
Phil. 'Tis great pity *Rhodophil's* a married man, that you may not have an
    honourable Intrigue with him.
Mel. Intrigue *Philotis!* that's an old phrase; I have laid that word by: *Amour*
    sounds better. . . . Oh, Count *Rhodophil!* Ah mon cher! I could live and
    die with him. [II, i, 1-17]

"Amour" does sound better than "intrigue"; it is remote and foreign.
The homelier English word lies too close to the facts of experience.

A word where lovers are constant to the death is the romantic heart's desire, but it suffers in translation to the stubborn facts of experience that show "amours" to be plain old intrigues and glittering lovers, married men. The sheer brilliance of the comic surface here is so overpowering that it can distract us from the underlying satiric comparison that structure is making. Of course, Melantha is wonderful simply as a comic portrait of the fashionable Francomaniac of 1670 London, but placement of the passage immediately after the end scene of act 1 makes a sharper point. In the literary imagination bred by French romances, lovers are constant, adoring, and bereft of words by powerful emotion. But the purity and stability of their elegant formalism is shattered and things fly apart when we leap from the remote pastoral world to the experiential. Stately verse explodes into patchwork prose, an oleo of cliché slang ("let me die"), homely English ("Aesop's Ass"), and misused tatters of French. Transcendent love becomes multifaced and duplicitous—both amour and intrigue. Men are no longer fairy-tale princes, whose radiance emanates from humble cottages; they are "pawing" animals, clumsily *doing,* making left-hand imitations of the courtly postures they only imagine they enact. Constancy ("I could live and die with him") is a pretty affectation and a sexual pun. And time, while it is still measured to the rhythms of human desire, moves at a frantic pace in pursuit of a beauty that is always changing, never attained, but always anticipated in the new.

This small sample illustrates the method by which transitions are effected throughout the play. Act 2 ends with Palmyra's elegiac lament for the world that she and Leonidas have lost and for her impending loss of him:

> **Palm.** In Woods and Plains, where first my love began,
> There would I live retir'd from faithless man;
>
> . . . .
>
> Thus would I live: and Maidens when I die,
> Upon my hearse white True-love-knots should tie
> And thus my Tomb should be inscrib'd above,
> *Here the forsaken Virgin rests from love.*
>   [II, i, 479-80; 485-88]

And immediately act 2 begins with Doralice and Rhodophil playing at being constant lovers for the benefit of Artemis. Doralice's words replay Palmyra's lament in a lower key for the sake of ironic comparison:

Rho. My own dear heart!
Dor. My own true love!
I had forgot my self to be so kind; indeed I am angry with you, dear; you are come home an hour after you appointed; If you had staid a minute longer, I was just considering, whether I should stab, hang, or drown my self. [III, i, 1-6]

As soon as Artemis has left them, "*they walk contrary ways on the Stage; he with his hands in his pocket, whistling; she singing a dull, melancholy Tune,*" poxing each other and each openly anticipating the relief he will feel at the other's death.

Act 4 ends with Palmyra's dilemma; she is caught between love and loyalty to Leonidas and duty and honor to her newly discovered father, Polydamas: "What Honour bids you [Leonidas] do [lead a revolution against Polydamas] / Nature [the bond of filial piety] bids me prevent." In sharp contrast, act 5 begins with Palamede's servant announcing the arrival of his father: "Yes, Sir; both my old Master, and your Mistress's Father the old Gentlemen ride hard this journey; they say it shall be the last time they will see the Town, and both of 'em are so pleas'd with this marriage, which they have concluded for you, that I am afriad they will lie some years longer to trouble you, with the joy of it," (V, i, 2-7). The presence and position of this speech makes the intention of satiric comparison between the two acts obvious, for the speech serves absolutely no purpose in the action. It exists solely to set a contrast between filial obligation as Idea in the high plot and as cumbersome, galling necessity in the low.

The structural design we have observed in the transitions is mirrored in the design of the whole. Scenes are juxtaposed for conceptual contrast with one another—as the act 2 of duet of remembrance between Palmyra and Leonidas is set against the scene of conjugal quarreling between Doralice and Rhodophil, or Leonidas's recognition of Palmyra's "Divinity. Disguis'd and silent" at the masquerade is set against the slapstick failures of Palamede and Rhodophil to recognize their disguised mistresses. Juxtaposed scenes form a running series of contrastive perspectives upon such ideas as love, marriage, filial duty, imaginative and sensual knowledge. As a line of action neither plot is particularly impressive; the high is a love-and-honor debate without the dialectical refinement of the sixties, while the low is the simplest of two-couple comic intrigues. The plots themselves are unimportant; both are used to *frame* modes of perceiving. Meaning rests in the interplay between the opposing perceptual modes that the plots frame.

As in *The Humorists,* act 1 exists to establish the basic terms of satiric opposition that the whole play will amplify and explore. Doralice's song functions in much the same way as Crazy's rhetorical confusion. It captures in capsule the opposition between stability and change, unity and diversity, oath and appetite, and it launches the action that will provide occasion to develop that oppostion. The world of experience is totally governed by change; in love or in political life no bond, oath, or idea can maintain itself. Love is the instant call of appetite; marriage is a mechanism of greed; and wit is the regurgitation of bits and snippets from the "sew'd up Gullet" of cormorant man. A whole half year is the furthest extent of passion's life, and after passion dies, "we are alone, we walk like Lions in a room, she one way and I another." Time is flux, and human beings, caught in the current, are both its victims and its agents. We long for union with the beautiful, but once in possession, we can neither know nor sense it ("Ask those who have smelt to a strong perfume two years together, what's the scent,"). Moreover, wherever on the wheel of time we are, matter is our only medium ("My old man has already marry'd me; for he has agreed with another old man, as rich and covetous as himself").

In the course of act 1 we make a condensed and symbolically significant passage from the low world of matter and change to the high world of imaginative vision. As soon as Rhodophil and Palamede have concluded that the only escape from marital entrapment is the pursuit of change, Almathea and Argaleon, a mixed pair—she all goodness and he a Machiavel—come upon the scene. Their entrance lifts us to a midplane, which is halfway between the position of the two comic couples and the pastoral plane. We learn from Almathea that Polydamas has usurped his throne and has threatened the rightful heir. Political life in the world of experience, like private life, is unstable and is governed by the lust for power and change. However, the course of Almathea's exposition leads us from the Polydamas who *was,* a lawless usurper, through the Polydamas chastised by heaven ("See how heav'n can punish wicked men / In granting their desires"), to the Polydamas of the play's present, a good king. The course of the account leads us out of "that country," where change and confusion reign supreme, and into the pastoral landscape, where Leonidas and Palmyra, the fairy-tale lost children of the king, appear as in a vision of imagination, and Polydamas's language leaps a full octave upward to describe them:

> Behold two miracles [*Looking earnestly at Leon, and Palmyra*
> Of different sexes, but of equal form:
> So matchless both, that my divided soul
> Can scarcely ask the Gods a Son or Daughter
> For fear of losing one.
>
> [I, i, 330-35]

Leonidas lifts our gaze still further upward to an ideal above earthly majesty. Urged by Polydamas not to be dazzled by the court, he proves himself a true prince by acknowledging allegiance to an authority above the court:

> I need not this incouragement.
> I can fear nothing but the Gods,
> And for this glory, after I have seen
> The Canopy of State spread wide above
> In the abyss of Heaven, the Court of Stars,
> The blushing Morn, and rising Sun,
> What greater can I see?
>
> [I, i, 394-400]

In the course of the first act Dryden has led us from the low radical of Doralice's opening song to the high radical of romance vision, where vows are inviolable and miracles are revealed to kings. Once this ground has been traversed, however, we have measured the distance of human perception; we are ready to move from high romance to the city between, the court, in which the contrastive opposition will be played.

Melantha is to *Marriage à la Mode* what Sir Fopling Flutter is to *The Man of Mode* or Crazy is to *The Humorists.* She moves in the action of the play, but she is also a symbol of significant import, an embodiment of its central meaning. The very crack-brainedness of Melantha is an exaggeration of the condition to which we all are heir. Melantha yearns for contact with majesty that will confer glory upon her, for love that will elevate her, and for language that is rare, exotic, and ever new. She pursues the fitful glimmers of these that are available to her in the confining world of experience. Of course, she is ridiculous in her attempts to make the visionary happen in the real, but in the disparity between the ideals for which she yearns and the clumsy machinery that life affords for getting at them, Melantha symbolizes the disjunction within us. For instance, Melantha would worship majesty if only the phenomenal world would stop changing long enough for her to be sure where it is, once it has been embodied in a human figure. Just as Leonidas, once out of the world of romance, finds himself "wandring in a maze of Fate / Led by fires of fantastic glory / And the vain lustre of imagin'd Crowns" (IV, i, 7-9), so too Melantha runs in the maze of the world, at a giddy pace in vain pursuit of "fantastic glory" and "imagin'd Crowns." However, while on the high plane of romance the anguish of change is resolved by a total and unwavering commitment to ideas of virtue, on the low plane of experience the uncertainty induced by change is resolved by an absolute fidelity to change itself. For instance, at the beginning of act 5 when Leonidas has been declared no king, Melantha cannot understand how she could ever have seen majesty in him: "Out upon him, how he looks . . . now he's found no Prince, he is the strangest *figure* of a man; how could I make that *Coup d'étourdy* to think him one?" (V, i, 115-17).

At the end of act 5, when Leonidas has once again been revealed to be a king, Melantha must once again revise her perception to accommodate the change:

Mel. Let me die, but I'le congratulate his Majesty: how admirably well his Royalty becomes him! . . .
Pal. How? does it become him already? 'twas but just now you said he was such a *figure* of a man.
Mel. True, my dear, when he was a private man he was a *figure*; but since he is a King, methinks he has assum'd another *figure*: he looks so grand and so August. [V, i, 493-500]

The portrait of Melantha is a portrait of us and of the cognitive dissonance that makes us the absurd creatures we are. Dryden was able to paint us so well because, as Samuel Johnson observed, "He delighted to tread upon the brink of meaning, where light and darkness begin to mingle; to approach the precipice of absurdity, and hover over the abyss of unideal vacancy."[21]

As the seventies advanced, a curious branching occurred in dramatic imitation. On the one hand, disjunctive unity was refined to perfection in dramatic satires that were closer to the compositional manner of Roman verse satire in the subtlety with which they blended satiric antithesis, the ideal value, into the context of satiric thesis, the fallen or ridiculous world-as-it-is. On the other hand, complete disjunction often occurred: the ideal was rendered in much more extravagantly heroic plays like Settle's *The Empress of Morocco* (1673), while downward exaggeration was rendered equally obviously in counterpart parody plays, like Duffet's *The Empress of Morocco: A Farce* (1674). Playwrights were aware of a double perspective in consciousness that caused the split. Duffet seems almost to have been reading Earl Miner or Jean Hagstrum: "Farce and Heroick Tale use but one fashion, / Love and Affection Lays the first foundation / Then Giant noise and show set Cheating Glass on."[22] His parody mocks not just *The Empress of Morocco* but the whole heroic mode and the theoretical assumptions that gave rise to it. For example, act 1 ends with an epilogue that takes a swipe at Dryden the playwright and Dryden the critic as well: "An Epilogue spoken by Hecate and Three Witches according to the Famous Mode of MAC-BETH—the most renowned and melodious Song of *John Dory* being heard as it were in the air sung in parts by Spirits, to raise the expectation and charm the audience with thoughts sublime, and worthy the Heroick Scene which follows."[23]

The very notion that art imitates metaphysical truth or that metaphysical truth has human relevance is soundly debunked in broad mock-heroics:

> You know [Jove] once came down a Trulling,
> The shape of beastly great Town Bull in:
> And so in twenty other dresses;
> In Villages to find out Misses,

> Which shows no Game i' th' upper Region,
> Can be compar'd to the sweet Pidgeon,
> Who'er disputes this is a Widgeon.   [II, i]

When a theoretically sensitive playwright like Shadwell chose the direction of ideal imitation, he undercut himself in an apologetic preface. Superficially considered, *Psyche* (1675) seems to be the same kind of love-and-honor tragedy-with-a-happy-ending that, as we have seen, was quite common in the sixties. Closer examination, however, reveals that elevation is not effected, as it had been before, by dialectic or ideational refinement. Rather, Shadwell attempts to arouse the admiration of the audience *directly* by music and spectacle that are extraneous to the rhetorical structure. Language has become the handmaiden of spectacular effects, much to the embarrassment of the author: "The great Design [of this play] was to entertain the Town with variety of Musick, curious Dancing, splendid Scenes and machines; And . . . I do not, nor ever did intend to value my self upon the writing of this Play. For I had rather be Author of one scene of Comedy, like some of Ben Jonsons than of all the best Plays of this kind that have been, or ever shall be written."[24]

Imitation of the ideal has become intolerable by itself; it can no longer stand without a balancing, antithetical downward pull toward the actual, without the "other" perspective. "Notes and Observations on *The Empress of Morocco,*" by Dryden, Shadwell, and Crowne, is criticism in the satiric mode, a long and extremely funny prose satire on literary affectation. It functions in much the same way as mock-heroic, deflating Settle's elevated style by reduction to the banal physical mechanics of experience. For example, consider their treatment of a Settle passage of only three short lines:

'Tis now our Royal Mother's Breath must bind / That Sacred tie of Love, my King has sign'd / And Providence has seal'd; make her but kind." The King has sign'd it, and Providence has seal'd it, how is his Mother to bind all with her Breath? Is she to set her mark with her Breath? or, in witness that it is sooth, is she to bite the Wax with her Tooth? for why may not Breath mean Tooth, as well as Royal Power, etc, but perhaps she is to bind all with her Breath; that is, to deliver the Deed with her Breath; that is, to puff the Parchment into his Hands.[25]

As Settle makes clear in his reply, "Notes and Observations on *The Empress of Morocco* REVISED . . . to be Printed . . . with the next edition of *The Conquest of Granada,"*[26] his style in *The Empress* is no more abstract, his idealizing imitation of nature no more elevated than Dryden's was in his heroic plays of the sixties; certainly his characters are no more "improbable" than Crowne's in *Juliana.* But aesthetic sensibility has changed in two major ways since the early sixties. On the writer's side was the desire to elevate the wonder of the audience instantly, to induce admiration by gorgeousness of style for its own sake and by use of music and spectacle that were unrelated to rhetorical structure and that therefore appealed directly to sense, bypassing understanding. On the critic's side was the development of a new consciousness of the nature that art must imitate, a growing awareness of reality as paradoxical, which made imitation of ideal truth, by itself, seem inadequate, insufficiently complex.

However, escape into spectacle was not the only alternative to dramatic satire. The serious drama too, especially that of Dryden and Lee, attempted to capture perspectival ambivalence in a single linear form. *Aureng-Zebe* (1675) was Dryden's response to the need to accommodate the new perceptual mode to heroic drama. Frederick M. Link has made two important observations about the play: first, it is not "affective" drama: "The rhetorical purpose is everywhere apparent. It lies behind the elaborate diction and imagery, behind the formal, distanced pattern of the lines. . . . When Aureng-Zebe is at the height of passion, the language becomes more informal and the rhythms more turbulent, but the distance and the sense of calculated art remain."[27] Second, and correspondingly, the play does not imitate an internal arena in character; it is, rather, a complex design held up to understanding: "*Aureng-Zebe* is not an exploration of character developing through inner conflict toward self-knowledge, but a play demonstrating the proper conduct of a prince. We are not to identify with the hero as a realistic figure; we are to admire him as an ideal. . . . He is essentially a static character."[28]

I do not agree that the play demonstrates the proper conduct of a prince only or centrally. It is, as Dryden tells us, "a tragedy of wit";[29] like the satiric drama, it demonstrates a paradox that is intrinsic in the human condition:—that is, "Desire's the vast extent of human mind," but desire is shackled to a dying animal; "It mounts above and leaves poor . . . [man] behind" (II, i, 55-56). In the world of experience, man is "to slavery design'd" (II, i, 43), "bounded with things possible" (II, i, 53). Nevertheless, man cannot accept his confinement in the limitations that his material nature sets upon him because he is "cheated with a free born mind" (III, i, 44). The whole, complex design of the play is a demonstration and amplification of this central paradox. As in the case of *Marriage à la Mode,* though less obviously, the design comprises discrete scenes that display conceptual opposition. As in the earlier play, the linear action here exists as a frame to support a series of contrasts that are the real center of our attention. It therefore does not matter that the city falls into different hands three times in one act; each fall executes a "turn" that provides occasion for a regrouping of conceptual oppositions. Characters, as in the drama of the sixties, are almost scaled conceptual counters. One could scale them to the measure of ideas of passion (Aureng-Zebe = transcendent, prophetic passion; Arimant = passion as heroic friendship; the Emperor = passion in the world, extravagant in will but impotent in possibility; Morat and Nourmahal = passion as "mad rage" and lawless lust). But one could as well scale them to the measure of greatness, regulated or irregular, or to virtue—Indamora's haughty, heroic virtue, Melissinda's passive virtue, and Nourmahal's weirdly heroic egoism. The design of the play does *not* scale them but, rather, uses them as pieces to be grouped and regrouped in various patterns of conceptual contrast.

The best evidence that the play does not imitate what happens to a group of people and how events affect them is that characters appear at the necessity of the structure to delineate one or another idea within a particular contrastive scheme. For example, Melissinda does not appear in the play until act 3 when the idea she embodies is required by a set scene that contrasts Melissinda's stoic acceptance of fate with Indamora's heroic defiance of it, while it emphasizes their similarity in virtue and constancy. Morat also does not appear until act 3, to set a contrast between the rough heroic valor that "desires no mistress but the wars" and the higher heroic valor that is spurred by love, and also to function in a contrastive design that balances the tyranny motivated by self-interest against the selfless stewardship that true kingship must be. Furthermore, a character changes in accordance with the contrast he or she is called upon to set. The Nourmahal of act 2, a termagant whose only goal is power in marriage and in the state, is not "consistent" with the Nourmahal of act 4, who throws away her newly won imperial power and that of her son for the tender seductions of incestuous love, if we think of consistency in post-seventeenth-century terms of character development.

The play is structured as a series of double perspectives upon ideas of love, honor, law, power, and majesty. The opposing angles of envisagement strike upward and downward in a variety of configurations, and the whole design they shape is an intricate web of contradictions. For example, honor is both "the mere raving madness of romance" (II, 534) and is also an unwavering adherence to ideas of virtue and "Presence of mind and courage in distress" (II, 555). Love is both "an airy good opinion makes," a "gaudy dream" of "strong imagination" (I, 372-75), and it is also a vision of the absolute that "young prophets does inspire," (I, 379). Beauty can be thought either "a monarch . . . which kingly power magnificently proves" (II, 175) or it can equally be conceived as a taking bait, a dangerous lure dangled by that "sex invented first to damn mankind" (IV, 101). Virtue may be the tutor of "honor's praecepts," or it may just as well be no more than a "barren airy name" (II, 503). Loyalty may be a constant reverence for majesty, or, on the other hand, it may be the wavering response of self-interested villainy to power: "t'each changing news they changed affections bring" (I, 50). The state may be conceived as the reflection on earth of nature's law, or it may just as easily be thought the enemy of nature: "nature's laws are by the state destroyed" (I, 43). Political man may, on the one hand, be a "character of valour," an "Altas who must . . . the sinking state uphold" (I, 104); on the other hand, he may be no more than "a crawling insect . . . [who is] kindled into man" only in the fitful light cast by a fading majesty in its failing hours. Finally, just as in *Marriage à la Mode,* marriage is both "a mysterious pow'r" (II, 356), the crown of constancy and valor, and it is also a galling yoke, for "when we lay next us what we hold most dear / Like Hercules invenomed shirts we wear" (II, 311). All values are dubious; all ideals are ambivalent.

Although structurally *Aureng-Zebe* is a refinement upon *Marriage à la Mode,* it nevertheless shapes the same disjunctive unity. It is irresolute even in its resolution. The play ends with a quarrel between Aureng-Zebe and Indamora about loyalty in this world and the next that illustrates the abrasion of egos that must attend the marriage of even the truest minds in the world of experience. However, their quarrel is followed immediately by the calmly heroic self-immolation of Melissinda "mount[ing] a glorious bride" to a renewal of her marriage bond with Morat. This heroic spectacle is in turn immediately followed by an opposing pair of scenes: in the first, Nourmahal is shown mad and dying, the victim of intemperate lust; in the second, the Emperor, who has been cured of his love madness, at last confers a crown and a mistress upon the deserving Aureng-Zebe. While these rapidly shifting scenes do not cancel each other, they do form a final contrastive pattern that brings the whole design of the play to a suitably bifocal conclusion.

Link's tempered response to King's interpretation of *Aureng-Zebe* is sound, but it does not, in my judgment, go far enough. He says, "Although the two scenes between Aureng-Zebe and Indamora, and the latter's exchanges with Arimant, suggest the influence of contemporary comedy, I cannot agree with Bruce King (*Dryden's Major Plays* [New York, 1966], Chapter 7) that the audience is to take scene, character, or play as comic in any important sense." [30] I would go further. In *Aureng-Zebe* we see not a serious play that has been influenced by contemporary comedy but, rather, a heroic play that offers an alternative to contemporary comic satire's way of shaping the double perspective that dominates dramatic imitation in the seventies. The play is precisely what Dryden called it: "a tragedy of *wit.*"

Nathaniel Lee has another method of accommodating the heroic to the demands of a paradoxical conception of reality. Lee has been linked with those playwrights who exaggerated emotion and spectacle for their own sakes or in order to increase response from a somehow emotionally more vulnerable audience. Rothstein, however, first pointed the way to a recognition that the central problem in Lee's drama is the conflict between overreaching imagination and impotent will. [31] John Armistead extended Rothstein's suggestion, arguing that when we examine Lee's designs and the variation he makes upon his sources, we become aware that his is a "fresh assessment of the conventional subjects of heroic drama, love and valor . . . [which] shows the frustration of old-style heroism in an alien socio-political environment." [32] I agree with Armistead, but I would suggest that the breakdown of the old-style heroic ideal is not attributable to a particular set of sociopolitical circumstances. The "alien" environment in which idealism fails is the human experience itself as it was conceived in the seventies.

The *Rival Queens* (1677) is similar to *Aureng-Zebe* in that it, too, explores the ambiguity of our condition.[33] Whereas Dryden achieves bifurcation of perspective in contrastive rhetorical and structural configurations, Lee embeds the ambivalence in the ideational counters themselves. Characterization is still the imitation of ideas, and plot still consists in a series of discrete scenes displaying various ideational juxtapositions. However the idea that any particular character embodies is itself complex rather than homogeneous, ambivalent rather than uniform. The rival queens who contend for control of the heroic human soul are the Neoplatonic queen of the realm of mind, Statira, and the Epicurean queen of the realm of matter, Roxana (composed of "such majestic *atoms* / [as] First made the world, and must preserve its greatness" [IV, i, 120-21]). Roxana, however, and not Statira, is made to express the central paradox that the play explores: "My soul is pent, and has not elbow room . . . / O, that it had a space might answer to / Its infinite desire, where I might stand / And hurl the spheres about like sportive balls" (IV, i, 123-27).

Statira is the constant object of Alexander's soul's love, as Roxana was once temporarily the object of his body's desire. She figures an *Il Penseroso*-like conception of the human mind as it yearns for retreat from the busy world to a *schola* of contemplation, a tower where "I in darkness hide me from the day / That with my *mind* I may his form survey, / And think so long 'till I think life away" (III, 208; italics mine).

However, Statira achieves neither retreat nor transcendence. She is no more ideationally absolute than Roxana is. Statira most often describes the ambivalence in Alexander in oxymoronic phrases like "dear, precious, faithless Alexander" (I, ii, 36) and "that great, that glorious man . . . / Is bravely false" (II, i, 10-12). Her character is paradoxical in itself. "Vast is [her] mind," but that mind is inextricably tied to earthly life and passion, and it is prisoner to a vacillating will. Great is her virtue, but it is a "sickly virtue" (III, 211) in the arena of the world, too weak to act and helpless to transcend. Like Statira, every character in the play figures ambiguity and illuminates the play's central, governing image of the two-sided human condition: the human spirit great in its desire to leap beyond the confining boundaries of the world and yet "pent without elbow room" in its little space and incapable to act. The terrible ambivalence is figured not just in the characters but in every aspect of the play. It dominates the structure, the language, and even the relation between characters and the words they speak. For instance, in the speeches of Cassander, the leader of the band of "silkworms" that threaten to undermine Alexander's power, and the worshiper of Roxana, the Epicurean queen, we find the only unequivocally heroic, exalted descriptions of Alexander as "a god, to give / The infinite assembly glorious audience" (II, 82-83), who comes "on a crowd of kings in triumph borne" (II, 53).

Characterization still imitates ideas in figures, and meaning is still realized in the structural juxtaposition of those ideas, but the ideas themselves have become complicated. For example, the rival queens are respectively ideas of mind and antimind. Their direct confrontation forms the structural center of the play. The curious nature of the confrontation shows us how far and in what way dramatic composition here differs from that of the sixties. Statira declares her plan to conquer herself and her rival by retreating from the world. She will "hide . . . from day," train her "mind" upon Alexander's "form," and "think [her] life away" (III, 208-10). That in itself is an odd position for a figure of heroic virtue to assume; normally, as in St. Catherine, heroic virtue is assertive. Roxana's response to Statira's planned retreat is odder still and is a clear index of the ideational complexity of both figures. If Roxana were merely a figure of lust like Zempoalla or a rendering of the *animo ferus* like Maximin, Statira's capitulation would signal victory for her principle. But Roxana figures a more complex idea than those. She replies to Statira, *"Thy no thought I must, I will decree"* (III, 215; italics mine). The idea Roxana figures is a power intrinsic in the human soul that wills *against* mind, a force that is not subject to mind and that is inescapable. The rival queens of mind and antimind seem to be not only rivals but necessary complements. In other words, the forces or impulses that contend for possession of the heroic human soul are equally ambivalent, and, most significantly, have equally valid claims upon the human spirit.

Curiously enough, the old heroic scale of love and honor is still faintly discernible in *The Rival Queens:* Alexander = heroic majesty, Lysimachus = heroic love and honor, Statira = beauty that inspires honor, Roxana = beauty that tempts from honor. However, that scale of values is a very far distant backdrop. It is comparable to the antithesis in satire that flickers behind the scene as a shadowy reminder of the unattainable ideal. The old idea of love as an uplifting drive toward metaphysical truth is a mere background shadow for the Burtonian madness that love is in the dramatic foreground. The old heroic ideas and ideals are not attainable graces; rather, they are a dimly recollected standard against which present attempts at heroic greatness are measured and found wanting. Using the terms and conventions of heroic drama as his instruments, Lee nevertheless comes very close to the conceptual mode of satire. In *The Rival Queens* the ideal is a longed-for "should be" that falters in the paralyzing presence of the human "is";

> So the pale Trojans from their weeping walls
> Saw the dear body of the God-like Hector,
> Bloody and soiled, dragged on the famous ground,
> Yet senseless stood, nor with drawn weapons ran
> To save the great remains of that prodigious man
>   (I, i, 234-38).

Dramatic imitation in the 1670s, then, as it had been in the sixties, is the imitation of emblematic figures operating within an ideational design. Both the design and the figures that move in it, however, now reflect a bifurcated conception of reality. What in the sixties had been an epistemological problem on the middle plane of action only (that is, the confusion between Idea and image that occurs in the descent from the plane of pure idea to the plane of matter) has become the drama's central focus in the seventies. Moreover, as the seventies advance, we move increasingly from observing cosmic man dangling in his middle state between earth and heaven to observing worldly man caught in the conflict between his heavenly and earthly natures. The angle of envisagement in drama is rapidly turning toward experiential reality.

Nevertheless, while ideality exists in the background rather than the foreground of particular plays, it is, and must be, present to consciousness if only by association to moral or literary contexts outside the play. Lee's ambivalent, problematic figures, for example, play against the background of a heroic tradition that conditions the audience's expectations and perceptions. For drama in the 1670s, the ideal is part of the emotional luggage that the audience brings to the theater; it stands in contrast to, and, thereby, as commentary upon, the scene that unfolds before the audience on stage.

While drama of all kinds in the seventies—heroic, tragic, and comic—often had perspectival ambivalence at its central core, it is nevertheless true that satire was the most felicitous vehicle for designing the ambiguous conception of reality that dominated consciousness in the decade. The new conception of nature that began to emerge in the seventies was a conception of nature as matter: "Contrary to the antecedent view of nature, the conception of nature as 'matter' entailed that nature was entirely without qualitative features. . . . its features were entirely quantitative: shape, size, etc. And further, matter qua matter was itself changeless, always remaining just what it was."[34] The genre best equipped to capture the vision of weakly fluttering spirit caught in the quicksand of obdurate, senseless matter is satire.

FOUR

The Varieties
of Dramatic Satire
in the 1670s

In "An Essay upon Satyr" Dacier says, "This the reader may observe, that the name of Satyr in Latin is not less proper for Discourses that recommend Virtue than for those which are design'd against Vice."[1] We might think of this observation as marking one extreme of the satiric spectrum, where "gentile satyre" recommends virtue and laughs at the silliness and affectation that make us deviate from standards "so easy to be kept." Here satire is almost indistinguishable from comedy. At the other end of the spectrum is the satire that Alvin Kernan describes, "Somewhere in his dense knots of ugly flesh the satiric author or painter usually inserts a hint of an ideal that is either threatened with imminent destruction or already dead."[2] Here satire is almost indistinguishable from bleak, unredeemed irony. However, the distinguishing mark of satire is its double, ambivalent vision. However dark or bereft of decency the scene a satire presents, in order to be satire it must suggest an idea of virtue, an ideal, however remote or romantic, for "only the presumption of a good state enables us to call the present satiric one bad."[3] Satire depends upon conceptual contrast and requires the reader or audience to entertain antithetic perspectives simultaneously to arrive at meaning;[4] it was therefore the best vehicle for shaping reality, or Nature, as it was conceived in the 1670s.

Earl Miner has said, "It is not true that Utopias are simply satires in reverse or satires failed Utopias, but by setting out extreme versions of each other, they depend upon each other's existence to keep them in being. It is this kind of interplay that is the fundamental 'Natural Rhetorick' of satire."[5] The range of interplay in a particular satire, the distance its rhetoric must cover to shape the "city be-

tween" Utopia and the city of dreadful night, determines the position that work takes upon the satiric spectrum I have posited.
Literary critics, particularly critics of Restoration drama, have
often failed to recognize a work as satire because they have not
understood the fundamental interplay that Miner describes. The
classicist H. A. Mason, for instance, recently broke with over a
thousand years of traditional understanding to argue that Juvenal is
not a moral satirist but a morally neutral composer of lightly comic
pieces that resemble Martial's *ioci* in intention. Samuel Johnson's
imitations of Juvenal *are* moral satires, Mason argues, *because they
hold up an ideal for emulation*; Juvenal's are not because they make no
positive assertion of good.[6] This misunderstanding has prevented
critics of Restoration drama from recognizing the satiric mode in
"Restoration Comedy." It has led Robert Hume to assume that the
presence of an unstated ideal or a satiric antithesis in that drama is a
mere hallucination suffered by critics who are "profundity zealots."
"If Harcourt and Alithea," he says, "are supposed to represent a high
moral norm in the play . . . then Wycherley made a mess of things,"
or "Harriet is too good a schemer to stand comfortable as a spotless redeemer."[7] But the point is that satiric antithesis need not consist in a "high moral norm" that is present in the play and certainly
need not center in a character who is drawn as an immaculate
redeemer.
I have no desire to debate so thoroughly dead an issue as "the
immorality of Restoration comedy." To my mind it was settled in
two sentences written over fifty years ago: "The morality of Restoration drama cannot be impugned. It *assumes* orthodox Christian
morality, and laughs (in its comedy) at human nature for not living
up to it."[8] Critics apparently cannot understand the obvious fifty
years after it has been pointed out to them. It is interesting though, to
examine the reasons *why* they cannot—which, in my opinion, can be
directly attributed to the change in the conception of dramatic
imitation that occurred during the last forty years of the seventeenth
century. The idea that a poem or a play in order to be satire or merely
to be moral must positively assert a moral good and hold that good
up for emulation rests upon a post-seventeenth-century conception
of the nature and aesthetic effect of art. In works written before the
1690s, satiric antithesis is usually *not* a stated moral or philosophical

position; quite simply, it is the *implied,* very rarely stated, alternative
to thesis. As Howard Weinbrot has so brillantly demonstrated, the
conception of satiric antithesis as a declared moral good that is held
up for emulation begins in criticism with Gildon in 1692 and in
practice with Young's *The Love of Fame* in 1728. Gildon, Weinbrot
says, "made clear the requirement that satire praise the virtue opposed to the vice attacked . . . [because, he argued that] the *Satires* [of
Juvenal] merely expose vice and define virtue by the uncertain path
of negatives. The reader is left rambling in the dark, and so may take
an opposite road."[9]

To Gildon's mind, panegyric is a more reliable force for moral
amendment than satire because it "has the effectual force Satyr
pretends to, in chasing away Vice and Folly, by discovering the
Properties and Beauties of their contraries."[10] As Weinbrot says, the
aim of Young's *Satire Four* is to arouse emulation of the behavior of
particular, actual people like Queen Caroline. In formal verse satire
as well as in dramatic satire, the imitation of actuality and the
presentation of ideal behavioral models that are meant to arouse the
emulation of an audience are a development of the last decade of the
seventeenth century and the first decades of eighteenth. Before then,
and most certainly in the verse and dramatic satire of the seventies,
satiric composition takes its character not from the personal ethical
or moral preferences of the writer but from the conceptual demands
of the genre. As we have seen, the conceptual design of this genre
contrasts ideality and actuality. It is not concerned to discriminate
between "good" and "bad" kinds of behavior. For example, Shadwell's *The Virtuoso,* a brilliant satire on the folly and affectation of
pretenders to the new science, is *not* philosophically antiscientific.
Quite the contrary, the play begins with an exordium upon Lucretius, the poet of atomistic materialism, and it is dedicated to
William Cavendish, the Duke of Newcastle. The ideal is right philosophical reason, but like Rochester's *Satire against Mankind,* the play
extols right reason only obliquely, as the *understood* antithesis of
intellectual pretentiousness and pride.

In the drama of the seventies the range of satiric expression, from
lightly comic to darkly ironic, is wide. On the extreme positive end,
very closely adjacent to comedy, is a play like Fane's *Love in the Dark*
(1675).[11] Fane figures thesis and antithesis in double strains, much as

Dryden had in *Marriage à la Mode*. High modes and low are further apart, however, and more obviously exaggerated than they are in Dryden's play. High consists in outright Platonic philosophical disquisition or in masquelike spectacle, while low is broadly mock-heroic caricature and farcial slapstick.

In the high plot Pharhelia, the Doge's daughter, tests the constancy of the heroic Sforza (who has never seen her) by surprising him, masked, in unpredictable encounters. Her purpose is to transform him into a perfect Platonic lover: "Now will I appear to him in Dreams and Visions and make him love by Inspiration" (I,i). Sforza is already promised to Parhelia by the Doge, but in order to test his capacity for the most elevated love, Parhelia becomes her own masked rival and pushes Sforza to the trial of choosing death and her masked self over marriage to her public self. The masked Parhelia and Sforza engage in exquisitely refined Platonic debate. Love is their subject and their vehicle to the metaphysical absolute:

> **Parh.** The beauty of the Soul's the ground of Love,
> And her Ideas in the face do move:
> For no Man is to White and Red inclin'd
> But to the Air, the Picture of the Mind:
> Then if the Soul will show it self as clear
> Without the Face, her weak Interpreter;
> Sure he is wise that with the Sov'reign Treats.
>   [I,i]

Sforza and Parhelia are Platonic adepts, set as far apart from the herd of lovers as Theander and Eurithea are in Davenant's Caroline play, *The Platonick Lovers*.

> **Sfo.** Religion's veil'd in Types from vulgar Eyes,
> None e'er return'd to tell Celestiall joys.
> If Heav'n were left for everyone to see
> Heav'n would be Hell, with too much company.
>   [I,i]

In contrast to Sforza, "the very Soul and Quintessence of Honour," are the mock-heroic figures, Intrigo and Cornanti. Intrigo is a pointed caricature of heroic idealism: "As others at their Festivals have Lords of Misrule; so too he has his Muster-masters of the Moveables, and his Clarks of the Uniformity. . . . If a Dish comes to

his Table out of its rank and file, he will eat no meat that day" (II,i).
Cornanti, in addition to being a jealous old husband (in that respect,
the antithesis of a Platonic lover), is a mock-hero in valor. He shouts
exaggerated heroic threats while he hides behind his servant to avoid
fighting, and he is finally driven off with a pillow:

> **Cor.** Death and destruction, and a thousand torments
> Attend thy sinful Carcas, thou Planet-struck
> And misbegotten Mortal! Have at thy lecherous Chine
> [Makes at Trivulto when his back is turn'd,
> who takes up a Cushion and makes him run
> to the end of the Stage.
>
> [II,i]

High action is static, philosophic disquisition; low action is very
broadly played intrigue and slapstick. The two styles alternate within a single linear design until the end scene when the lovers coming
together at the Doge's palace to be married are accused of treason and
conspiracy, are arrested, and are brought before the Senate. The play
then descends into farce and topical satire on the inadequacy and
anti-heroic perversity of parliamentary government.

The contrast between thesis and antithesis in Fane's play is quite
strong, but it is not delineated structurally (as it is, for example, in
Marriage à la Mode). Episodes in the low mode do not comment
specifically upon episodes in the high. The play lies so close to
comedy, in fact, that it appears to be the three-tiered design of the
sixties with the middle plane removed. Nevertheless, simply the
presence side by side of high heroic/philosophical and low mock-
heroic/slapstick makes the necessary perspectival contrast. If the
play is not quite satire, it rests on the thin edge that separates satire
from comedy.

Aphra Behn's *The Feign'd Courtezans* (1679) conforms much more
closely to the design and conventions of formal verse satire.[12] Behn's
targets are the conventional targets of the Roman satirist: first and
foremost among them a debased age that has lost its aristocratic
ideals:

> **Galliard.** Away with your Antiquated Notions . . .
> Examine the whole World *Harry*, and thou wilt find a Beautiful woman
> the desire of the Noblest, and the reward of the Bravest.

Fill. And the common Prize of Coxcombs; times are alter'd now, *Frank,*
why else shou'd the Virtuous be Cornuted, the Coward be carest, the
Villain role with Six, and the Fool lye with her ladyship.

[I, i]

In the view of the satirist the decay of the times is consequent upon
the willingness of the aristocratic class to forget itself and upon the
corrosive influence of base-born parvenus. Galliard, who is one of
the play's three satiric spokesmen, says of Sir Signal Buffon: "Our
Knights Father is even the first Gentleman of his House, a fellow,
who having the good Fortune to be much a fool and knave, had the
attendent blessing of getting an Estate of some eight thousand a year,
with this Coxcomb to indent it; who (to aggrandize the Name and
Family of Buffons) was made a knight, but to refine throughout and
make a compleat Fop was sent abroad under the Government of one
Mr. *Tickletext* his zealous Fathers Chaplain, as errant a block-head as
a man wou'd wish to hear Preach; the Father forseeing the eminent
danger that your Travelers are in of being perverted to Popery" (I, ii).
Money has replaced virtue and honor as the highest social value.
Knavery and chicanery are the ways to preferment in the fallen age.
Most often Behn launches her thesis attack in the manner of a verse
satirist, as commentary upon the scene that is spoken directly to the
audience by a type of the traditional satiric spokesman. This direct
satiric commentary is aimed at upper-class shortcomings, at the
nouveau nobility, at the corrupt and clearly Puritan clergy (Tickletext is a lecher and a hypocrite)—all the traditional targets of verse
satire. In a topical vein, it even takes a swipe at the Popish Plot
hysteria that was still raging in 1679.

The play has two conventional satiric spokesmen. Galliard is an
honnête homme man of sense, who is not above the frailties he attacks
and who addresses the audience in set pieces that often imitate, or at
least call to mind, their classical sources, as these lines recall Juvenal's
Satire Six:

Gall. O Women! Women! fonder in your Appetites
    Than Beasts, and more unnatural!
    For they but couple with their kind, but you Promiscuously shuffle your
    Brutes together The fop of business with the lazy Gown-man—the
    learn'd Asse with the Illiterate wit. The empty Coxcombe with the
    Politian, as dull and insignificant as he; from the gay fool made more a
    beast by fortune to all the loath'd infirmities of Age. [IV, i]

Petro is a parasite-satirist, one who ridicules his gulls behind their backs even as he takes their money. As is traditional of this figure, he is a man of many faces: "He is capacitated to oblige in any quality; for, Sir, he's your brokering Jew, your Fencing, Dancing and Civility-Master, your Linguist, your Antiquary, your Bravo, your Pathetick, your Whore, your Pimp, and a thousand more Excellencies he has to supply the necessities of the wanting stranger" (II, ii). Usually the parasite-satirist makes his commentary in asides that act as glosses upon the ridiculous actions of his victims, but occasionally his commentary is aimed at the audience. For example, Petro explains that his basic disguise is that of a barber because the role is a particularly good one in which to test the suitability of his pigeons for plucking. In the process of explaining himself, however, he indirectly attacks one of the perennial targets of satire—flattery as the means to preferment in a debased age—for the benefit of the audience. Playing a barber, Petro says, enables him,

> the sooner to take the heights of their judgements, it gives handsome opportunities to commend their faces, for if they are pleas'd with flattery, the certain sign of a fools to be most tickled when most commended, I conclude 'em the fitter for my purpose; they already put great confidence in me, will have no Masters but of my recommending, all which I supply my self. I doubt not to pick up a good honest painful livelihood, by cheating, two Reverend Coxcombs.
> **Gall.** How the devil got'st thou this credit with 'em?
> **Pet.** Oh easily, Sir, as knaves get estates, or fools employments. [I, i]

The gulls are also caricature types conventional in satire: the pretender to nobility and the religious hypocrite. Sir Signal bears some resemblance to Sir Fopling Flutter in being the very ape of fashion: "[of his suit] Made for me—Who Sir, he [Petro] swore to me by the old Law, that 'twas never worn but once, and that by one high-German Prince—I have forgot his name—for the Devil can never remember these damn'd Hogan-Mogan Titles" (I, ii). Like Sir Fopling, Sir Signal also aspires to international, cafe society manners: "How I long for my Civility-Master, that I may learn to out-compliment all the dull Knights and Squires in Kent, with a *Servitore Hulichmo-No Signora bellisima, base la Mane . . .* and so I'l run on, hah Governor, hah! won't this be pure?" (I, ii). Tickletext bears close resemblance to Wycherley's Alderman Gripe and Jonson's Zeal

O'the Land Busy, but by 1679 the hypocritical, lecherous Puritan
divine is so conventional a type that the caricature is hardly attributable to any particular source—indeed, it seems a bit old-fashioned
and creakily theatrical. Satiric antithesis is presented with greater variety in this play than
is usual in a single work. Sometimes it appears in a close juxtaposi-
tion of romantic and antiromantic strains that both states and deflates
the ideal in an instant. The "feign'd courtezans" are Marcella and
Cornelia, the romantic and antiromantic pair of female characters we
find in *Flora's Vagaries* and *She Would If She Could*. Here their function
is both to embody the idea of virtue hidden behind a tawdry exterior
(the inner virgin, the outer courtesan) and to give voice to satire's
double perspective:

> **Mar.** The Evenings soft and calm, as happy Lovers thoughts;
> And here are Groves where the kind meeting Trees
> Will hide us from the Amorous Gazing Croud.
> **Cor.** What should we do there, sigh till our wandering Breath,
> Has rais'd the gentle Gale amongst the boughs;
> To whose dull melancholy Musick, we
> Laid on a bed of Moss, and new fall'n leaves
> Will reade the dismal tale of Eccho's Love!
> —No, I can make better use of Famous Ovid.
>
> [II, i]

Antithesis recalls the golden world of Ovid to set the contrast
with thesis's vision of a world where beauty is "the common prize of
coxcombs" and the "fool lyes with her Ladyship." The golden world
is no sooner evoked by Marcella however, than it is mocked and
undercut as a poetic fancy by Cornelia. Nevertheless, its very evocation sets the necessary contrast essential in satire. Moreover, despite
the better use Cornelia thinks she can make of Ovid and because she
is at heart virtuous (and in fact *embodies* the play's antithesis emblematically), antithesis in this satire is firmly set *within* the thesis context.
That is, the ideal is envisioned as attainable, though rarely so, in a
fallen world.

A more sharply contrastive statement of antithesis is made in
mock-heroic allusions. For example, when Galliard comes upon the
slapstick battle in which Tickletext is beating Petro-as-Fencing-

Master with an old-fashioned English broadsword, he exclaims:
"Why how now *Mr. Tickletext*, what mortal wars are these? *Ajax* and
Ulisses contending for *Achillis* his Armour?" (I, ii). Galliard's allusion
to the *Iliad* sets a heroic standard by whose light we mark the mock-
heroic intention of the farcical scene. There are less specific allusions
to epic and romance throughout the play; their function, typical in
satire, is to draw the ideal into the thesis context indirectly.

One expression of antithesis in the play, however, is quite unconventional and may be unique in Restoration drama, namely, Behn's
portrait of a Herculean heroine of irregular greatness, Laura Lucretia. Laura Lucretia is great souled in exactly the manner of heroic
figures of the sixties; indeed, in her defiance of conventional boundaries and inadequate definitions, she resembles a secular St. Catherine:

> **Lau.** . . . I can know no fear, but where I love!
> **Syl.** And then that thing that Ladys call their Honour
> **Lau.** Honour, that hated Idoll, even by those
>   That set it up to worship; No,
>   I have a Soul my Boy, and that's all Love!
>   And I'le the Tallent which Heav'n lent improve.
>   [II, ii]

Because thesis is somewhat distanced in *The Feign'd Courtezans* (that
is, the scene is set in Rome and the action is decidedly romantic) and
because antithesis is figured as a virtue that *does* exist, though disguised, in the fallen world, the play stands toward the comic end of
the satiric scale.

With Etherege's *The Man of Mode* (1676) and Wycherley's *The
Country Wife* (1675), we come to the center of that scale. The scene
presented by thesis is familiar and immediate. Heroic antithesis is
carefully blended into a realistic thesis context—for example, in
Dorimant's quotations from Waller's Odes and in the gently romantic pastoral songs that provide chiaroscuro shading for the modish
foreground follies under consideration; or in the clever mock-honor,
mock-love, double-entendre debates between Lady Fidget and
Horner. Antithesis is also presented in single figures like Harriet and
Alithea, whose moral and intellectual integrity sets them slightly
apart from the scene of fools and hypocrites. These characters are

neither heroic, perfect, nor emblematic; they exist as part of the thesis context and yet they embody ideals of virtue. The ideal has become less obvious, and the closeness of thesis to antithesis makes satire more pointed; however, while in Wycherley's play virtue is indeed "threatened with destruction," in both plays virtue is still alive in the fallen city, still a realizable possibility. Consequently, satire has not yet descended to the ironic end of the spectrum. Because I have dealt with Wycherley's satire so often in the past,[13] I shall use *The Man of Mode* as my example here. In this play thesis and antithesis are hardly separable. They are not presented in separate lines of action or separate styles, nor in any simple opposition of ideational counters. Characterization has tipped quite far in the direction of imitation of the actual, but characters still retain a degree of metaphoric identity. For instance, Bellinda is introduced as a "mask" because her function as a character is to figure an empty *form* of seeming virtue or respectability; Old Bellair is a *Senex Amans;* Nan, the Orangewoman is a figure of La Vieille, who stands in relation to Harriet as the play opens in a configuration that, as I have argued elsewhere,[14] is as old as *Sir Gawain and the Green Knight*. It is important to note that in as refined a realization of the satiric conceptual mode as we find in this play, contrast is not achieved by simple panegyric/burlesque, upward and downward reflection. Rather, characters, who are themselves complex, cast light upon one another or slightly refract each other's light. Here satire's "distortions in the artist's mirror of the norm of nature" are very subtle distortions. They are masterpieces in literature of what Hagstrum calls "mock-portraiture:" "The invention and practice of mock-portraiture was vastly more than a mere trick of line and illusion. It was the attempt to grasp the truth beneath the surface through superficial distortion, to create a new comic art by a new vision of deformity."[16]

In *The Man of Mode* satiric contrast lies in the opposition between the surface and what, if anything, lies beneath the surface, which is exposed through very subtle, superficial distortion. It is almost as though the juxtaposition among characters caused hairline cracks in the surface of a particular character, through which we get the slightest glimpses of what lies below. I do not mean to imply that Etherege is a precursor of those authors in the nineties who attempt to plumb the depths of characters who stimulate "real people." In this play, as in the other dramatic satires we have examined, the center of our attention is *perspectival ambivalence*. The interplay we watch is that between nature and artifice in the human condition. Just as Dryden figures the human paradox in interplay between "literary" imaginative truth and stubborn experiential "facts" in *Marriage à la Mode* or Lee figures it in the conflict between the mighty human soul struggling for freedom and the paralyzed will confined in the world, so Etherege figures it in the distance between natural man and surface man. To "prepare a face to meet the faces that you meet" is neither foolish nor immoral; it is one half of our inescapable humanity. Man is the only creature who is simultaneously fashioned by the hand of nature and self-fashioning.

The central question the play poses for us is: What is the difference between self-fashioning artifice that serves, imitates, or embellishes nature, and the artifice that inhibits, distorts, or substitutes for nature? Throughout the play the artifices of man the image maker are examined. Characters stage deliberate scenes for one another, sometimes to deceive others, as Harriet and Young Bellair play the roles of fashionable lovers to the audience of Old Bellair and Lady Woodvil. Sometimes the parts that characters play to deceive others prove to be double-edged, deceiving the observer but also exposing aspects of the player that he would rather conceal or of which he is not aware. For example, Dorimant plays Mr. Courtage, one who dotes upon the forms of the last age, in order to deceive Lady Woodvil. In the process, however, *we* become aware that Dorimant has been playing a hero of the last age in Mrs. Loveit's scenarios and a great-souled libertine in his own. Etherege uses Harriet to point out this satiric double play to the audience:

Lady Wood. What have you to except against him
[Dorimant disguised as the admirable Courtage]
Har. He's a fop.
Lady Wood. He's not a Dorimant, a wild extravagant fellow of the times.
Har. He's a man made up of forms and commonplaces sucked out of the remaining lees of the last age. [IV, i]

Dorimant affects to be, and, when we regard only one surface of his figure, *we* think him to be, an "extravagant fellow of the times," a free-flying libertine. However, seen in the context of slightly distorting comparisons in which the play sets him, he may also be seen from a totally different perspective to be a mere scarecrow effigy of the intoxicating hero of irregular greatness, a papier–mâché image of the great-souled hero that has been patched together from imagination's leftover scraps and tatters.

Characters "play" literary stereotypes to expose or to influence one another, toward the greater end of illuminating the central idea of the play, which is that self-dramatization and artificing are inescapable human tendencies. Mrs. Loveit, for instance, is always at full tilt playing a Caroline heroine who inspires love and honor in the breast of her Herculean hero. She stages him for herself as an "angel yet undefac'd" and pictures herself in relation to him as a beauteous spur to greatness. Then, failing to inspire heroic love and valor, she rages in high heroic style; her language is straight out of Davenant or Fletcher. Indeed, her exchange with Dorimant that begins "Is this the constancy you vowed?" is taken from the key passage of one of the best-known plays of the former age, *The Maid's Tragedy.*

Bellinda too is a play-maker. She stages a scene that will separate Dorimant from Loveit and capture him for herself:

Dor. [to Medley] She means *insensibly* to *insinuate* a discourse of me, and *artificially* raise her jealousy . . . the quarrel being thus happily begun, *I am to play my part.* [I, i; italics mine]

Harriet acts Dorimant's affectations to him in the Mall, arranges the playlet in which he enacts a Caroline beau, and, even as she acknowledges to herself that she loves him, uses theatrical images to expose his and the world's affectations:

Dor. What have we here, the picture of a celebrated beauty giving audience in public to a declared lover?
Har. Play the dying fop and make the piece complete, sir.
Dor. What think you if the hint were well improved—the whole mystery of making love wrought in a suit of hangings?
Har. 'Twere needless to execute fools in effigy who suffer daily in their own persons. [V, ii]

Sir Fopling Flutter, an English booby, plays at being a French chevalier, for "varnished over with good breeding many a blockhead *makes a tolerable show"* (III, i). Sir Fopling is, of course, an exaggerated emblem of the central question the play raises: Is heroic man in any age an honnête homme libertine enlarged to his heroic dimensions by "the force that through the green fuse drives the flower" or is he a fopling flutter, a set of postures, a shape without substance? The genius of Etherege's subtle satiric style is that as it puts Sir Fopling into contrast with Dorimant, his glaring foppishness slightly refracts Dorimant's fashionable glow and makes us reassess what we have been admiring. For instance, the first mention of Sir Fopling is made when our attention is fixed upon Dorimant in the act of dressing:

Handy. You love to have your clothes hang just, sir.
Dor. I love to be well-dressed, sir; and I think it no scandal to my understanding.
Handy. Will you use the essence, or orange flower water?
Dor. I will smell as I do to day, no offence to the ladies' noses.
Handy. Your pleasure, sir.
Dor. That a man's excellency should lie in neatly tying of a ribbon or a cravat! How careful's *nature in furnishing the world with necessary coxcombs?*
Bell. That's a mighty pretty suit of yours, Dorimant.
Dor. I'm glad't has your approbation.
Bell. No man has a better fancy in his clothes than you have.
Dor. You will make me have an opinion of my *genius.*
Med. There is a great critic, I hear, in these matters lately arrived piping hot from Paris.
Bell. Sir Fopling Flutter, you mean. (Italics mine) [I, i]

Our "fancy," "genius," or imagination makes us conceive images of ourselves, which we then create and play for the world. Dorimant is not more a libertine and less a fop than Sir Fopling because he chooses to smell like himself, as some critics have argued, for even the decision to smell as one does, to be *natural,* is a choice in the creation of an image by artificer-man. Every male character in the play plays at being a man of mode (with the possible exception of Young Bellair, who is a romantic lover), from Tom the Shoemaker to Sir Fopling, because in the satiric vision of the play to *be* that ridiculous but charming thing—a human being—is to be a player and a shaper of scenes. The only question is how successful and pleasing a correspondence one makes between the image one creates of oneself and the underlying nature it imitates and decorates.

The surface realism of the play is itself a satiric device; we the audience are the people of mode that the play really exposes. Etherege's mock-portraiture probes the surface of *our* common and universal human nature. As Dryden said in his epilogue to the play,

> Most modern wits such monstruous fools have shown
> That seem'd not of Heaven's making but their own.
> These nauseous harlequins in farce may pass,
> But there goes more to a substantial ass,
> Something of man must be exposed to view,
> That gallants, they may more resemble you.[16]

Harriet, who expresses satiric antithesis both in what she is and in what she says, is aware that it takes a fine critical judgment to discriminate between what is "natural," or comfortable to nature, and what affects to be so:

Har. He [Dor.] is agreeable and pleasant I must own, but he does so much affect being so, he displeases me.
Y. Bell. Lord, Madam, all he does and says is so easy and natural.
Har. Some men's verses seem so to the unskillful, but labour 'i the one and affectation in the other to the judicious plainly appear. [III, iii]

It is not accidental that Etherege associates judgment of poetry with judgment of a man of mode, for poetry is the product as well as the sign of man as a maker of images that may prove to be empty forms or that may prove to be valid imitations of nature. Artifice is not a vice when it knows itself and presents itself to be artifice. Harriet, who embodies "nature," is an archdesigner of images. But she uses them as a comic poet does, to strip Dorimant of pretentions and to bring him to self-knowledge. Unlike Loveit, who uses scenes for self-aggrandizement, and Bellinda, who uses them for self-gratification and protection, Harriet uses them openly, to call attention to the truth that all human behavior is in some degree playacting: "Women now-a-days have their passions as much at will as their complexions, and put on joy and sadness, scorn and kindness, with the same ease as they do their paint and patches—Are they the only counterfeits?" (V, i).

Antithesis in the play is untempered nature, virtue, and decency, and it is embedded in Harriet, nature's instrument and agent. Medley's initial description of her emphasizes her natural beauty: "a fine, easy, clean shape . . . hair in abundance . . . lips . . . that look like the Provence rose, fresh on the bush, ere the morning sun has quite drawn up the dew" (I, i). In reply to Dorimant's "Where had you all that scorn and coldness in your look?" Harriet says, "From nature, sir, pardon my want of art, I have not learnt those softnesses and languishings which are now so much in fashion." The fashions, modes, and affectations of the "present" are, as they invariably are in satire, "unnatural." Old-fashioned virtue and simplicity are the values the play extols. And Harriet is decidedly virtuous as well as old-fashioned. She refuses to defy her mother to marry Dorimant because she "[has] not done, nor never will do anything against [her] duty." She openly declares for "the rules of decency and honour," to the extent that, though her mother does not control her fortune, she will not disobey her to marry Dorimant without her mother's consent. Despite decades of critical opinion that have understood Etherege's play as a celebration of libertine values, the *ideals* it gives us upon which to measure the value of life à la mode are natural grace, filial obedience, and virtue.

The play is, of course, open-ended. The honnête homme may choose nature's way and take a journey into the country where Harriet and the traditional image of a man's fate in nature await him:

Har. . . . my mother, an old lame aunt, and myself, sir . . . sitting moping like three melancholy birds in a spacious volery. [V, ii]

On the other hand, he may choose against nature and may fully become his doppelgänger, Sir Fopling Flutter; Sir Fopling is the "other" reflection in satire's double-faced mirror, a slight distortion that reveals the libertine to be a scarecrow of empty forms.

Shadwell's *The Virtuoso* (1676) crosses the midpoint on our imaginary satiric scale and begins the move toward the ironic end of the spectrum. Like *The Humorists*, but more successfully, it is an attempt to render Juvenalian satire in the dramatic mode. In structure, tone, and mock-portraiture it comes close to capturing the Roman style. Its thesis presents examples of real moral deformity, as well as mere folly, as, for example, the sexual deviance of Snarl, the satyr-satirist, whose pleasure is to be whipped by Figg-up, his whore. It has the economy of Roman verse satire in that it lashes one vice principally, false knowledge, and other vices and follies only as they are subordinate to the primary target. Finally, it is self-consciously satiric, and, like Wycherley's *The Plain Dealer* and Juvenal's *First Satire,* it questions the usefulness of satire as an instrument of moral reformation: "The Beastly Restive World will go its own way; and there is not so foolish a Creature as a Reformer" (I, i).[17]

In his preface Shadwell says that he has "endeavored in this Play at Humour, Wit, and Satyr." He defines humour as "an affectation, as misguides men in Knowledge, Art, or Science, or that causes defection in Manners, and Morality, or perverts their Minds in the Main Actions of their lives."[18] His central target in the play is the form of intellectual pride that misdirects men's understanding of the uses of knowledge, art, and science and that breeds in them improper self-love and inaccurate self-knowledge, which in turn perverts their manners and morals. The play begins with an open statement of antithesis: a declaration of right knowledge and sense that is the standard upon which we are to judge the perversions that follow. (This kind of initial declaration, ironically expressed, is common in Juvenal.) Bruce is reading Lucretius, the favorite poet (and, with Epicurus, the favorite philosopher) of the new scientific learning or "natural philosophy" that was so much admired by Shadwell's patron, the Duke of Newcastle. Antithesis in this play is pointedly *not* heroic or literary; Lucretius is invoked as "thou profound Oracle of Wit and Sence! Thou art no Trifling-Landskip-Poet, no Fantastick Heroick Dreamer, with empty Descriptions of Impossibilities and mighty sounding Nothings. Thou reconcil'st Philosophy with Verse, and dost, almost alone, demonstrate that Poetry and Good Sence may go together" (I, i).

Satiric thesis is presented both in dramatic scenes of vice and folly and in rhetorical set pieces aimed at the audience. Scene is mainly used to demonstrate the extravagances of pretenders to knowledge, as, for instance, the scene in which Sir Nicholas Gimcrack is learning to swim in his laboratory rather than in water because "[He] care[s] not for the Practick. [He] seldom bring[s] any thing to use, 'tis not [his] way." But scene is also used to expose the vice and hypocrisy to

which a virtuoso may be brought by ignorance or denial of the
"practick," appetitive component in his nature: "What! is my florid
Fool catch'd with a Whore? an ugly Whore? does your noble Soul
operate clearly, without the clog of your sordid humane body now?
You are a fine formal Hypocrite" (V, i).

The sharpest satiric attacks, however, are presented rhetorically in
diatribes aimed at the audience. Two kinds of satiric spokesmen
appear in the play: the honest "gentlemen of wit and sense," whose
style is pointed but urbane, and the satyr-satirist, Sharl, who is
himself morally deformed and who spits out venom under the hue of
moral chastisement. Snarl is a "brute," like Wycherley's Manly, "a
great Disclaimer against the Vices of the Age, a clownish, blunt,
Satyricall Fellow, a hater of all young People and Fashions . . . [who]
should be Wormed like a mad Dog" (I, i). His rough and bitter
attacks upon the age are invariably aimed at the vice of which he
himself is guilty: sexual depravity. As Alvin Kernan has shown, the
constellation of traits, hypocrisy/deformity/spite, as well as a harsh
revulsion at bodily processes, is a hallmark of the traditional satyr
spokesman who dominated in English verse satire from Chaucer's
Pardoner to Marston's and Hall's spokesmen in the seventeenth
century.[19] The satyr-satirist hates the age in which he lives not
because he is morally superior to it but because some incapacity, like
age, cowardice, or impotence, prevents him from indulging his own
beastliness:

Snarl . . . the last Age was an Age of innocence, you young Sluts you; now
a company of Jill-flirts, flaunting, vaine Cockatrices, take more pains to
lose Reputation, than those did to preserve it. I am afraid the next Age
will have very few that are lawfully begotten in't, by the Mass. Besides,
the young Fellows are like all to be effeminate Coxcombs, and the young
Women strumpets . . . all Strumpets, by the Mass.
Clar. *You are a fine old Satyr indeed; 'twere well if you decri'd Vices for any reason
but that you are past them.* [I, i; italics mine]

Snarl's rough railing and his sexual aberrations with Figg-up create
the atmosphere that Kernan describes above—"ugly knots of dense
flesh" with only hints of an ideal—and do much to push the play
toward irony.

Longvil and Bruce, however, are *vir bonum* satiric spokesmen.

They are driven to lash the age by their own commonsensical morality. Their style is, of course, much lighter in tone than Snarl's, but it is nevertheless distinctly Juvenalian. Their comments are restricted to the principal vice under attack, false learning, and foundations of miseducation in the rearing and the conduct of youth:

Long. . . . Gentlemen care not upon what strain they get their Sons now, nor how they breed 'em, when they have got 'em . . . you shall seldom see a young Fellow of this age that does not look like those over-grown Animals newly manumitted from Trunk-Breeches.
Bruce . . . before they can Conster and Pearce they are sent into *France* with sordid, illiterate Creatures, call'd Dry'd-Nurses, or Governors . . .
Long. . . . or they are sparks that early break loose from Discipline, and at sixteen forsooth set up for Men of the Town.
Bruce Such as come Drunk and Screaming into the Play-house . . . and toss their full Periwigs and empty Heads, and with their shrill unbroken Pipes, cry, *Dam-me, this is a Damn'd Play; Prithee let's to a Whore, Jack.* [I, i]

This exchange between Bruce and Longvil functions in exactly the manner of Juvenalian satire; that is, satirist and adversarius survey contemporary life and conjure the satiric scene (of pox-ridden, adolescent blockheads at a playhouse) by means of their rhetorical exchange.

Satire in *The Virtuoso* is multitextured. Some of the scenes set before us are broadly comic and lightly ridicule the affectations of pretenders to knowledge—like the scene in which the scientific virtuoso, Sir Nicholas, who sees worlds in a dish of vinegar, and the oratorical virtuoso, Sir Formal, who embroiders Sir Nicholas's achievements in fine language, show Bruce and Longvil around Sir Nicholas's laboratory; or the scene in which Lady Gimcrack juggles with words (like "honor") as she attempts to seduce Bruce. Still other scenes are superficially farcical but carry a dark undertone— like the whole of act 4. On the surface the usual confusion of illicit lovers trying to meet and yet to avoid detection is farcical, while beneath the surface the gross sexuality of Figg-up and Snarl and the homosexual almost-union between Sir Samuel and Sir Formal is much uglier in tone. On the third level the spoken satire of Snarl is harshly obscene. Finally, the spoken satire of Bruce and Longvil operates directly upon the audience and turns the whole thrust of satire into their lives in Brechtian style.

As we move further toward the ironic pole of our spectrum, we find that antithesis is almost invariably oblique. In this play *understood* right reason and sense is the opposite of the virtuosos' extravangance, while old-fashioned chastity and love stand in opposition to the moral deviance that false understanding breeds. The only open statements of antithesis are the short initial invocation of Lucretius and two act 5 statements of the young sensible lovers, which together comprise about eight lines:

Mir. I love Bruce . . . and could venture any thing but honour for him.
Clar. I'd lose my life a thousand times before my virtue. [V, 1]

While the young women value their virtue above their love, the young men value the minds of their mistresses above their bodies:

Long. . . . I would not have the body without the mind.
Bruce A man enjoys as much by a rape as that way. [V, i]

In the world of *The Virtuoso* right knowledge is common sense and honor is simple virtue, but very little direct attention is given them. We understand these values only as implied alternatives to the negatives of them that are set before us.

With *The Libertine* (1676) we come to the last extreme, where satire is indistinguishable from bleak, unredeemed irony.[20] Hume has said: "As in *Timon* . . . Shadwell imports the moral code of contemporary libertine comedy into a tragic structure, and the result is sober-faced burlesque."[21] As we have seen in examining *The Man of Mode*, it is questionable a comic form existed in the 1670s, that *celebrates* libertine values; it is equally questionable, I think, that the structure of *The Libertine* is "tragic" in either our own or the Restoration senses of the term. "Sober-faced burlesque," seems far too mild for the atmosphere we find in this play; however, the description might be valid if we mean to suggest by it the furthest extent of downward exaggeration to which satire can reach. The play fails because what we find here is the darkest vision of which satiric thesis is capable and the *total* absence of the "other," antithetical perspective.

In style the play is a morality play; figures are abstract images of Vice, uncomplicated, uniform, and homogeneous; the figures are not conceptual counters of different kinds of vice, or of different aspects of the human soul, or even of different aspects of libertinism. Don John equals libertine, and no more is made of that equation than of the equation that follows from it: libertine equals evil. Scenes exist, as in romance or as on the heroic plane of the works we have examined, as a series of discrete display boxes. However, they do not display the various faces of evil; they simply pile enormity upon enormity. The scenes do not juxtapose ideas or figures in conceptual configurations, nor do they develop or explore character. Don John begins as an evil libertine, and he ends as an unrepentant, evil libertine. The play is not tragic in the Restoration sense because it does not end in passage through death to metaphysical truth; it is not tragic in a twentieth-century sense because Don John comes to no anagnorisis. His end-scene speech as his companions are being carried off by devils is fustian; it moves nowhere rhetorically:

These things [devils carrying his companions away] I see with wonder, but no fear.
Were all the Elements to be confounded,
And shuffl'd all into their former Chaos,
Were Seas of Sulphur flaming round about me,
And all Mankind roaring within those fires,
I could not fear or feel the least remorse.
Here I stand firm, and all thy threats contemn,
The Murderer stands here, now do thy worst.   [V, i]

The speech may seem defiant out of context, but it is no more elevated, no further enlarged, no more conceptually refined than any other speech in the play. Like the long series of unconnected scenes that precede it, the end scene is one more display in a vision of unrelieved cruelty, depravity, and moral vacuity. Throughout, satiric thesis presents a world already come to chaos.

Antithesis is not merely lost or threatened with destruction; it is destroyed before our eyes. For example, act 4 presents us with a highly "literary" pastoral scene of nymphs and shepherds singing the delights and beauties of untempered nature. We would expect this to comprise the antithesis, for it is untempered nature rightly understood in opposition to the libertine's false understanding of untempered nature:

1 Shep. Nature is here not yet debauch'd by Art,
'Tis as it was in Saturn's happy days:

Minds are not here by Luxury invaded;
A homely Plenty with sharp Appetite,
Does lightsome health and virgorous strength impart.

[IV, i]

The remote, literary vision of Saturn's golden days, the breath of pastoral simplicity, is quite common in dark satire (compare Juvenal's *VI* and *IX*). In fact, as I have argued elsewhere,[22] the darkness of the thesis scene is functionally related to the remote unreality of the antithesis in classical satire. However, not even in Juvenal do we find anything to compare with Shadwell's treatment of the fate of innocence in the fallen world; no sooner have the nymphs and shepherds finished their song than Don John and his companions enter to rape and slaughter them.

So bleak is the total vision of the play that the small infrequent passages of direct social satire it affords cannot stand in its withering atmosphere. For example, in act 3, scene 1, in the exchanges of two young virgins, we are given the kind of bantering ridicule of English society that we found in *The Humorists* and *The Virtuoso:*

Clar. Oh that we had those frank civil English-men instead of our grave dull *Spanish blockheads* . . .

Flav. In England if a Husband treats his Mistress openly in his Glas-Coach: the Wife for decency's sake, puts on her Vizer, and whips away in a Hackney with a Gallant, and no harm done. [III, i]

The light ridicule of the passage is totally incongruous in the context, however, for the virgins no sooner meet the Englishmen whom they long to see than they are raped and mutilated by them.

In a context where murder, rape, and the violation and mutilation of nuns in their convent form a Bosch-like nightmare vision of reality, satire cannot maintain its necessary balance, its perspectival ambivalence. Shadwell's adaptation of Shakespeare's *Timon* is just as dark as *The Libertine* in thesis. In that play, however, Shadwell maintains satiric balance by adding to the original the faithful Evandra, whose honesty, fidelity, and generous love provide at least a slight contrastive pull upward from the dark scene.

As we have seen, the reality that satire captures in a form is double faced, exaggerating upward and downward at the same time to imitate the "nature" that lies somewhere between those two reflections. When one reflection is completely obliterated, the intention of this conceptual contrast is blurred or even lost. Dryden attributed the failure of *The Kind Keeper* (1678) to his audience's inability to perceive its satiric intention. His attempt to justify the play provides us with a clue to his understanding of the balance that satire demands: " 'Twas intended for an honest *Satyre* against our crying sin of keeping. . . . The Crime for which it suffer'd, was that which is objected against the *Satyres of Juvenal,* and the *Epigrams of Catullus,* that it express'd too much of the Vice which it decry'd."[23]

Dryden thought that posterity would vindicate him, and in his claim that the play was intended as moral satire, posterity should. The play is problematic not because it makes sin delightful but because its mock-heroic antithesis is too slight to carry the weight of its thesis—so slight and so scattered that it is hardly even the "hint" that Kernan observes in dark, knotted satire. At most we get hints of hints. For instance, Woodall's reply to his servant Gervase, who has been describing Woodall's prowess in drinking and fornication, is a mere tint of mock-heroic: "*Gervase,* thou shal't be my Chronicler, thou losest none of my Heroick Actions" (I, i), or Gervase says of the obscene Aldo: "My old Master wou'd fain pass for *Philip of Macedon* when he is little better than Sir *Pandarus of Troy.*" The hints are never reinforced; neither Woodall nor Aldo are shown to be mock-heroic in their action (as Sir Frederick Frolick is in *Love in a Tub*) or their in rhetoric (as Crazy is in *The Humorists* or as Cornanti is in *Love in the Dark*). Mock-heroic satires like *The Man of Mode* or comical satires like *The Country Wife* can sustain a very lightly drawn antithesis because their thesis mockery and caricature are light. In *The Kind Keeper* images of vice are too heavily wrought to be balanced by a random scattering of one-liners like "Tricksy hath murder'd sleep."

We must take another factor into account when trying to understand the failure of *The Kind Keeper.* As we near the end of the decade, another change in sensibility is becoming apparent. In my opinion audiences found the play scandalous, in part because they were gradually beginning to understand drama as imitation of the actual. There is, of course, a great deal of obscenity in the play but no more than in *The Virtuoso.* There is a great deal of topical satire on the proto-Whigs, and the question of whether Limberham is Shaftesbury has yet to be finally decided, but there had been satire of the Left since *The Committee,* and Liberham is certainly not as obviously a portrait of Shaftesbury as Otway's Antonio is. Both the way in which audiences understood the play and the argument that Dryden offers in attempting to justify it foreshadow another change apace in the conception of dramatic imitation of nature: "It has nothing of particular *Satyre* in it; for whatsoever may have been pretended by some Criticks in the Town; I may safely and solemnly affirm that no one Character has been drawn from any single man; and that I have known so many of the same humour, in every folly which is here expos'd, as may serve to warrant it from a particular Reflection."[24] When we compare this observation with the observations upon satiric portrayal that Shadwell makes in his preface to *The Humorists* with which we began our discussion of dramatic satire, we discover that in the course of the 1670s a very subtle but profoundly important change has occurred in the playwright's conception of what the reality is that he imitates. We will remember that Shadwell says his reasons for avoiding imitation of a real fool are *aesthetic*, because, he argues, the making of a play consists in "the invention of remote and pleasant thoughts of what kind so ever; and there is as much occasion for such imaginations in the writing of a Curious Coxcomb's part, as in writing the greatest Hero's."[25] Shadwell argues further that for a playwright to imitate empirically observable actuality on the stage would present the audience with that which they would find "unnatural." Dryden's reasons for not presenting a "particular Reflection" are altogether different; they are social and perhaps moral, but they are not aesthetic. Shadwell argues in 1671 that a poet *cannot* present the actual particular onstage; Dryden argues that he might have presented any number of particular individuals but that he has chosen not to. Whereas Shadwell conceived of a vice or folly as an abstract quality, a "Character of the Mind," which the poet must detach from the *encumbrance* of actual events and particular persons, Dryden eight years later understands the picture of folly to be a composite drawing of the actual behavior of particular people. The delicate balance of ideal with actual has tipped. In the decades to come we shall still be concerned with patterns of ideal truth, but we shall look for them in the material world as signs of divine Providence and at last shall seek them in the very center of man's hidden, idiosyncratic life.

FIVE

Nature as the Experiential Actual, 1680–1700

At last the cleerest, best and most certain Knowledg that mankinde can possibly have of things existing without him is but Experience, that is noe thing but the Exercise and observation of his Senses about particular objects, and therefore Knowledg and Faith too at last resolve themselves into and terminate somewhere or other in Experience either our owne or other mans.

Locke, *An Essay concerning Human Understanding*

I cannot imagine, nor do I understand what is meant by *Beautiful Extravagance;* for if it is something beyond nature, it is so far from being admir'd by Men of Sense, that it is contemn'd and laugh'd at. For what there is in any Poem, which is out of Nature and contrary to Verisimilitude and Probability can never be beautiful, but abominable. The Business of Poetry is to copy Nature truly, and observe probability and Verisimilitude justly; and the Rules of Art are to show us what Nature is, and how to distinguish its Lineaments from the unruly and preposterous Sallies and Flights of an irregular, and uninstructed Fancy.

The Art, Rise, and Progress of the Stage

'Tis certain that our Manners are in great measure form'd by our Education, and Monsieur *Pascal* had reason to say, *That whereas Custom is stil'd a second Nature, he doubted whether Nature were anything but a first Custom.*

Motteux, Gentleman's Journal

Hume has quite rightly observed that because there is no sharp break in the continuity of theatrical history from the 1670s through the 1680s, we have been led to underestimate the drastic changes that occurred in drama in this decade: "The full extent of the change during the eighties is apparent only when the plays of 1678 are set against those of 1688. One can, of course, similarly contrast the plays of 1668 with those of 1678, but with this difference: in the seventies the drama seems to be fulfilling an inherent potential, working in a natural direction from the potentialities developed in the sixties. In the eighties a reversal of direction is obvious; new types are being explored while the achievements of the seventies are suffering rejection."[1]

In the eighties a direction begins in dramatic imitation that does indeed end in the rejection, or drastic revaluation, of the achievement of the sixties and seventies; in my view, however, that direction is not a reversal but an inevitable evolution from the past. Just as the drama of the seventies fulfills potentialities inherent in plays of the sixties, so too does the drama of the eighties fulfill and extend upon the seventies' foreshadowings. In examining the plays of the seventies we discovered in them the necessity for a downward pull toward the actual, toward the other-than-idealizing perspective, which arose from a new paradoxical conception of reality. Once the metaphysical absolute was no longer believed to be directly capturable, both the hypsos and bathos radicals in mimesis were drawn into a middle plane where interplay and contrast between them composed a disjunctive unity in form and meaning. The 1680s begins a further thrust into the actual that comes to full flower in the nineties and, at last, penetrates the surface actual to establish interior, psychological truth as the new locus of reality. During these twenty years our gaze is brought down to earth to a revelation of truth embedded in human experience and the patterns of Providence, and then further down into particular "manners" and into idiosyncratic "sentiments." Drama presents to understanding the only truth of which human understanding is believed to be capable, the truth of "Experience," which is "noe thing but the Exercise and observation of [man's] senses about particular objects."[2]

Eric Rothstein has observed that one of the critical differences between plays of the sixties and those of the eighties lies in where they locate the truth they imitate: "In the heroic play 'reason' and 'nature' essentially refer to the genre and its procedures. . . . The criterion of 'reason,' applied to language, means the rationalizing of feeling into artful paterns, while 'nature' as something to be imitated is established by the rules of the genre. The pathetic play, however, refers reason and reasonableness, nature and the natural outside the play itself."[3] In my opinion Rothstein is not right about the heroic play. As we have seen, it is not merely self-referential. Rather, it attempts to imitate a nature that lies outside the reach of ordinary perception. He is quite right, however, about the object of imitation in drama of the eighties and nineties, which he calls "pathetic." The representational idiom of these plays refers outside the works themselves and finds meaning in the justice with which the "reality" in them corresponds to the reality evident to our ordinary perception.

Early in the eighties Banks makes the point in a generatlization: "We on the Stage stand still and are content / To see you act what we should represent."[4] Ten years later Southerne says to Thomas Skipworth, to whom *Sir Anthony Love* is dedicated, that if his friend wants to judge the merit of the play, he needs only to compare it to the particular, known reality it paints: "You know the Original Sir *Anthony,* and therefore can best judge how the Copy is drawn."[5] Progressively in the last two decades of the century, the nature that drama is thought to imitate is "actual"—phenomenal reality, that which is available to our most common understanding—and the merit of a work is judged upon the closeness with which it conforms to the apparently real. "Dramatic Poetry indeed aims at a just Representation of Nature, and that which deviates least from our *common apprehensions of Nature's force,* has the greatest Beauties and must take best with a judicious Auditory."[6]

This aesthetic assumption creates a curious problem for criticism. From Artistotle it has been a critical dictum that the mimesis of tragedy is somehow "high" and the mimesis of comedy "low." The 1660s resolved the question by interpreting this as a difference in "essence"; the essence of tragedy was conceived to be "admiration" and the essence of comedy to be "satire."[7] Admiration lifts us to an apprehension of metaphysical truth, while satire reminds us of the disparity among the parts, spiritual and animal, that comprise our being. When the object of dramatic imitation is conceived to be ordinary experience, differentiation between high and low is measured by *degree* in intensity among *probable* kinds of behavior, and the rules are discovered and insisted upon to the creation of a delusionist "realism." (That the action of a play should be confined to the number of hours we spend in the theater is merely an extreme expression of the desire to make perfect correspondence between what occurs in a play and in our actual experience.) Peter Motteux, whose observation upon dramatic representation is quoted above, says, "Comedy seems most concern'd in close adherence to that Rule [that drama represents our common apprehensions of nature], for a thousand various humours are the proper Subject of it; nothing ought to appear forc'd there, for humane Follies should not be represented beyond their genuine standard."[8]

Comedy's excellence lies in its ability to imitate the wide variety of kinds and instances of particular human behavior that is observable all around us; consequently, we have for the first time in English true "comedy of manners." Tragedy can afford to be more extravagant than comedy but only because the *probable* human experiences it imitates are more extreme in expression than those actions are to which our follies drive us: "The Subject of Tragedy being generally Grave, Majestic and Melancholic, so, mournful Passions there to be represented are usually in themselves very extravagant; and *it is not uncommon* to hear persons in the violent pangs of intense Grief, break out into expressions bold and irregular, and sometimes impious, as the most daring Tragedian e're could reach to. This gives the Poet a vast scope for Fancy to move in, which, when guided by an exact Judgement, produces thoughts equally proper pleasant and surprizing. The Judgement shows itself in reducing its most eccentric thoughts to *somewhat of a probability*" (italics mine).[9]

These observations are significant for a number of reasons. First of all, they insist that both tragedy and comedy imitate probable, experiential reality. Tragedy is no less "realistic" than comedy. Second, in the same way that Mrs. Evelyn's response to *The Conquest of Granada* provides us an invaluable clue to the unconscious aesthetic sensibility of the sixties, so do Motteux's observations reflect the unconscious sensibility of the nineties. The *Gentleman's Journal* was aimed at moderately well read and cultivated readers, not at playwrights or theorists. Therefore, we can assume that the critical pronouncements made in it rest upon widely held and largely unquestioned aesthetic assumptions; what Motteux says, we may safely assume, is what most members of the audience would think if they gave their minds to it; his understanding of the reality that art imitates matches most audiences' understanding.[10] If we grant that proposition, the "affective" theory becomes questionable, for it is clear that Motteux is not at all concerned with affect. Indeed, he is oblivious to the overall effect of drama upon the emotions of the spectator. He is keenly interested rather, in the justice with which a play *represents "nature"*: the probable, experiential truth that our common apprehensions assure us is reality. If the tragic poet is allowed a greater scope for fancy than the comic poet, it is not because he is more interested than the poet of the sixties was in moving *our* emotions. Rather, it is because apparent reality in the probable experiences he represents—situations of terror, pain, and grief—display a deeper degree of intense emotion and a more broadly extravagant mode of gestural and linguistic expression than appears in the foolish behavior that the comic poet imitates. This view strongly suggests that the drama of the nineties is not intentionallly pathetic; its primary aim is not to evoke the tender emotions of a somehow more feeling new audience.[11] A far more exciting and aesthetically revolutionary change was afoot.

I submit that in the 1680s and 1690s in both tragedy and comedy, playwrights are *inventing a completely new aesthetic conception:* namely, "character" as we now understand it—or, more precisely, a fictional internal arena in dramatic figures.

The new literary historicans and semioticists have been sensitive to the problem of "character" in fiction for some time, but, except for Shakespeare's, they have not yet turned their attention to seventeenth-century drama to any large extent. Helene Cixous poses these fascinating questions: "What exactly is 'character'? How is it possible to think of the 'concept' of 'character'—if it is a concept? Assuming that this concept has a history, how far are we along now in this history or in examination of this history? What does 'character' name?"[12] Patrick Coleman says that "by general agreement the notion of character in art and criticism began to command sustained attention in the eighteenth century." He argues that the change from seventeenth- to eighteenth-century usage of the term by philosophers is from meaning the distinctive "mark" or position of an entity within a schematic design of reality to meaning a psychological reality interior to human individuals: "The idea of character as the discrimination of an object's peculiar essence, as the discursive 'placing' of an entity in the spectrum of being, still remained [in the eighteenth century], although the emphasis shifted from character as a self-evident mark to the characterizing activity of the human mind and the qualities of its language."[13]

In the drama of the 1680s and 1690s we find the first and most subtle evidences of this change. In my opinion, prose fiction becomes a serious literary mode in the eighteenth century precisely because it can represent "the characterizing activity of the human mind" more fully and more delicately than the drama can. Before the 1680s, figures in drama are placements within a dialectic or entities within the design of a spectrum of reality. We read an internal arena of mind into Shakespeare's characters for exactly the same reason that Dryden and Davenant read a dialectic refinement of Idea into *Macbeth* or Tate found justification for a providential design in *King Lear,* namely, because our own perceptual set has been conditioned by a deep, unconsciously held *belief* in the interiority of dramatic figures. But the conception of "character" is not a given in human consciousness, as the new literary historians have been showing us. It has a history. I would put the beginnings of that history earlier than they have done and would center its origins in English literature with Hobbes and Locke rather than with the French philosophers. In Shakespeare criticism, for example, we find the conception that "mind" operates within a highly individuated, "conscious" dramatic character as early as 1711 in Shaftesbury's observations upon *Hamlet:*

That piece of his, (the Tragedy of Hamlet) which appears to have most affected *English* hearts, and has perhaps been oftenest acted of any which have come upon our Stage, is almost one continu'd Moral: a series of deep Reflections, drawn from *one* Mouth, upon the subject of one single Accident and Calamity. It may be properly said of this Play, if I mistake not, that it has ONE *Character or principal Part.* It contains no Adoration or Flattery of the *Sex*; no ranting at the Gods; no blustering *Heroism*; nor any thing of that curious mixture of the *Fierce* and *Tender*, which makes the hinge of modern Tragedy, and nicely varies it between the Points of *Love* and *Honour*.[14]

The great philosopher of benevolism is not an admirer of the tender in drama. He does reject the heroic, but equally he rejects the pathetic. What interests him is the singularity of the "ONE Character" and the deep reflections emanating from that character's "mind." (I suspect that we should look to Shaftesbury rather than to the German romantic critics for the origin of the notion that *Hamlet* is a play about Hamlet.) By 1711 the revolution in sensibility that we have been tracing is already complete in drama and drama criticism.

The movement through the eighties and nineties toward closer and closer imitation of the actual, with the consequent emphasis upon character, occurred in two stages. In the first stage—roughly the decade of the eighties—the design of a play, still paramount, was thought to be the design of Providence operating within human affairs. This stage clearly is midpoint between dramatic design as the shape of reality, even the paradoxical reality of the seventies, and design as what Coleman calls "a cogent account of concrete human experience."[15] Characterization, too, is midway between placement within a scheme of abstract concepts or literary types and the probable behavior of people like ourselves. Perhaps most important, however, is that the presumed effect of drama upon the minds of an audience is different. Drama is no longer thought to demonstrate an ideational construct to understanding but rather is thought to *prove* a generally accepted moral dictum—divine justice working in human affairs—to *experience*.

As it was conceived by the best critical minds of the late 17th century and as it was employed by the best playwrights of the same period . . . the concept [of poetic justice] was considered fully referential to *an ontological reality that was truly immanent in all earthly events*. If poesy were to reflect the essential realities of man and his world, it had to image forth, they thought, the order of cosmic justice which they and the majority of persons in their age believed in. . . . Poetical justice is not a mere didactic or dogmatic precept; it was initially at least a phrase designed to express a necessary connection between art and reality.[16] [Italics mine]

However, the "reality" to which conceptions like poetic justice and providential design point is *experiential* reality, not transcendent, metaphysical reality. Providence is a sign of divine wisdom operating in the world, and the conception of poetic justice is attendent upon the idea that the nature art imitates is human nature as it is revealed in human history and experience.[17]

The relation of art to reality as it is conceived in a conception like poetic justice is one among many manifestations of a sweeping movement in epistemology, history, and aesthetics toward a new valuation of experience. In the eighties there is a burst of interest in history and biography, and there is even a new way of understanding ancient literature. Classical study and the use of classical sources, for instance, are no longer simply aristocratic adornments, the assumed intellectual equipment of a gentleman. "In the first half of the 1680s both tragic and satiric uses of classical sources were popular; larger numbers of pamphlet buyers and playgoers were absorbing the didactic results of neoclassical stress on history teaching by example."[18]

In the eighties the primary function of art is not to feign "another," higher reality, as it had been in the sixties and earlier, but to show exemplary patterns of divinity operating in *this*, our experiential reality. The great works of ancient literature that a hundred years earlier Sir Philip Sidney had thought revealed such truths as nature "shews she would faine make"[19] but *cannot* make, are now thought to show patterns of divine wisdom that nature and human experience *have* made: "By the mid-eighties classicists in general were agreed that the great virtue of ancient learning was that it threw light on eternal human nature and *provided patterns of experience*, individual and collective, which might guide both private and public behavior" (italics mine).[20]

Indeed, by the 1690s, if the patterns discernible in a work of art did not have relevance to actual facts and actual human experience, the value of the work seemed doubtful. Even the *Aeneid*, considered for centuries the model of epic perfection, was tested upon the grounds of truth to human experience:

M. Bochart asserts that *Eneas* never went into Italy. If this is true the *Eneis* of *Vergil* is a Fiction much exceeding what we call Poetical License. . . . at the least the ground of a Poem ought to be founded in Truth; . . . though the Circumstances may be feign'd 'tis somewhat too much for the chief Subject to be so too . . . our mind takes no interest in a relation where we are sensible that we are imposed upon in every particular, since we love at least to see the Image of Truth. . . . If the Hero never went out of *Asia* his achievements in Italy seem too Romantic.[21]

This new aesthetic conception of the relation between art and human nature had a profound effect upon the conception of dramatic imitation. Extending upon the bifurcated vision of reality of the seventies, the playwright of the eighties looks upward for the "moral" of his piece but *downward* for his "fable." The "moral" of a play is the eternal truth or wisdom toward which it points; the "fable" is the example that realizes that truth in terms of our experience. In "On the Grounds of Criticism in Tragedy" Dryden reverses the conception of imitation he held nineteen years earlier (that is, that "Images and Actions" must be "rais'd above the Life") and argues for the primacy of fable in composition: "The moral . . . directs the whole action of the play to one centre; and that action or *fable is the example built upon the moral which confirms the truth of it to our experience*; when the fable is designed, then, and not before, the persons are to be introduced with their manners, characters and passions" (italics mine).[22]

Fable shapes Providence using human affairs as its medium. The new primacy of fable—and, indeed, the neo-Aristotelian renaissance that began in the eighties—reflects a new understanding of the nature that drama imitates. We are midway between imitation of Idea (the cosmic principle of justice) and imitation of particular human behavior (the more extreme probability and particularity for which drama strives in the nineties). In the eighties, as Dacier says, the playwright's aim is to imitate *exemplary* not *particular* action, for his purpose is not pathetic. His aim is not to arouse emotion but rather, by means of fable, to demonstrate universal truth to experience. "According to the Rules of Aristotle," Dacier argues, "a Tragedy is the Imitation of an Allegorical and Universal Action." It is not "imitation of some particular Action, which affects no body and is only invented to amuse Spectators, by the Plot and unravelling a vain Intrigue." This latter practice, because it is intended to "stir up . . . [the audience's] Passions, instead of rendering them calm and quiet," is not only not tragedy; it is not art. "In a word 'tis not a Fable, and by consequence, is in no wise a Tragedy, for a Tragedy cannot subsist without a Fable."[23]

In addition to bringing truth down to earth, the playwright of the eighties also brings exemplary designs that have already been realized in art or history into present time and space, into immediate experience. Tate says that his purpose in adapting *Coriolanus (The Ingratitude of a Commonwealth* [1681]) was to bring the exemplary design he found in Shakespeare to bear upon current events: "I saw no small Resemblance with the busie *Faction* of our own time. And I confess, I chose rather to set the Parallel nearer to Sight than to throw it off at a further Distance."[24] Dryden and Lee think of *The Duke of Guise* as a double demonstration of the workings of Providence. Their play imitates in art what Charles's victory demonstrates in life, that is, "the unsearchable Providence of Almighty God." And in doing so, their play itself becomes an instrument of divine will, for "we are to trust firmly in the Deity, but so as not to forget that he commonly works by second causes, and admits of our endeavors with his concurrence."[25]

When we consider the highly political nature of the drama and, even more pointedly, of prologues and epilogues in the eighties, we are to some extent faced with a chicken-or-egg dilemma. Whether the frantic atmosphere of the Popish Plot and the Monmouth Rebellion caused the tide of political allusions in plays and the open polemic in prologues and epilogues is impossible to determine. It is certain, though, that in the 1680s the prologue and epilogue become media for allusion to and discussion of current events. In the sixties and seventies, prologues primarily discussed aesthetic issues (for example, whether the playwright was following "Fletcher or Ben" and to what extent) or they praised the playwright for capturing such "exact images of Virtue" or attacked or defended the use of rhyme. Epilogues were usually playful banterings with the audience, however serious the play they appended (consider Nell Gwynn as St. Catherine, for instance). In the eighties prologue and epilogue are used to comment on political events occuring outside the playhouse and often to underscore in red pencil the relation between the reality imitated in the play and the experiential reality of the moment (as in Dryden and Lee's prologue to *The Duke of Guise,* Dryden's prologue to Southerne's *The Loyal Brother,* Behn's prologue to *The City Heiress,* or Otway's prologue and epilogue to *Venice Preserved).* Use of the prologue as a political forum began slowly in 1679, first as a gentle chiding of the audience for its avidity for news (as in Dryden's prologue to Lee's *Caesar Borgia)* or as a mockery of them for their fearful fantasies and malicious suspicions (as in Behn's prologue to *The Feign'd Courtezans).* As the political atmosphere thickened and political passions became more intense, prologues and epilogues correspondingly became more direct and more biased. Crowne's *The Misery of Civil War* was reissued in 1681 with a prologue and epilogue that brought home the resemblance between the events of the play and the current crisis, while his prologue and epilogue to *Thyestes* attacked Papists directly. Settle entered the political war on the Whig side with his prologue to *The Heir of Morocco* (1682). Banks abjures politics in his epilogue to *Virtue Betray'd; or, Anna Bullen* (1682), but he cannot forbear attacking the politicization of the theater:

> No matter for the *Play,* nor for the *Wit,*
> The better Farce is acted in the *Pit.*
> Both Parties to be cheated will agree,
> And swallow any Non-sence, so it be
> With *Faction* guilt, or fac'd with *Loyalty.*
> There's such a Rout with *Whigging* and with *Torying*
> That you forget your dear lov'd sin of Whoring.[26]

Southerne's *The Loyal Brother* (1682), which Clifford Leech has described as a "thinly disguised political allegory which exalted James, Duke of York at the expense of Shaftesbury and even of Charles,"[27] carried a paid prologue by Dryden that attempted to deflect attention from the presumption of an attack upon the king and aim it mockingly at the corrosive effects of factionalism itself:

> In one poor Isle, why shou'd two Factions be?
> Small difference in your Vices I can see.
>
> . . . .
>
> Mean time you see what Trade our Plots advance,
> We send each year good Money into *France;*
> *And they that know the merchandize we need*
> *Send o're true Protestants, to mend our breed.*[28]

Whatever impetus the exciting events of the time gave to the playwrights' engagement in public affairs, the movement of drama (indeed, of literature generally) toward imitation of the actual none-theless precedes the Popish Plot (it is clearly foreshadowed in the seventies) and would have occurred, though perhaps more slowly, no matter what the experiential reality was to which the drama referred. For example, Aphra Behn's *The City Heiress* (1682) is obviously and pointedly political, but when we put this play into the context of the nonpolitical *The False Count* (1680) and *The Lucky Chance* (1687), written after the political crisis was over, and when we compare these plays of the eighties with Behn's plays of the seventies, we find that very significant changes in compositional method have occurred. The plays of the eighties first slowly redirect satire from abstract and literary typological targets to actual targets. Then, with increasing subtlety, they transform satiric typology into comic *portraiture:* more individuated, more dependent upon particularity of detail, more closely correspondent to familiar, contemporary experience. Moreover, a comparison of Behn's conception of the purpose of drama in 1673 (preface to *The Dutch Lover*) with her conception fourteen years later in the dedication to *The Lucky Chance* indicates a drastic revision in aesthetic sensibility. In the seventies Behn at her best is a light-handed satirist, and she assumes the conventional, literary satirist's stance, saying that figures in the drama are not meant to be models for imitation and that plays "have not done much more toward the amending of men's Morals or their Wit, than hath the frequent Preaching, which this last age hath been pester'd with."[29] By 1687, shortly before five of her novels (including the two most popular, *The Fair Jilt* and *Oroonoko*) were written, Behn's conception both of the nature of drama and of its effect upon an audience has been transformed. Plays, she says "are secret Instructions to the People, in things that 'tis impossible to insinuate into them any other way," an argument that strongly suggests interiority as the locus of reality. Furthermore, she argues that " 'tis Example alone that inspires Morality, and best establishes virtue," an opinion that finds her in perfect accord with the neo-Aristotelian critics she had so roundly mocked in the preface of 1673 as those "who discourse as formallie about the rules of it [the drama], as if 'twere the grand affaire of humane life."[30] Behn has moved from the position of a playwright who *demonstrates* the absurdity of our paradoxical condition to reason (to the end of tickling our wit) to the position of a playwright who instructs us in morality by proving eternal truth to our experience and, more surprising, who *"insinuates"* secret instructions to our subconscious. And this in only fourteen years!

As dramatic imitation moves closer and closer to experience, character of necessity moves further and further to the forefront of attention, and the conception of an interior reality in character develops apace. As we have seen, Tate's primary aim in writing a happy ending for *King Lear* was to design a fable that would exemplify the justice of Providence, but the expedient he chose for doing so, a love between Edgar and Cordelia, had the additional benefit of providing familiarly understood motivation for Lear's rage and Edgar's disguise. Grounding ideal truth to experience goes hand in hand with a naturalization of character and leads by the nineties to the primacy of character over fable or action and to the attempt to imitate the depths of "mind." The vast change that occurred in the eighties and nineties and the rapidity with which it occurred is vividly revealed when we compare Dryden's priorities in 1679, when imitation of the actual was just beginning—moral, to fable, to action, and, last of all, to persons—with Gildon's priorities in 1702, when imitation of the actual was commonplace: "As Tragedy is the Imitation of an *Action* . . . so there is no *Action* that does not proceed from the *Manners* and the *Sentiments;* therefore the *Manners* and *Sentiments* are essential Parts of Tragedy. For nothing but the *Manners* and *Sentiments* can distinguish and Characterize an *Action;* the *Manners* form and the *Sentiments* explain it, exploring its Causes and Motives; and those being the Producers of *Actions* are the Causes of Good and Evil in Mankind."[31] In a little over twenty years the laws of causality and providential justice had been interiorized, and the existence of an internal arena in fictional characters was an unquestioned assumption.

In 1662 Theophilus Gale had written that the name of a thing represents its essential metaphysical nature and also the Idea of it both in our minds and in the mind of God: "[God] *instituted* certain *Names* and affixed them as *appendents* to the things themselves, thereby to *represent* their proper *Natures, Offices,* peculiar *Respects* unto, and *Differences* from, each other. For, look as our *Conceptions* are . . . the resemblances and *images* of things; so *names* and *words* are the *images* both of our conceptions, and also the things themselves. . . [and] as in the *mind* there is a certain . . . *Character* or *Idea* of things; so likewise in *oration* or speech there is a *Character* or *Idea* of the *Mind.*"[32]

By the time that Locke wrote his *Essay* in 1698, the essential connection between word and thing had been lost and the epistemological connection between word and idea exploded. The name of a thing was no longer thought to be instituted by God but—often carelessly—given by men. Furthermore, it was thought that since new simple Ideas are not available to human apprehension and since any idea is necessarily a composite drawn from manifold sensory impressions, words *cannot* "character" metaphysical Ideas and consequently there can never be certainty about the connections between word and idea or word and mind. "Words being suited to common apprehensions, and made use of for quick dispatch, are called so united in one subject, by one name; which by inadvertancy we are apt afterward to talk of and consider as one simple *Idea*, which is indeed the complication of many *Ideas* together."[33]

As Novak has argued, a strong distrust of language permeates thinking in the 1690s.[34] Language is considered a concealer as often as it is a revealer of truth, and it is at best a hieroglyphic pointing toward hidden mysteries it is inadequate to reveal. In the sixties dramatists thought that a vision of metaphysical reality could be attained by the "harmony of words," since words could character concepts and could therefore figure Ideas *in* the mind and *of* the mind. In the seventies dramatists believed that Idea was at least available to imagination by the powerful medium of language: "Characters in Plays being representations of the Virtues or Vices, passions or Affections of Mankind, the idea of these can no other way be received into the imagination of a Poet, but either from the Conversation or Writings of Men."[35]

By the last two decades of the seventeenth century, the realm of pure Idea was lost to human view. As early as 1684 the shapes of visionary truth that had been the very end of drama in the sixties and that in the seventies were conceived as revelations to literary imagination are considered aberrations ("Extravagant and monstruous Fancies are but sick dreams") unfit for any dramatic imitation other than farce, because only "Farce extends beyond Nature and Probability."[36] By the nineties prophetic vision is represented in the quack prognostications of a Foresight (*Love for Love*), for truth is to be discovered only in the tangible—in objects or in gestures: "For Gestures have that advantage over Voice, that whereas Voice and Writing are signs by institution only, the others are understood by all Nations, being lively and natural Images of Things and Actions."[37]

Truth is also imagined as lying hidden in some mysterious inner region of mind and spirit where language cannot reach.

The effects upon dramatic composition of the epistemological changes we have been discussing were many and profound. The most salient were: a greater concern for probability and causality in plot, portraiture rather than typology in characterization, and the replacement of declamatory rhetoric by dialogue, with the accompanying conception of soliloquy as "the realistic representation of the improbable act of thinking out loud."[38] In the eighties plot is fable and it images the ways of a just Providence; in the nineties, because imitation is closer to experience, providential design is conceived as mysterious and inscrutable. Moreover, as character becomes more central and more particular, Providence is more often conceived as "Fate" than as an exemplary pattern in history (as, for example, in *Don Sebastian*).

The new characterization consists in closer, more detailed portraiture and results in individuality of person rather than individuation by type (the fop, the hero, the satyr–satirist, and so forth). As a result, while it is almost impossible to remember the names, no less the identities, of any but the title characters in plays of the sixties and seventies, in later plays Jaffeir, Loveless and Amanda, Mirabell, Fainall, and Lady Wishfort all have distinct and memorable identity. The consequence is the first manners drama in English and, by the end of the century, the primacy of manners and sentiments as the key elements in dramatic composition: "The Manners therefore of the principal Persons at least ought to be so clearly and fully mark'd, as to distinguish them from all other Men; for Nature has made as great a Distinction between every individual Man by the Turn of his Mind, as by the Form of his Countenance."[39]

The most important change, however, is in language, the instrument by which all the other changes are wrought. The new dramatic language, rather than shaping ideational constructs, *simulates* discussion, for since ideas are believed to exist nowhere but in the thoughts and impressions of men, they can be found nowhere but in the conversation of men. As Novak says "Writers like Congreve, Southerne and Vanbrugh aimed their comedies at the audience that read *The Gentleman's Journal,* an audience that . . . liked serious dialogue on contemporary problems. As a result the critical center of

Restoration comedy shifted drastically in the direction of dialogue."[40] Language, and especially failures of language—stuttering, extended pauses, verbal tics—are the means by which an imagined subterranean "reality" is brought to the surface to reinforce the apparently real: "The *Sentiments* are the Discourses or Speeches of the *Dramatick Persons,* discovring their *Thoughts* and making known their Actions; by which they speak agreeably to their *Manners* or Characters, that the Auditors may know their *Manners* before they see their Actions."[41]

I shall briefly examine some plays of the eighties to demonstrate the first evidences of change and shall then explore a few plays of the nineties to measure its magnitude.

Sutherland has said that although the significance of *The Orphan* (1680) is "little more than 'Alas, how easily things go wrong,' " Otway "may be praised for his *touching simplicity,* and for his avoidance in general of that *declamatory utterance which describes rather than expresses emotion*" (italics mine).[42] His assessment is an interesting twentieth-century "map of misreading." The modern critic finds "a mournful threnody of broken hearts" in a work that its author calls a satire—"Satyr's the effect of Poetries disease / Which, sick of a lewd age, she vents for Ease"[43]—a play that openly mimics Wycherley (Acasto's "No Flattery, Boy" speech in act 2, scene 1), Juvenal (Polydor's "Your sex was never right" speech in act 1, scene 1, Castalio's "Woman the Fountain of all Frailty" speeches in act 3), and Rochester (Polydor's "Who'd be that foolish thing call'd man" speech in act 1, scene 1). More important, Sutherland's statement reveals how readily and unselfconsciously twentieth-century sensibility *assumes* an inner space in characters from which the meaning of the play surfaces to be expressed. We praise what we find familiar (an expressive mode) and damn what we find unfamiliar ("declamatory utterance"), despite the fact that over a third of the play is written in the declamatory style. (Polydor's diatribe on the vanity of woman [I, i], Polydor's exposure of love as animal lust [I, i], Acasto's attack upon hypocrisy [II, i], Polydor's and Acasto's exchanges on the corruption of courts [II, i], Castalio's diatribe against women [III, i], Castalio's evocation of the world of pastoral innocence [IV, i], and Castalio's final curse upon the whole fallen world of man are a few of the most obvious examples.)

Sutherland's response to the play is interesting because it demonstrates an interesting quirk in twentieth-century critical consciousness; Otway's play is interesting because it demonstrates an equally illuminating seventeenth-century oddity: a drama caught between two conceptual modes of imitation, not yet ready to abandon the older, nor to fall in squarely with the newer, representational conception. Like Cavendish's plays of the sixties, this play, by its very awkwardness, reveals the subtle aesthetic conditions that underlie it more fully than a perfectly constructed play would do. Its confusion both in method and intention shows the uncertainty that perforce must have accompanied so rapid a transition from one imitative mode to another.

The Orphan falls between two stools. On the one hand, it is studded with rhetorical set pieces of formal Juvenalian satire, but it is not conceptually satiric. On the other hand, the real world of 1680 consistently intrudes upon the play, but it is nevertheless not *dramatic imitation* of the actual. It is a jarringly inconsistent play that by its very inconsistencies and incongruities quite clearly demonstrates the movement of drama at the beginning of that decade that, as Hume said, encompassed such drastic changes.

Let us first consider the play in relation to the drama that precedes it. *The Orphan* is not dramatic satire because it neither juxtaposes nor contrasts opposing perspectives upon reality; rather, it vacillates between the heroic and the satiric and confuses them. This uncertainty is readily apparent if we examine only the first act and restrict our attention to the shifting stances and voices of a single figure. Polydor, one of the twin sons of the heroic old solider Acasto, has been described in the exposition in conventional heroic terms, as "of nature mild and full of sweetness." His first appearance does nothing to belie the description. He is the heroic friend as well as brother of his twin, Castalio, and, in a style that would not be inappropriate in the context of a play by Tuke or Howard, he challenges his brother/rival into a declaration of love for Monimia. Castalio, equally heroic, admits that he loves; yet, in a gesture typical of heroic drama, he arranges for Polydor to declare his own suit to Monimia. Polydor's declaration of love to the virtuous Monimia is delivered in high romantic style:

Who can behold such Beauty and be silent?
Desire first taught us words; man when created
At first alone long wander'd up and down,
Forlorn and silent as his Vassal Beasts,
But when a Heav'n-born Maid, like you, appear'd
Strange pleasures fill'd his eyes and fir'd his heart,
Unloos'd his tongue, and his first Talk was Love.
[I, i, 305-11]

In a play of the seventies the figure of Polydor and the words he speaks would clearly belong to the elevating, heroic/romantic perspective, the antithesis. Labeled noble, heroic, and generous even before he comes upon the scene, Polydor would remain a figure in the high perspective throughout. Moreover, the style of speech given him would be consistent with his place in the high context. If his language descended to satire at all, it would never descend below light-handed social criticism. Consider, then, the generic confusion here. Less than twenty lines after this romantic, Edenic speech, Polydor is given the voice and posture of a libertine: "Hence with this peevish Vertue, 'tis a cheat, / And those who taught it first were Hypocrites, / come, those soft tender limbs were made for yielding." (I, i, 330-32).

Monimia's response to Polydor's entreaty is, again, conventionally heroic; it is virtue's defiant stand against lust in despite of Fortune: "For though to Fortune lost, I'll still inherit / My Mothers Vertues and my Fathers Honour" (338-39). Instead of eliciting a heroic response from Polydor, even the egoistically heroic repsonse that St. Catherine's defiance evokes from Maximin, Monimia's words trigger yet another and wholly inconsistent change of voice and mode. Polydor's response to Monimia's assertion of virtue is a set satiric diatribe against the vanity of women:

Intolerable Vanity! Your Sex
Was never right, Y'are always false,
Or silly; even your dresses are not more
Fantastick than your appetites! You think
Of nothing twice! Opinion you have none.
To day y'are nice, to morrow not so free,
Now Smile, then Frown; now sorrowful, then glad,
Now pleas'd, now not; and all you know not why!

> Vertue you affect, Inconstancy's your practice,
> And when your loose desires once get dominion,
> No hungry Churle feeds courser at a Feast;
> Every rank Fool goes down.
>
> [I, i, 335-41]

The voice is the harsh voice of a Juvenalian satirist, but it exists in a vacuum, having no relation either to the speaker or to the scene before us. The speech bears no relation whatever either to Monimia's declaration of virtue or Polydor's own declaration of love. It clearly echoes Juvenal's *Satire Six* but has no connection to anything in the action or language that comes before or after it. Unlike a satiric set piece of the seventies, it neither undercuts nor comments upon a heroic mode of envisagement. Quite simply, it bears no relation to the heroic (and this in a play that is largely heroic): not to Polydor as he has been described in the exposition, nor to Polydor in his first appearance as heroic friend and brother, nor to Polydor as romantic lover nor, indeed, even to the Polydor of the libertine speech ten lines earlier.

Act 1 ends with another set piece in an even darker, ironic tone: Polydor's "Who'd be that sordid foolish thing call'd man" speech. These two highly conventional pieces of satiric declamation are in the manner of formal verse satire, the style of Oldham, Rochester, and Juvenal. When we find such declamation in the drama, it is given to a speaker like the maddened moralist Manly, or the deformed satyr-satirist Snarl. It is *never* voiced by a romantic or heroic, antithesis figure. More glaring, however, than the inconsistency between satiric language and speaker is the incongruity between satiric diatribe and scene. In the plays of the seventies some scene of vice or folly, however comically drawn, would justify the satiric spokesman's wrath. *Saeva indignatio* at the lust and fickleness of women, however, is inappropriate to the romantic behavior of the virtuous Monimia, and lashing exposure of the sordid nature of man is a jarringly inappropriate ending for a scene in which we have witnessed the quite conventional heroic scene of an heroic friend courting his brother/rival's mistress.

The confusion persists throughout the play. Act 2 begins with Acasto, whom we already know is a noble old soldier, a generous master, and a loving father, describing a boar hunt in herioc style. The admiration that the description elicits from Castalio abruptly and incongruously triggers a satiric declamation from Acasto upon flattery—"No flattery, Boy! an honest man can't live by't" (II, i, 15)—which develops into a full-scale attack upon hypocrisy and social corruption that is unmistakably copied from *The Plain Dealer* ("the superstitious States-man with his sneer . . . a hot-brain'd Atheist / Thanking a surly Doctor for his sermon . . . A Grave Councellor meet a smooth young Lord and praise his good Complexion" and so on [II, i, 21-30]). Not only is a satiric attack upon the court not particularly appropriate to the speaker, who is a nobleman loyal to his king, it is totally inappropriate to the scene before us, which is entirely in the heroic mode. The action of act 2, heroic and increasingly romantic, consists in the noble Chamont's return from the war, his questioning of the safety of his sister's virtue in Acasto's house, and Acasto's assurances of his honor and pledge to protect Monimia at all cost:

> if th'offence be found
> Within my reach, tho' it shou'd touch my Nature
> In my own Off-spring, by the dear remembrance
> Of thy brave Father whom my heart rejoyc'd in,
> I'd prosecute it with severest Vengeance.
> [II, i, 187-91]

This outburst is followed by Chamont's confrontation of Monimia, her confession that Castalio has won her "Soul / By generous Love and honorable Vows," and Chamont's satisfaction that his sister is spotless in virtue. The act ends with a series of exchanges between Monimia and Castalio that play the conventional windmill turns on love, jealousy, constancy, and reconciliation with which we are familiar from the heroic drama. Castalio's end-scene speech after Monimia has forgiven him (for what it is not certain) could be inserted untouched into any heroic play of the sixties or into any Scudéry-derived high plot of the early seventies:

> Where am I? surely Paradise is round me!
> Sweets planted by the hand of Heaven grow here,
> And every sence is full of thy Perfection.
> To hear thee speak might calm a mad-man's Frenzy,
> Till by attention he forgot his sorrows;
> But to behold thy Eyes th'amazing Beauties
> Might make him rage with Love as I do.

To touch thee's Heav'n, but to enjoy thee oh!
Thou Nature's whole perfection in one piece!

[II, i, 401-9]

There is nothing of "touching simplicity here"; this style is the declamatory style of romance. The play confuses two highly conventional declamatory styles throughout, varying between high heroic and harsh satiric to no logical, conceptual end. Acasto's farewell to his sons (heroic) is abruptly followed by his attack upon religious and political corruption (satiric); Acasto's granting the hand of his virtuous daughter Serina to the noble Chamont (heroic) is followed within ten lines by his unwarranted attack upon the wantonness and falsity of women (satiric). Chamont delivers a harsh attack upon the corrupt hypocritical clergy to the Chaplain, who has just demonstrated his love for and loyalty to his king, his master, Acasto, and all noble soldiers (III, i, 210-40). Act 2, as we have seen, ends with Castalio's romantic celebration of love and beauty; act 3 ends with his bitter diatribe against women ("I'd leave the world for him that hates a Woman / Woman the Fountain of all Humane Frailty" [III, i, 579-80]); and Castalio enters act 4, only eighty lines later, uttering a conventional romantic speech in the pastoral style—"Wisht Morning's come." Nothing occurs between the satiric attack and the pastoral aubade that offers the slightest explantion for the change. There is not even a heroic drama "turn," however improbable, to justify it. But more significantly for our purpose, no logical *juxtaposition* of satiric and pastoral perspectives is made. In the conceptual design of the seventies pastoral and satiric would comment upon one another; upward and downward tilting of the mirror would reflect *one* norm of nature. In this play heroic and satiric bear no relation to one another. Changes in style reflect neither changes in a character's aspect nor his position within a configuration Whether language is heroic or satiric is completely arbitrary and has no bearing upon the formal design of the whole play.

These failures are very revealing. They indicate that in *The Orphan* Otway is using the superficial styles of the seventies but is ignoring the conceptual vision that they were used to figure. The play does not design a paradoxical *idea* of reality; its satire has no meaning in the internal fictional design. Rather, it uses satire—both praise and blame—only in reference to real conditions and actual people in

London in 1680. It points to (but does not imitate) actual experiential reality. For example, we have seen that references to corruption at court and the corrosive effects of hypocrisy upon the social fabric have no referents within the play. The scene is not set at court but in Acasto's house, and the behavior of its characters is uniformly heroic and unquestionably loyal. Moreover, neither king nor court appear in the play or have any bearing upon the characters or their actions. The king to whom the play refers, is not Acasto's king but Otway's, Charles II.

> He merits more than man can do!
> He is so good, praise cannot speak his worth;
> So merciful, sure he ne'er slept in wrath;
> So just that were he but a private man,
> He could not do a wrong.
>
> [II, i, 122-26]

Similarly the "Atheists . . . [who] make use of Toleration" (III, 93) and "Knaves of Conscience" (III, 95) are Charles's real Protestant enemies, while the "Tribe" and "Trade" of "loathsome sneaking servile . . . Priest[s]" are real papist subversives, Otway's contemporaries. "The quaint Smooth Rogue, that sins against his Reason: / Calls sawcy loud Suspicion publick Zeal / And Mutiny the Dictates of his spirit" (III, 81-83) has no existence or reference in the fictional world of the play. He is, of course, Shaftesbury. *The Orphan* refers us outside the play and outside the realm of literary tradition or imagination for meaning.

However, if the play has left "that country" where dramatic imitation designs Idea, it has not yet arrived at the place where dramatic imitation simulates "a cogent account of concrete human experience." I have argued that the three most salient characteristics of the new mode in imitation are exemplary plot, particularity in characterization, and dialogue rather than declamation in language. *The Orphan* attempts the first two of these. Otway clearly is attempting to create a "mills of the gods" effect in his fable. He does not succeed because he has not yet given sufficient attention to probability. Our response to his failure is itself indicative of the halfway state of his composition. The plot of this play is strikingly different from those of the sixties and seventies because its end is not a just and final placement of conceptual counters. It is a *narrative,* and therefore our interest is in what happens and why. Because the play is strong in addressing the former question and weak in dealing with the latter, it raises expectations that it does not satisfy.

As unlikely as it may seem for a modern reader to discover that he has anything in common with Thomas Rhymer, our dissatisfaction when the complexity of *The Orphan* boils down to "Alas, how easily things go wrong" marks our hankering for poetic justice. We long to see some cause beyond mere accident for all those sorrowful effects. We are dissatisfied when a dramatic design that promises to be a fable ends up by showing us the face of blank-eyed "Dilitory Fortune." We want justification for Castalio's not telling Polydor that he is married; we want some explantion for Polydor's willingness, or even his ability, to trick Monimia (beyond the mere accident that her bedroom is next door to Acasto's and Acasto has suddenly and for no reason gotten sick). We want to know why the marriage was kept secret from Chamont and Acasto, since they both approve the match. In short, we want causality and probability. These are demands that we would not make of a play of the sixties or seventies because they hold up various ideational configurations for our inspection; we make them of *The Orphan* because it leads us to expect a design of experience or, more precisely, a design of cause and effect, of just reward and punishment that even such confirmed absurdists as we are would like to believe governs our experience. We want some notion of Providence.

Just as the play reaches toward but does not quite attain the eighties' ideal in fable, so, interestingly enough, it reaches toward an imitation of human experience in extremity, that which will constitute the tragic in the nineties. In that attempt the play is hampered by a time lag in the developing conception of characterization. Dramatic imitation in the nineties requires particularity, even idiosyncrasy in characterization; in *The Orphan* Otway's characterization is still typological. However, once again the play points the direction drama will take. Characters vacillate with disconcerting rapidity among a variety of types. For example, Polydor is now a heroic youth chafing for glory, now a heroic friend/brother, now a romantic lover, now a libertine, now a satyr-satirist, now a Machiavellian villain, now a generous, dying hero. Many types compose the figure, but they retain their rigid conventionality as types; their variety in a single figure merely bewilders us. Theoretically, however, the attempt to create character as a composite of types shows the ideal for which Otway was aiming: Dryden's "composition of qualities not contrary in the same person."[44]

Two years later in *Venice Preserved* Otway advanced considerably further in the direction toward which *The Orphan* points. The prologue and epilogue of this play are more detailed in reference to particular current events than is usual even in these years of intense political paper war (for instance, the reference to the "picture mangler" who destroyed a portrait of Charles I and in so doing, in Otway's view, spiritually remurdered the Royal Martyr). The events of the play, too—conspiracy, betrayal, the evils of republican government—are aimed at issues uppermost in the public mind in 1682. The play illustrates the transformation that is occurring in dramatic imitation of nature, however, not in these respects but in the changes that have occurred in techniques of composition. Its double structure—heroic in the high mode and grossly satiric in the low—seems at first glance to be the double perspective design of the seventies. However, the low does not bear a contrastive, thesis-antithesis relation to the high; rather, high and low stand in causal relation. Plot is a cause-effect chain of relations: because Antonio keeps Aquilina, Pierre is driven to the extreme of revolution; because Pierre is driven to that extreme, Jaffier is drawn into the conspiracy; because Jaffier conspires against her father, Belvidera betrays him, etc. It is true that the Antonio scenes magnify a suggestion of sexual excess that runs undercurrent in the relation of the lovers, but that effect is ancillary to its primary purpose of creating the atmosphere of corruption in the body politic. In the new imitative mode, structure is a complex design that is exemplary of the way of Providence with conspirators, republicans, and intemperate lovers. Poetic justice is not as straightforward nor apparent as a purist like Rhymer might wish, but it is nevertheless clear that the events of *Venice Preserved* design a fable whose purpose is to show us that "The seal of Providence is upon [us]" (IV, ii, 524), working its will in human life and history. Though the precise nature of the moral that the fable realizes to our experience has puzzled critics for centuries, the theoretical relation of fable to moral is as Dryden understood it in "The Grounds," and fable is clearly the primary compositional element.

A growing naturalization in character is also evident in *Venice*

Preserved. Figures retain much of their typological identity—Pierre as Herculean hero, Jaffeir as heroic lover caught between love and friendship, Belvidera as a heroine caught between filial piety and love, and Antonio as a grotesque senex amans. However, the characters not only are complex in themselves but are invested with particularity. Jaffeir and Belvidera are too complicated to act as ideational counters in the formulaic configurations their situation suggests. Moreover, though they are heroic lovers, their love does not exalt them or the audience; its excess is not elevating but peculiar, especially in married lovers. Complication in the characters is itself complicated. For instance, Belvidera is not merely ambivalent, as Statira and Roxana are in *The Rival Queens,* nor does her aspect change in response to the situational turn in which she is placed, as Nourmahal's does in *Aureng-Zebe.* Her characterization is never uniform or lucid and can therefore never "character" a concept—heroic love, inspirational beauty, or even lust. The ambiguities in characterization exist for their own sake. They are mysterious; like qualities in real people they are never altogether explicable or knowable. Complexity itself becomes the constant in this kind of characterization; it does not alter with one or another turn in the design, and its very elusiveness creates an illusion of depth.

The most interesting and illuminating character in the play is Antonio. Antonio is satiric *portraiture* that is built, detail by detail, upon a typological base. A comparison between Antonio and Snarl of *The Virtuoso* can be useful. The same type is the foundation for both characters, namely, the sexually perverted, impotent old man. In Snarl the type is adjusted slightly to fit the demand of another type, the satyr–satirist speaker of vitriolic abuse; in Antonio the type is made the foundation of a detailed and, consequently, realistic and individualized portrait. We cannot, of course, know how closely Antonio resembled the real Shaftesbury. It is evident, though, that the fictional character itself is particular, individual, and unforgettable. The character of Antonio clearly shows that characterization in 1682 is well on the way to imitation or simulation of "real" people— in this case, hopefully, *not* like ourselves. Most of the language of the play is love and honor declamation strongly flavored with Shakespearean overtones, but Antonio's language is in the new imitative mode; it is the instrument by which the new characterization is made. The verbal tics, senile baby talk, and nicky-nacky blathering are used to create the illusion of a diseased mind. Here, at last, is expressive rather than declamatory language. It is interesting that in the eighteenth century, when emulation psychology had fully taken hold, the Antonio episodes were removed from the play. After three hundred years, the psychopathology depicted by this brilliantly employed language is still shocking. We still feel uncomfortable when our minds are touched by the fictional "mind" of Antonio.

Aphra Behn's method in *The City Heiress,* she declares, is a *demonstration* designed to make "Whigism . . . a Jest where'er 'tis met with." In 1682 she no longer thinks plays are as ineffectual "toward the amending of men's Morals" as boring preaching is, as she had in 1673, but, on the other hand, neither has she come to think of them as "secret Instructions" to be insinuated into the hearts of the audience, as she will in 1687. The function of drama is still to her mind "demonstration" to understanding, but the understanding she addresses is common understanding, the ordinary apprehensions of ordinary men, and the truths she would demonstrate are both derived from, and directed toward, their ordinary experience: "seditious Fools and Knaves that have so long disturb'd the Peace and Tranquility of the World, will become the sport of Comedy, and at last the scorn of that Rabble that fondly and blindly worshipt 'em; and whom nothing can so well convince as plain Demonstration, which is ever more powerful and prevailent than Precept, or even Preaching it self."[45] *The City Heiress* (1682) is dependent upon the actual, but it is not yet imitation of the actual. Like *The Orphan,* the play demonstrates reality by reference to systems of meaning outside itself, outside the playhouse, and outside a literary context. Moreover, the demonstration is satiric, as Alan Roper has so well put it, ". . . satires are usually more concerned to *interpret* than *approximate* life. They are accordingly issue-directed, classifying individuals as fool or knave. Satiric event takes the form of illustrative example, and individual fool or knave must also represent folly or knavery."[46]

The City Heiress is not in the conceptual mode of dramatic satire that we examined in the last chapter, however. It does not imitate nature as the city between or juxtapose conflicting perspectives upon an idea of reality. It functions in the way that verse or prose satire or the rhetorical set pieces embedded in a play of the seventies function.

It is aimed at the audience, and contemporary life is its object. Therefore, while the play is not an approximation of experiential reality, its satire *depends* upon experiential reality to complete its meaning. Satiric attack is aimed at actual external reality: the activities and behavior of Whigs, which is downwardly exaggerated, of course. But satiric antithesis is also externally located—in the activities and behavior of Tories, which is upwardly exaggerated but is *not* idealized and is not literary. There are neither panegyric nor burlesque "distortions in the artist's mirror of the norm of nature" because the *nature,* and even the distortions, upon which satiric meaning depends, lie outside the confines of the play. The vices of Whigs (hypocrisy, greed, sedition) as well as the more attractive vices of Tories (drinking, whoring, gambling) are exaggerated representations of the activities of real people or, more precisely, are conventional cliché traits that real people, Whigs and Tories, *historically* attributed to one another in actual political slanging matches. Moreover, we differentiate between the constellations of traits morally—thinking the Tory's charming follies and the Whig's despicable vices—on the basis of our own and Behn's real political prejudices.[47] Like the *Drapier's Letters* this satire needs the reader's knowledge of immediate actual behavior and events to be understood. Let us consider the following speech, in which Sir Timothy, the Whig speaker, attacks Tory vices: "Sir *Charles,* thanks to Heaven you may be lewd, you have a plentiful Estate, may whore, drink, game, and play the Devil . . . but for such Sparks as this [a "Man of Birth," friend to Wilding] and my Fop of Fashion here [his nephew and heir, Wilding, a Tory] why with what Face, Conscience, or Religion, can they be lewd and vitious, keep their Wenches, Coaches, rich Liveries, and so forth who live upon Charity and the Sins of the Nation," (I, i).

To understand the satire here we must be aware that in 1682 a source of Whig complaint and a primary Whig justification for attacks upon the government was Charles II's generosity to his mistresses. Without that information we might very well mistake this passage for an attack upon Tory extravagance and lewdness, when it is intended as the very opposite, an attack upon Whig hypocrisy and greed. This passage is designed to show us that Whigs hate lewdness not because it is a sin but because it is expensive. The mockery of Tories in it is superficial and gentle; we are made to undersand that Tory dressing up, drinking up, and acting up are acceptable, even desirable, in any young man worth his salt. Whigs would do it if they could, but they are too old, too stingy, and, above all, too canting hypocriticial. They prefer to take their pleasures behind a respectable façade, as in the "Days of old Oliver" when "a man might Whore his heart out and no body the Wiser" (I, i). Our knowledge of real events and quarrels outside the play allows us to understand where the satire is aimed in this speech and throughout the play. The collision necessary in satire, then, is not a clash of perspectives within a fictional design that is held up to our inspection but a collision between fictional figures on stage and their real counterparts outside the playhouse. At this step in the progress toward imitation of the actual, the poles of satiric interplay lie one in art and one in life.[48]

Rhetorical set pieces in the seventies were aimed at the audience, it is true, but their targets were general types inherited from the literary tradition—the mercenary upstart, the flatterer, the wanton, the hypocrite of virtue. Characterization in *The City Heiress* is no less typological than it was in the dramatic satire of the seventies or in its ancestor, Roman verse satire, but the types are composites of famil iar, contemporary stereotypes. In 1682 Behn had not yet developed a style of satiric portraiture, as Otway had. It is interesting, since Shaftesbury is the model for both Antonio and Sir Timothy, to compare the two characters. Otway's figure is drawn from particulars, and the language given him further individuates him and creates the illusion of a real and "conscious" man. The character's own language creates our impression of him. Behn's figure is described in declamatory style by another character rather than being revealed by his own words. The caricature actions and traits ascribed to him *demonstrate* vices and follies typically associated with Whigs (earlier with Roundheads, earlier still with Puritans) for over sixty years. We have here not a grotesque portrait of Shaftesbury but a political cartoon, under which we can almost envision a headline: Wealthy Whig Politico Swaps Hospitality for Clout: "You keep open House to all the Party, not for Mirth, Generosity or Good Nature but for Roguery. You cram the Brethern, the pious City-Gluttons, with good Cheer, good Wine, and Rebellion in abundance, gormandizing all Comers and Goers, of all sexes, Sorts, Opinions and Religions, young half-witted Fops, hot-headed Fools and Malcontents: You guttle and fawn on all, and all in the hopes of debauching the King's Liege-people into Commonwealthsmen" (I, i). The generalized traits associated with Whigs and Tories are century-old clichés. Tories are known for feasting, mirth, and generosity. Whigs are gluttons (already a cliché in Jonson's time), malcontents, hot-brained zealots, and treasonous hypocrites. Tories are dashing and sexually gifted; Whigs are impotent wittols. Honnête homme Tories have "the honest Reputation of lying with the Magistrates Wives, when their Reverend Husbands [are] employ'd in the necessay Affairs of the Nation, seditiously petitioning" (II, iii). Whigs are so unnatural that they would murder their kin for profit and reputation in the City and their king for sheer, seditious bloodimindedness:

> **Sir Tim.** [of his nephew] I am content to be so much a Parent to him . . . to see him fairly hang'd. . . . He has deserv'd it, Madam: First for lampooning the Reverend City with its noble Government, with the Right Honorable Gown-men . . . charging us with . . . the sins of our Fore-fathers . . . [whereby] the Sins of Forty-One are receiv'd again in Eighty-One . . . Secondly, Madam, he deserves hanging for seducing and most feloniously bearing away a Young City-Heiress. [III, i]

Character in this play, then, is the composite of a host of rigid stereotypes drawn from the common prejudices of everyday life.

Plot does not imitate Providence in *The City Heiress*. As in the previous decade, plot exists merely to provide a frame for satire. The comic intrigue, drawn from Massinger's *The Guardian* and Middleton's *A Mad World, My Masters,* is carelessly thrown together, certainly with no conceptual intention of fable. In fact, the haphazard construction of the action causes unintentional confusion in characterization. For example, it is inappropriate for a Cavalier lover like Wilding to offer love to two mistresses at the same time, particularly since one is a romantic type, (Charlot) and one a witty madcap (Lady Galliard). The female types require different formulas, which causes Wilding's type to waver uncertainly. In the seventies his duplicity would make him either a target of satire, like Dorimant, or a parasite-satirist, like Horner. In a Providential, or

experiential design of the late eighties and nineties, it would make
him a villain. Here it seems merely a confusion of types from two
different modes—a modern type (the bold, open-hearted Tory) and
an older, literary type (the passionate romantic lover, driven to
intrigue by overpowering love of his lady). Language, too, is in the
older imitative mode It is the declamatory rhetoric of satire, with no
movement toward dialogue. To sum up, *The City Heiress* in its
dependence upon external referents and in the immediacy of its
setting, indicates a strong movement toward the actual; it is not,
however, imitation or simulation of the actual.

Behn's *The Lucky Chance* (1687) represents a giant step in that
direction—in its close approximation of the actual (for instance, the
depiction of Gayman's poverty, which by its probability and use of
particulars builds realistically upon a typological configuration of
City landlady and aristocratic tenant); in its probability (for instance,
the financial realities that press Lucretia into a hateful marriage with
Sir Feeble, or Gaymans' complete disbelief in a supernatural agent of
his good fortune); and, most especially, in its use of language and
failures in language to create the illusion of interiority in characters
(for instance, Sir Feeble's senile, lustful baby talk, or the pauses and
silences that express Lucretia's revulsion, or Bellamour's "thinking
out loud" arguments with himself). By means of these compositional devices the central issue of the play, which a satiric treatment
would damn by mockery and exaggeration, is presented for serious
consideration and sober discussion as a real social problem:

> L. **Ful.** Oh, how fatal are forc'd Marriages!
> How many Ruins one such Match pulls on!
> Had I but kept my Sacred Vows to *Gayman*
> How happy had I been—how prosperous he!
> Whilst now I languish in a loath'd embrace,
> Pine out my Life with Age—Consumptions Coughs.
> [II, i]

The marriage of May and January, a stock subject for broad,
fabliau satire since Chaucer, is now an occasion not merely for farce
but for serious reflection as well. We are made to see such a marriage
as it *really* might be, as it might make *real* people feel. Senex amans
himself if given new, serious consideration. Sir Feeble Fainwoud is

still ridiculous, but he is quite different from the foundation stock type upon which he is built. First, and most important, though the language given him reveals his folly, it also naturalizes his character. By its very pauses, its tics, its baby-talk blathering, Sir Feeble's language creates a realistic overlay, the impression of a *real* old man talking, to clothe a stock figure and to create the illustion of inner space: "Hah—hum—how's this? Tears upon the Wedding Day? Why, why—you Baggage, you, Ye little Ting, Fool's face—away, you Rogue, you're naughty. *[Patting and playing and following her* Look— look—look now,—buss it—buss it—buss it—and Friends; did'ums, did'ums beat its none, silly Baby—away, you little Hussey, away, and pledge me—" (I, iii).

To appreciate fully the power of failures in language, verbal tics, and gestures ("For Gestures have that advantage over Voice," and so forth) in creating the realistic illusion of actuality and interiority in character, we must compare Sir Feeble here with Old Bellair in *The Man of Mode*. Old Bellair's "Away, ye Rogue, I can't abide ye" to Emilia is a linguistic tag that immediately classifies him as a senex amans type, but it is not developed extensively enough or par- ticularly enough to create the illusion of language as it is really spoken. (It is, of course, not intended to do so.) We can imagine a dirty old man in real life sounding like Sir Feeble; we can even imagine what he is feeling as he speaks so. For precisely that reason Otway's Antonio is still disturbing.

Sir Feeble takes on further texture from the realism of Lucretia's portrayal and from the complexity of Lucretia's response to him. For a young wife to feel sorrow or pity for her old husband at the moment she is running away from him with a young lover is unthinkable in a satiric drama of the seventies. Here at two situa- tional cruxes—just after Lucretia has agreed to run off with Bell- amour at the end of act 3 and when Bellamour, disguised as a ghost, frightens Sir Feeble away from the marriage bed—Behn gives Lu- cretia a dimension of serious reflection that complicates the texture of the character and the play and brings it further into the new imitative mode. The act 3 end-scene verse tag, even though it is rhymed and even though a verse tag at the end of an act is highly conventional and artificial, works to naturalize the characterization both of Lucretia and of Sir Feeble: "Old Man forgive me—thou the

Agressor art, / Who rudely forc'd the Hand without the Heart. / She cannot from the Paths of Honour rove, / Whose Guide's Religion, and whose End is Love" (III, iii).

The idea expressed here is antique; it is the Caroline Platonic Love conception that we find in Ford's *The Broken Heart.* The context and style of *The Lucky Chance* put an old idea to a quite new use and thereby transform it into "sentiment" or thought process. Lucretia here is made to *muse* about the morality of an act she is about to commit. That musing forces us to penetrate beyond the stock comic turn of juvens tricking senex and beyond the January–May formula. We are made to think about the moral dimension of an action that would not have engaged our attention beyond the surface level ten years earlier. We would give no more reflection to a young wife tricking an old husband in a play of the seventies (*The Country Wife*, for example) than we would consider the problem of overpopulation or the psychological effects of overcrowding when we watch twenty clowns climb out of a Volkswagen at the circus. In a comedy that *demonstrates* a schematic, metaphoric design of reality or in a circus trick that *demonstrates* the clowns' challenge to physical law, it is the very conventionality and invariability of an old chestnut trick that is satisfying. Behn's play asks us to bring an additional dimension of thought to bear in considering the situation. We are not asked to think how a given *part* fits into a pattern or scheme; rather, we are asked to consider what a given *human action* means morally.

In act 5 Bellamour comes disguised as a bloody ghost of himself to frighten Sir Feeble and prevent him from consummating his marriage. We the audience have been awaiting this conventional, eleventh-hour reprieve as nervously as Lucretia has. But, once again, Behn complicates Lucretia's response in a totally new way. She says, "Blest be this kind Release, and yet methinks it grieves me to consider how the poor old Man is frighted. (V, iii) By investing Lucretia with sympathy for the old man, Behn not only creates the illusion of interiority in Lucretia and, because the response is multi-textured, makes her character a closer imitation of the actual, but by having Lucretia pity Sir Feeble's fright, she draws Sir Feeble and the stock comic scene in which he is engaged closer to us and makes a totally improbable situation *probable.*

Throughout the play Behn uses a new style in language (that is, simulation of real speech instead of declamation, heroic or satiric) and a new complex multidimensionality in character to build realistic overlays upon conventional types and stock situations. The situations are, indeed, borrowed wholesale from earlier plays. Lady Fulbank's pleasant deception of Gayman, of course, is taken from Shirley's *The Lady of Pleasure,* and Bredwell's wooing Diana in Bearjest's presence and seemingly in Bearjest's behalf is taken, move by move, from *The Country Wife.* But Behn uses the bricks she has borrowed to construct an altogether new kind of edifice. Let us consider two examples, one a borrowed character and the other a borrowed situation.

Bearjest, as his name implies is a bear-garden natural to whom Sir Feeble, with typical Alderman greed, has betrothed his daughter, Diana. Bearjest, the Alderman, and the relation between them are taken from *Bartholomew Fair:* Bearjest is Bartholomew Cokes, Sir Feeble is Adam Overdo, and Diana is Grace Bornwell (whose last name, with a slight alteration, has been given to Diana's true lover, Bredwell). Bartholomew Cokes is an emblematic figure—"the natural." He is not realistic; the speech and actions given him are exaggerated bold strokes used to delineate the type of a Cokes, or a booby. Bearjest retains a Cokes-like foundation; for example, he delays joining the bride he is in the process of abducting in the hope of catching a glimpse of the devil. But the language Behn gives him *simulates* language as it is spoken, especially in its breaks and haltering, and, once again, the language creates an illusion of depth and realism in characterization: "I never knew but one way to a Woman's Heart, and that road I have not yet travelled; for my Uncle, who is a wise Man, says matrimony is a sort of a—a kind of a—as it were, d'ye see, of a Voyage, which every man of Fortune is bound to make one time or other; and madam—I am, as it were—a bold Adventurer" (II, ii). Bearjest, because he is made to speak as he does, makes himself a Cokes. The language seems to surface from a confusion and stupidity *within* the character.

Behn builds a similar realistic overstructure upon the situation she has borrowed from Shirley. In *The Lady of Pleasure,* Aretina, as her name indicates, is a type of the libidinous adulteress, and Kickshaw, her dupe, is a fop. Kickshaw believes that he is being bought by the devil, and the probability of such an event is of no consequence to the character or the audience. (Gayman is made to assert the improbability of supernatural intervention and to speculate about "real" reasons even as the action takes place.) Kickshaw's inadvertent disclosure of distaste at the voracious sexual appetite of the hag he has ridden tricks Aretina out of her humor, and that is that. Behn first slightly alters the situation itself. She makes Gayman the true lover of Lady Fulbank, betrothed to her before her forced marrige to Sir Cautious, and we are given Lady Fulbank's serious reflection upon forced marriage as preconditioning preparation for the trick. We see the trick, that is, through a lens that has forced us to look beyond the surface and to ponder how the marionettes *feel*. We also learn that Gayman is poor because he has given all for love of Lady Fulbank. That Gayman has bankrupted himself for love merely makes the Aretina-Kickshaw formula romantic. Behn does much more than that. She naturalizes her characters and gives them interiority. She renders Gayman's poverty in a completely new compositional style, making it approximate experiential reality. Moreover, we are not just made to see poverty as it really is; we are *drawn into* the scene and made to experience what the character has "experienced" for love's sake. The method by which we are drawn in and "secretly instructed" makes *The Lucky Chance* a landmark in the progress we are following.

Behn can achieve the closeness of detail, the particularity, the creation of a realistic atmosphere that we fully enter, only by *narrative description*. Gayman's scene with his landlady and the trick Lady Fulbank plays upon him are stock comic formulas, but we do not respond to them as we do to stock scenes because we are prepared for them as we are prepared for events *in a novel*. Narrative description is the doorway through which we enter into the conditions of Gayman's life. Once we have been there, we perceive what happens to him from the *inside,* from a vantage that tempers their comic conventionality. It will be well to consider this descriptive passage closely (which, incidentally, is unusually long for drama and of which I quote here only a part):

Bred. . . . . at the door [I] encountered the beastly thing he calls a Landlady; who look't as if she had been of her own Husband's making, compos'd of

moulded Smith's Dust. I ask'd for Mr. Wasteall and she began to open—
and did so rail at him, that what with her *Billinsgate,* and her Husband's
hammers, I was both deaf and dumb—at last the hammers ceas'd, and she
grew weary, and call'd down Mr. Wasteall; but he not answering—I was
sent up a Ladder rather than a pair of Stairs. . . .
'Tis a pretty convenient Tub, Madam. He may lie a long in't, there's
just room for an old join'd Stool besides the Bed, which one cannot call a
Cabin, about the largeness of a pantry Bin, or a Usurer's Trunk; there had
been Dornex Curtains to't in days of Yore; but they were now annihi-
lated, and nothing left to save his Eyes from the Light, but my Landlady's
Blue Apron, ty'd by strings before the Window, in which stood a broken
six-penny Looking Glass, that shew'd as many Faces as the Scene in
Henry the Eighth, which could but just stand upright, and then the
Comb-Case fill'd it. [I, iii]

In discussing the three-tiered comic structure of the sixties in
chapter 2, we observed that the high plane is remote, abstract,
empty, and that descent to the middle plane is a descent into the
jumble and clutter of *things.* The most striking, new feature of style
in this passage is its close, detailed description of things—a room as
small as a tub, a bed like a pantry bin, tatters of bed curtain that were
of sleazy quality to begin with (Dornex), a joint stool, a cracked
looking glass, a combcase. This description is not the merely suggested "A Scene in Mrs. ———'s House" of drama; this scene is the
kind we find in a novel. We are made to notice particulars—the sizes,
colors, and shapes of objects—to imagine seeing and hearing as we
see and hear in life. We hear the smith's din and see the landlady's
smutty face at first hand, so to speak. Consequently, as in a novel, we
are made to *enter* the scene that Bredwell describes. Not only are we
made to enter and experience Gayman's poverty, but we are given the
illusion that Lady Fulbank, the fictional auditor of Bredwell's tale, is
also imaginatively entering the scene of poverty.

The effects of this description are manifold. It is first of all
imitation of the probable and the particular: reality as we ordinarily
experience it. Second, it creates the illusion that fictional characters,
Lady Fulbank and Gayman, are real people, who have a life like our
own. We imagine that, since they see and hear as we do, they must
also feel as we do. Third, by the style of description we are made to

enter the experience described. Once we "experience" his poverty, we feel sympathy for Gayman—*not,* as in earlier drama, approval or admiration. This feeling reinforces our sense of the character's interiority. We can see, then, that in 1687 the process of artistic imitation that would make "nature" familiar experience and relocate "reality" in the inner life of individual human beings was well under way.

The Lucky Chance is well advanced in the new mode of dramatic imitation as we have seen. This new mode came to full flower in the nineties. However, *The Younger Brother,* which was written at about the same time as *The Lucky Chance* and which employs many of the same devices, was hissed off the stage when it was produced by Gildon in 1696. Behn's plays retained too much of the old satiric style for the taste of the nineties. Gildon's defense of the play and of Behn herself (who Gildon believed, as I do, was one of the best dramatists of her time) is very revealing. He praises the play for its "Conversation," or *dialogue,* for the *probability* of its incidents, and for the *justice* of its plot, or fable: "The Play . . . had an Intrinsic merit [besides the high reputation of Behn, who died in 1689] for we find it full of Humour, Wit, and Variety; the Conversation Gay and Genteel, the Love, Soft and Pathetic, the incidents Natural and Easy, and the Conduct of the Plot very Justifiable."[49] The methods of composition that Behn and Otway were exploring in the eighties had become criteria for measuring excellence by the mid-nineties.

SIX

Imitation of the Inner Arena: Sentimental, Pornographic, or Novelistic?

In the course of writing this book, I have often thought that it would be quite possible to chart the revolution in dramatic imitation I describe had we no other works available but those of Behn and Dryden, so clearly does the outline of change appear in their canons. In *Don Sebastian* (1690) Dryden has left the old imitative mode behind entirely. I do not subscribe to Hume's view that this play or *Cleomenes* is a throwback to the heroic drama. There is little trace in them of either the methodology or the aesthetics of the sixties. *Don Sebastian* steps fully into the nineties and, indeed, stands squarely on our side of the great divide in sensibility, which is one reason we like it so well. The play is interesting for many reasons, but for economy's sake we shall restrict ourselves to those hallmarks of the new mode in imitation that we watched sprout in the eighties: probability, providential design, naturalization of character and language, and a certain straining toward the kind of realism and particularity that only the novel would finally be able to accommodate.

Because he was one of the great geniuses of literary criticism, Dryden, of course, anticipated us. He has himself addressed all the questions that a serious critic must put about the play in his preface. Primary among these is the question of probability: whether the kind of artistic imitation this play attempts is better answered by a work that is read or by a work that is seen; whether the realism it seeks is better achieved by close adherence to the unities or by throwing off their rule. Earl Miner, editor of the California *Dryden* edition of the play, calls our attention to "the wealth of detail found in

Don Sebastian concerning what was then referred to commonly as Barbary or the Moors."[1] Dryden himself, whether seriously or with feigned modesty, wonders whether it is "through a long disuse of Writing, that [he] forgot the usual compass of a Play" and "crowding it with Characters and Incidents, . . . put a necessity upon [him]self of lengthning the Action."[2] The wealth of detail and the crowded scene of characters and events mark not the rustiness of an old writer but the demands of a spanking new imitative mode.

Dryden is aware that the compass of drama is too confining for his new method. Betterton had "judiciously lopt" the play to fit it to the dimensions of playable drama, which must *show* everything. But a tightly confining dramatic design, though it can preserve the necessary connection among events, is not always sufficiently capacious to make them probable. For the new imitative mode to work, we must be prepared to accept that the events could really happen so in experience. Furthermore, we must *believe* in the motivation that would give rise to such events. We must have the illusion of exploring beneath the surface of the dramatic representation. Dryden worried about just this issue; he sees the necessity for Betterton's cuts but is not certain that the play as trimmed expresses his intention. He praises Betterton, "to whose care and excellent action, I am . . . oblig'd that the connexion of the story was not lost; but on the other side, it was impossible to prevent some part of the action from being precipitated and coming on without due preparation, which is requir'd to all great events; as in particular, that of raising the Mobile . . . which a Man of Benducar's cool Character could not *naturally* attempt, without taking those precautions which he *foresaw* wou'd be necessary to render his design successful" (italics mine).[3]

It is revealing to compare this insight into compositional method with the statement on priority among compositional elements that Dryden made in 1679 ("When the fable is designed, then, and not before, the persons are to be introduced"). The order of priority has been completely reversed. First in importance comes an *inner quality* of a character, coolness, that gives rise to the *consciousness* of the character, what he "foresaw." These inner qualities of sentiment and thought determine what the character would or would not *"naturally* attempt,"* which leads to his motivation in acting, which in turn generates the action or event itself. Here we understand a pattern of action, not as fable (a design of events that mediates between meta-physical principles and our experience) from the outside in, but rather as the outward manifestation of feelings and thoughts that arise from *within* individual human beings—from the inside out.

Dryden, moreover, is aware that drama is not the best medium for artistic imitation of this interior reality. His assessment of the dif-ference between watching a play and reading it is like a voice of prophecy announcing the advent of the novel as a serious literary form in the eighteenth century: "There is a vast difference betwixt a publick entertainment on the Theatre, and a private reading in the Closet; In the first we are confin'd to time . . . though we talk not by the hour-glass. . . . in the last every Reader can take up the book and lay it down at his pleasure; and find out those beauties of propriety, in thought and writing which escaped him in the tumult and hurry of representing."[4]

The reader can enter the reality of a book and explore at his leisure. By its attention to particularity and by its exploration of the inner life and motivation of its characters, a book prepares us to receive and understand its events differently from the way we receive and understand them in a dramatic representation. Dryden's need for a form that would allow him more time and space indicates a drive toward probability and the imitation of nature as experience. It makes him want a reader rather than a spectator, and it makes him chafe against the rules, for though the invention of the rules itself is a direct consequence of the movement toward understanding "nature" as equivalent to actuality, the rules are an obstacle to the artist who is attempting to *simulate* what is probable in actual life. That is, three hours spent in the theater are the *equivalent* of three hours actual time, and one day is a symbolic *equivalent* of actual time, but only the illusion that the actions and events one sees on the stage are real, are happening as they happen in our familiar experience, can *stimulate* the actual. Therefore, Dryden's drive toward further probability makes him opt for loosening the rules: "I must further declare freely, that I have not exactly kept to the three Mechanick rules of unity. I knew them and had them in my eye, by follow'd them only at a distance . . . . I have taken the time of two days because the variety of accidents, which are here represented, cou'd not *naturally be suppos'd* to arrive in one" (italics mine).[5]

Dryden is still interested in revealing the workings of Providence. However, his primary compositional device for imitating Providence is no longer fable, though he does acknowledge the wisdom of "Mr. Rhymer" and accept the regulation imposed upon poets by "Poetical justice." His method is to imitate the workings of Providence as they occur in human experience, mysteriously, rather than as they are pictured by a well-wrought exemplary design. Real history, as opposed to an example derived from or imposed upon history, provides his groundwork, but, he argues, the poet may build whatever he likes upon that foundation "provided he makes it of a piece and *according to the rule of probability.*"[6] Obedience to the rule of probability leads him to depict Providence in a series of revelations or unravelings. We become aware of Providence in the play as we do in life: in spots or epiphanic flashes of enlightenment, rather than by a neatly sewn seam of events. Therefore, in addition to the "general Moral," which Dryden gives us in the concluding verse tag—a capsule, rather than a fable, that underscores the truth that has just been proven to our experience by the whole play—Dryden also embeds the moral within the characters: "Beside the general Moral of it, which is given in the four last lines, there is also another Moral, couch'd under every one of the principal Parts and Characters, which a judicious critick will observe though I point not to it in this Preface."[7] Character has assumed primacy over fable as the medium through which moral truth is proven to experience. Reality has been interiorized; its locus is now the internal arena of characters who in their complexity and particularity are portraits of people like ourselves.

The "innerness" of Dryden's characterization has attracted critics from Scott to Miner. It caused Scott to prefer *Don Sebastian* to *All for Love*: " 'Don Sebastian' has been weighed with reference to its tragic merits, against 'All for Love'; and one or other is universally allowed to be the first of Dryden's dramatic performances. To the youth of both sexes the latter presents the most pleasing subject of emotion; but to those whom age has rendered incredulous upon the romantic effects of love, and who do not fear to *look into the recesses of the human heart* when agitated by darker and more stubborn passions, 'Don Sebastian' offers a far superior source of gratification" (italics mine).[8] Miner argues that the major difference between Dryden's play and its source—which, significantly enough, was a *"Historical Novel"*[9]—is the realism of its characters and the fidelity of their behavior to experience: "His Sebastian and Almeyda possess greater vitality, are more 'real.' Although Dryden takes up the story where history had left it off, as a man who had seen how a court behaves he was better able to give a convincing sense of what may be called political behavior. This is not to say that Dryden's hero possesses any greater historical accuracy than the hero of the romance."[10] Miner is quite right (and characteristically subtle) in the critical observation he makes. Dryden's character is not more convincing because it is more historically accurate than the figure in the novel or, as far as we know from any account of his life, more like the real Don Sebastian. What convinces us of the "reality" and "vitality" of the character is the illusion of complexity and interiority in the portrait Dryden draws. Once again, consummate critic that he was, Dryden was aware of his compositional means and the ends they served. He dismisses the "more ignorant sort of Creatures," who, too dull witted to see what he was about, "maintain that the Character of *Dorax,* is not only unnatural but inconsistent with it self." He sends them for enlightenment to "that Chapter of the Wise Montaigne which is intituled *de l'Inconstance des actions humanes."* The gap here in sensibility between Dryden's contemporaries and us is interesting. The very quality that makes a modern critic find the characters vital and real and a nineteenth-century critic find the deep recesses of the human heart revealed in them makes the less subtly minded of Dryden's original audience think that character "unnatural" and "inconsistent with it self." What does that mean? It suggests, I think, a slight and interesting time lag. In 1690 Dryden was using the new imitative mode, but Dryden was a playwright who was always in the vanguard (which is why some of his most penetrating critical essays, starting with the preface to *The Conquest of Granada,* were intended as explanations of his practice). Some of his audience, however, had not yet grasped the new imitative mode; consequently, the old way in characterization—uniformity and consistency within the Idea or type that a particular character embodies—seemed to those spectators more *natural* than the multivalence and mystery that makes characters seem *real* and *natural* to us. The reaction of Dryden's audience to Dorax is yet another bit of evidence that an aesthetic revolution did indeed occur during the last decades of the seventeenth century.

The characterization of Dorax bears close examination for other reasons; its components and their arrangement illuminate Dryden's new method in characterization. The typological foundation for Dorax's character is complex in itself. It is a combination of elements from three inherited types: the satyr-satirist, the plain-speaking honorable soldier, and the heroic friend. The complexity with which the types are combined and the particularity and probability in the overstructure built upon them make the finished portrait realistic, not an ingenious combination of types, but a man we might know.

When we first encounter Dorax, the satyr-satirist element in his foundation is the most prominent. He is "sullen of port"; he is an outcast, renegade from his own people and alien among the Moors. He has been injured in spirit and deprived of love, and he is governed solely by brutal rage. He hates his fellow men: "I kill'd not one that was his Maker's Image / I met with none but vulgar two-leg'd Brutes" (I, i, 96-97). He kills men carelessly and pitilessly: "I spitted Frogs; I crush'd a heap of Emmets" (I, i, 79). His speech is full of the satyr-satirist's sexual revulsion: "I hope she dy'd in her own Female calling / Choak'd up with Man" (I, i, 132-33). True to the type, he *is* what he accuses those he most hates of being: "outlaws of Nature."

In act 4 when he reveals himself to Sebastian, the most prominent of Dorax/Alonzo's foundation types is the blunt-spoken honest soldier, a man of honor whose relation to his king was undermined by fawning courtiers:

> thou hast stood besieg'd
> By Sycophants and Fools, the growth of Courts;
> Where thy gull'd eyes, in all the gawdy round
> Met nothing but a lye in every face . . . .
> . . . .
> when I spoke
> My honest homely words were carp'd and censur'd
> For want of Courtly Stile; related Actions
> Though modestly reported, pass'd for boasts:
> Secure of Merit if I ask'd reward,
> Thy hungry Minions thought their rights invaded,
> And the bread snatch'd from Pimps and Parasites.
> [IV, iii]

As Rhymer said, the type was a thousand years old before Shake-speare drew Iago.

When he refuses to betray Muley-Moloch, though he knows him a tyrant ("shall we betray him? / A Master who reposes Life and Empire / On our fidelity" [II, i], when he will not kill a defenseless Sebastian, though he has been wronged by him ("But how to right 'em [his wrongs]? on a Slave disarm'd, / Defenseless and submitted to my rage? / A base revenge is vengeance on myself" [II, i], or when, finally, he prevents Sebastian's suicide without humiliating him, Dorax's type is the hero of honor. Dryden's instrument for transforming a composite of distinct types into a single, integrated portrait is language.

In the essay to which Dryden directs his "ignorant" detractors, Montaigne says: "If I speak variously of myself it is because I consider myself variously. All contrarieties are there to be found, in one corner or another, or after one manner or another."[11]

But how to achieve the interiority in a character that will allow the reader or spectator to apprehend the contrarieties as "corners" within a single "self?" Dryden's most subtle device for creating the illusion is a language that in its rough cadences (as compared, for example, with the "harmony of words" in *Tyrannick Love*), its looseness, its heavy internal pauses, its deliberate breaking of verse patterns, *simulates* spoken language. As he warns us in the preface, when his language sounds most casual, there we shall find him most masterly: "And I dare boldly promise for this Play, that in the roughness of the numbers and cadences, (which I assure was not casual, but so design'd) you will see somewhat more masterly arising to your view, than in most, if not any of my former Tragedies."[12]

As we have seen, we react to such rough "dialogue" language differently from the way we respond to declamation. Because we receive it as we receive language in actual conversation, it creates the illusion of depth in the speakers. The characters are like the people we know; by extension, they must be like us; and, by further extension, they must "experience" the depth we feel within our-selves. They seem to be, as we are, self-conscious.

Declamatory language rigidifies type. The linguistic decorum of high heroic and the linguistic decorum of Juvenalian satire are in-stantly recognizable and are also distinctly different from one another. The oratorical style of a speaker in a play of the sixties immediately "places" him within the gridwork of the play's design or, in a play of the seventies, tags him as "lover," "satyr-satirist," "libertine," "soldier." Declamation sharply defines and differentiates among types. If we compare the style of Dorax's language in any of the three foundation stances he is made to assume, we do not find these sharp differences. In all three postures Dorax is given language that sounds like spoken language. Consequently, the demarcation among foundation types is blurred, and they are more easily combined as parts within a unified, rounded portrait. Our sense of the wholeness of the speaker reinforces our sense of his interiority.

Not only in sound (rough cadences, pauses, and so forth) does language naturalize the reality of the play to our experience. What the words make us visualize also fosters the illusion. Miner has amply demonstrated Dryden's extensive and careful use of travel books to create authenticity in every detail of his picture of life in Barbary: "From travel-writers, and especially from what seems a French tradition represented by Pidou de St. Olon, Dryden was able to take, then, numerous details comprising the Moorish milieu and specific details of names and characters for his play."[13] It is for this reason that the play cries out for a reader rather than for a spectator; its "reality" is created out of concrete particularity and probability, as in a novel, not from the brilliance of its dialectic nor its oratorical versatility. This scene is no heroic never-never land, no *Empress of Morocco* technicolor spectacle; we have, rather, an illusion of experiential reality constructed in particular detail by language.

I should like to conclude discussion of this play with a single, small example of the use to which Dryden puts a "fact." In *The Present State of the Empire of Morocco*, St. Olon provides a curious and no doubt erroneous detail of Moorish life: "The Reservedness and Restraint in which the Moors keep their Wives, serve . . . to quicken the Desire. . . . They are particularly fond of Christians because they are not *Circumscis'd*."[14] Dryden puts this detail into a speech of Dorax, who, full of hatred and wrath, is hoping that Almeyda has been raped as well as murdered in the course of the battle her side has lost: "I hope she dy'd in her own Female calling / Choak'd up with Man, and gorg'd with Circumcision" (I, i, 132-33). This sentence is obscene as no "sex comedy" ever was, as Rochester's bawdiest verse satire never is. It is obscene because the language in which it is formulated is dialogue, not declamation; because the visual image it creates is particular, not abstract; because it brings a detail from the actual world into the reality the fiction simulates; and because its particularity and style make its speaker seem realistic and thereby create the illusion of an internal "self" in him. We therefore perceive the speaker as a real person like ourselves, and when his "consciousness" touches ours, we are revolted.

Maureen Sullivan, the most recent editor of Colley Cibber's three best-known plays, calls them *Three Sentimental Comedies*; in her introduction, she describes the transitional character of the first play, *Love's Last Shift* (1696): "It is worth remembering . . . that this, Colley Cibber's first play, was transitional and experimental, imposing the attitudes of sentimental morality on the materials of Restoration comedy, playing up the new spirit, but unwilling to relinquish the successes of the past."[15] In a variety of ways over the past twenty-five years, scholars (Underwood, Williams, Kenney, Miner, Hume and myself) have seriously questioned whether "Restoration Comedy" *is* a genre, or even a useful category. One might have expected such a deal of scholarship to have dislodged so improbable a notion as that from 1660 to 1696 a comedy reigned that celebrated sexual license, adultery, and hypocrisy and that this "Restoration Comedy" was replaced overnight—Congreve and Vanbrugh to some extent excepted—by a new reigning queen, "sentimental comedy," which celebrated chastity, fidelity, and romantic love. Unfortunately, however insubstantial they may be, literary critical prejudices are harder to lay than Hamlet's ghost.

In examining the comedies of the sixties, we saw that the ideals they held up for admiration and attainment were exquisitely refined ideas of virtue. Whether they appeared in a rarefied atmosphere (as on the high planes of Etherege's *Comicall Revenge* or Tuke's *Adventures)* or whether they appeared in St. James's Park (as in Wycherley's *Love in a Wood*), the virtues celebrated as ideals were chastity, fidelity, and romantic love. In the seventies we found that the same virtues were celebrated in comedy and in dramatic satire: "the rules of decency and honour" (Harriet, in *The Man of Mode*). We found upwardly slanted, antithesis figures, as in *The Virtuoso,* to be young women who prized virtue above life—"I'd lose my life a thousand

times before my virtue" (Clarinda)—and young men who valued
minds above maidenheads:

Long. . . . I would not have the body without the mind.
Bruce A man enjoys as much by a rape as that way

Just as there is no evidence that immorality and profaneness ever
were made virtues in the comedies and satires of Charles II's reign, so
too there is not a shred of evidence for a new or sentimental *morality*
at the end of the century. Unquestionably, there is something new in
the comedy of the nineties, and that something new drew the charge
of immorality upon the plays. Moreover, once we have identified
what is new, it is not surprising that Vanbrugh and Congreve, who
(we like to think) broke away from the mad, bad "sex farce" of the
seventies and embraced a "sentimental morality," were the main
targets of Collier's attack (while he thought wicked old Wycherley a
moralist, forsooth!).

In Chapter 4 we recalled T.S. Eliot's assertion that "Restoration"
drama "assumes orthodox Christian morality, and laughs (in its
comedy) at human nature for not living up to it."[16] In the nineties,
however, comedy *assumed* nothing and realistically *portrayed* human
nature in the *process* of not living up to its moral values. What seems
to us a new morality is the same old morality, but it is no longer
assumed as a given; rather, it is stated and seriously discussed. Just as
the plays discuss moral issues extensively and in detail, so too they
represent immoral actions probably and in detail. What really
aroused the wrath of Jeremy Collier—though he never managed
quite to put his finger on it—was the *realism* with which the drama
depicted human beings in the process of being immoral: the probability of the characters and the familiarity of their language. Indeed, a
muddled attempt to get at delusionist simulation of the real makes
him attack Vanbrugh for not observing "the Rules of the Stage."
Oddly enough, Vanbrugh's defense unwittingly hits upon the same
crucial issue. Primary in his composition, he says, is not exemplary
fable but character and language, and he adds that were that not the
case, he could easily have avoided Collier's objections: "I believe I
cou'd shew, that the chief entertainment, as well as the Moral, lies
much more in the Characters and the Dialogue than in the Business

and the Event. And I can assure Mr. *Collier,* if I wou'd have weakened the Diversion, I cou'd have avoided all his Objections, and have been at the expense of much less pains than I have."[17] The combatants were standing on the same aesthetic ground, though Collier, being neither a playwright nor a theorist, was not as sure as Vanbrugh of the grounds on which he argued. What changed in the comedy of the nineties was neither morality nor sentiment but imitative mode.

Colley Cibber, who, indeed, was by no means a blockhead, said that his character, Loveless, was "lewd for above four Acts," and most critics, like Sullivan, assume that Loveless's being "an honest rake" until his fifth act conversion constitutes the "immoral" element in the play, a carry-over from earlier comedy. But Loveless as a rake is such a stereotype, and the situation in which we find him (starving, rake-tricky servant, and so on) is such an old chestnut formula, that they could not elicit any response from an audience other than the kind of automatic laughter triggered by sitcom. However, Loveless in the *bedroom*—where, if he appeared at all, a rake of the seventies would be treated in broadly slapstick style, as Horner is—is another matter

> **Lov.** Oh! lead me to the Scene of unsupportable Delight; rack me with
> Pleasures never known before, till I lie gasping with convulsive Passion.
> [IV, iii, 213-15]

The particularity of language here, the illusion of interiority in the character, and the *probability* which has already been infused into the bed-trick make even this snippet of dialogue more erotic than anything that appears in earlier comedies. It is not at all clear whether the drama in any age does or, indeed, can induce us to behave in one or another way, but if it is possible for drama to arouse erotic feeling in us, then we are moved in *Love's Last Shift* not by what is old but by what is new.

Cibber's way with the bed-trick, which had been a stock device in drama for at least eighty years before he used it, is worth considering in this respect. It illustrates perfectly what was happening in the comedy of the nineties that suddenly made it seem morally threatening. When we examined *The Orphan* we took into account that, though this was very much a half-way play, there was enough of the new imitative direction evident in it to make us want to question *how*

Polydor could have tricked Monimia, a question that simply does not obtain in *Measure for Measure*, for example. When we considered *The Lucky Chance* we were struck by the fact that whereas the question of probability never comes up at all in Behn's source, it is brought into her play by Gayman's speculations about the kind of "devil" who is most likely delivering him. Gayman's skepticism is one among many small touches that work to naturalize the scene to experience. In *Love's Last Shift* the bed-trick is *enacted* on the stage. Then it is made to fall apart for reasons of *improbability*, which, of course, makes it more probable and which, in turn, makes the trick-within-a-trick that substitutes for the conventional formula (that is Amanda's playing a libertine) more probable and, consequently, more erotic.

Cibber was the first playwright, to my knowledge, to bring the bed-trick on stage. But he goes further still. The trick is not just acted out; it is made to imitate probable experience down to the smallest details; for example, the steward, Sly, spends "this half Hour pretending to pick the Lock of the Garden-Door" (IV, ii, 6) to give the servants time to set up supper and music. Whole masques appear in Behn and Shirley without the slightest need for explanation, and Shakespeare, of course, leaves us in the dark.

Cibber uses the same methods we observed in *The Lucky Chance*. First he prepares us for a stock situation with a discussion of the morality of the act:

Am. . . . Can I justify, think you, my intended Design upon my Husband?
Hil. As how, prithee?
Am. Why, if I court and conquer him as a Mistress, am I not accessory to his violating the Bonds of Marriage? For, tho' I am his Wife, yet while he loves me not as such, I encourage an unlawful Passion; and tho' the Act is safe, yet his Intent is criminal; How can I answer this? [III, i, 29-35]

Love and Honor logic-chopping of the sixties and seventies has precision of *idea* as its end. Here the object of moral scrutiny is inner human motivation and intention. Amanda's speculations invest the bed-trick with psychological dimensions. Consequently, they prevent us from seeing the action they anticipate merely as a *design*, as a pattern of ideas or a configuration of ideational positions—as we perceive the love and honor debates of earlier plays. The speech gives probability to an improbable, stock situation and provides the illusion of interiority in the characters. We cannot think of Loveless as simply "the rake" or Amanda as simply "the virtuous wife" once we have been made to consider their action as we consider our own actions, as involving possible conflicts between intention and act, or between inner feeling and outer sign.

Second, Cibber enlarges the bed-trick to an extended encounter and exchange of dialogue between Loveless and Amanda. The scene is multitextured from the start because *we* know about Amanda what Loveless does not know—that she is a virtuous wife playing the part of a libertine. We have continuous awareness of two levels in the characterization as a given. Then, the language and gestures (in stage directions) that Cibber gives Amanda as she plays the libertine are so convincing that they add depth to Loveless's character as well as to her own. As we watch him being duped, we want Loveless to be more "aware," as we are aware, of how complicated Amanda is. And in wanting that in a character, we invest him with *consciousness.*

Cibber uses two methods to naturalize language: reduction from the romantic and elaboration of the particular. For example, Amanda's exclamation as she enters the room is conventionally romantic: "Where's my Love? O, let me fly into his Arms, and live forever there." Loveless's spoken response is in the same mode ("My Life! My Soul!"), but his aside transforms romantic language to language that describes particular physical attributes and sensations: "By Heav'n a tempting Creature! Melting, soft, and warm—as my Desire—Oh that I cou'd hide my face for ever thus, that, undiscover'd I might reap the Harvest of a ripe Desire, without the lingering Pains of growing Love" (IV, iii, 67-71). The method—reduction from the abstract to the mundane—is derived from the old satiric mode, except that here reduction is not downwardly exaggerated distortion; it ends in experience. That Loveless is hiding his face for the practical end of avoiding detection adds further probability to his speech. Throughout the scene language *states* in the declamatory style and then reduces abstract declaration into descriptions of physical sensation. Passion is thereby transformed from an idea into an experience in which, to some degree, the audience participates.

Finally, as Amanda moves from her initial role of romantic heroine to her role of libertine ("I have found the Man to please me now;

One that can and dares maintain the noble Rapture of a lawless love" [IV, iii, 187–88]), the illusion is created that layers of artifice are being stripped away, so that when we come at last to Loveless's final "rack me with Pleasures never known before, 'till I lie gasping with convulsive Passion," we feel that we have come to bedrock experiential truth. In all, the scene comes as close as a play can to representing the sexual act on stage without crossing the borderline into a Minnesota Strip "happening."

Vanbrugh's *The Relapse* (1696) was, of course, intended as a satiric commentary upon *Love's Last Shift,* and it does retain strong outlines of the satiric structure of the seventies. Interestingly, however, the basic satiric design itself is modified in ways that will appear in verse satire in the eighteenth century and that will give impetus to the turn from Juvenal to Horace as the favored ancient model. The first of these modifications is that satiric antithesis is openly stated as a positive moral standard from which the fallen world of thesis deviates; the second is that both upward and downward distortion are far less exaggerated and are brought into the compass of probability. Positive and negative are not rendered as opposing perspectives upon reality or opposing planes of being. There is one "nature" only— experiential reality—and both upward and downward distortions are in kinds of actual behavior that exist in the real world.

The Young Fashion-Hoyden subplot is more exaggerated in its satiric portraiture than the main plot and has more conventional situational comedy in it than moral discussion (younger brother tricks older brother and country bumpkin to win fortune, and so on). But it does not exist to comment upon the main plot satirically (as in *Marriage à la Mode*), and it contains its own positive, "antithesis" moral standard. Most importantly, evident in the subplot as well as in the main plot, is the drive toward probability. Young Fashion does not trick Foppington, Hoyden, and her father, out of simple clever knavishness, as a parasite-satirist of the seventies would. He is given "inner" motivation. He acts out of a desperate need that his brother is not generous enough to supply. By itself this is not too significant. Though the configuration is romantic rather than satiric, it falls well within the boundaries of an antithesis that might appear in the seventies. The "fable" of the subplot, too, is in the earlier, exemplary mode. Providence allows Foppington's own vanity to undo him, and Young Fashion is Providence's instrument, first to give Lord Foppington one last chance and then, when out of uncharitable self-centeredness Foppington refuses that chance, to fool him. Of course, like any comic poet, Vanbrugh treats Providence with tongue in cheek, but the biter-bit motif in comedy is an old and traditional expression of providential design. Collier misses the point because he is so relentlessly literal-minded, but we recognize that a comic poet can be funny and serious at the same time. For example, in act 1, when Young Fashion says that Providence is helping him to fool his brother, he is being ironic, but Vanbrugh is being both serious and ironic. Young Fashion *will* be helped by Providence because, despite his faults, he has a conscience; Foppington will be tricked by Providence because he has neither conscience nor charity:

Y. Fash. So *Lory.* Providence thou see'st at last, takes care of Men of Merit; we are in a fair way to be Great People.

Lo. Ay Sir, if the Devil don't step between the Cup and the Lip, as he uses to do.

Y.Fash. Why Faith he has play'd me many a damn'd trick to spoil my Fortune, and I'gad I'm almost afraid he's at work about it again now; but if I shou'd tell thee how, thou'dst wonder at me . . . . what woud'st thou say if a Qualm of Conscience should spoil my design?

Lo. I wou'd . . wonder more than ever.

Y.Fash. Why faith *Lory* tho' I am a young Rake-hell, and have plaid many a Roguish trick; This is so full grown a Cheat, I find I must take pains to come up to't, I have Scruples—

Lo. They are strong symptoms of death; if you find they increase, pray, Sir, make your Will.

Y. Fash. No, my Conscience shan't starve me neither. But this far I'll hearken to it; before I execute this Project I'll try my Brother to the bottom, I'll speak to him with the temper of a Philosopher, my Reasons (tho' they press him home) shall yet be cloak'd with so much Modesty, not one of the Truths they urge, shall be so naked to offend his Sight: if he has yet so much Humanity about him to assist me (tho' with moderate aid) I'll drop my Project at his Feet and shew him how I can—do for him, much more than what I ask, he'd do for me; This one Conclusive Tryal of him I resolve to make. [I, iii]

Initially the passage is satiric in the traditional sense; the twist lies in the devil giving Young Fashion a qualm of conscience. We, the

audience, carry a Faustus Good Angel/Bad Angel configuration in
our heads that we bring with us to the passage; the comic twist
depends upon the incongruity between what we know and what we
hear. Devils do not give tricksters qualms of conscience. That is the
"understood" value upon which the joke plays—all quite conventional. But as the passage continues it becomes unconventional. The
antithesis is not merely an assumption the audience carries to the
play. It is stated and reflected upon. It is not within the conventions
of the old satiric mode for a trickster to think about the moral
implications of his action before he executes it. It is also new to have a
satiric antithesis that is not only fully stated but also seriously
explored. Zimansky thinks this passage is irrelevant to the moral
stance of the play. However, what the moral stance of the play *is*
bewilders him: "The one sop Vanbrugh throws to conventional
morality is to have Young Fashion test his older brother to make
certain that he does not deserve fair treatment; even here the oppor
tunity for a comic scene was probably as important as any moral
consideration. Lord Foppington's attitude in the scene certainly
motivates Fashion's 'Conscience, I defy thee,' but the actions that
follow are directed less against his brother than against Hoyden and
her father, the ones permanently cheated by his imposture."[18]

In this observation (and Zimansky is not unusual in his ambivalence) I find it interesting that at the very moment that the critic
argues that the subplot is not morally serious, he is taking it far more
seriously than he would take a stock comic plot, certainly more
seriously than a conventional satiric design would permit him to do.
We must ask what makes the critic take Young Fashion and, stranger
still, Hoyden and Sir Tunbelly, who are one-dimensional stock
types, so seriously that he is driven to consider the moral implications of a comic trick? Does not his wondering about the "imposture" of Fashion and the long-range effects it will have upon his
victims suggest a degree of involvement with the characters that
would not be elicited by a comedy of the seventies? We do not give a
moment's thought to the effects being "permanently cheated" might
have upon Lady Woodvil or Old Bellair. Moreover, it is not the
"sentimentality" of the characters or their being "exemplary" models that moves the critic. Neither what happens nor the kinds of

characters to whom it happens is new. What is new is the mode of representation. When a trickster explores the moral implications of his proposed trick, even in so short a passage as the one I have quoted, it ceases to be a trick and he ceases to be a simple type. Moral speculation creates the illusion of interiority in the character who speculates and, by extension, even in the characters he dupes. Now, it is not at all unusual for the subplot to have a moral satiric antithesis—conscience and brotherly charity. It is quite safely within the bounds of satiric convention. It *is* unusual, though, for the trickster to *state* the antithesis at all, no less to reflect upon its fine points. We cannot imagine Dorimant musing upon the morality of disguising himself as Mr. Courtage, or Bruce and Longvil discussing the ethics of disguising themselves as virtuosi. I do not say that satire of the seventies is not moral; it most decidedly is. But its morality is presented obliquely, in thesis attacks upon vice or folly that appeal to our reason, not in interiorized antithesis reflections that we are invited to share.

In the subplot as in the overplot, both thesis and antithesis are softened because the new imitative mode draws them into the realm of probability and turns conventional figures and types into fictive "real people," as ambivalent as we ourselves are. As thesis and antithesis soften they are blurred, and we become uncertain of how to discriminate between the satiric and the exemplary:

Vanbrugh's main plot lacks the variety and action of the sub-plot and cannot entirely free itself from Cibber's sententiousness. Amanda we expect to speak sentimentally, but what of Loveless, the reformed rake now safely retired to the country? In poetry the theme of country retirement was popular, but Restoration drama showed few sensible gentlemen who preferred the country. Loveless is not one of these; at the beginning of the play he protests too much, and in such inflated language that one would probably take the scene as a satire on the theme of retirement. But the odd verse in which the scene is written raises questions.[19]

Retirement to the simplicity of country life as an expression of satiric antithesis is as old as satire itself (one thinks of Umbricius's decision to leave corrupt Rome for retirement in rural Cumae, for example), and, as we have seen in earlier chapters, seventeenth-century criticism did not distinguish between verse satire and dramatic satire. Furthermore, verse as the poetic style in which satiric antithesis is expressed is quite commonplace; in the drama of the sixties and seventies it is the usual device for heightening the upward perspective. It is the new mode of dramatic representation that makes the expression of satiric antithesis unsettling here. The antithesis statement, though it appears quite conventionally at the opening of the play (as it does in *The Virtuoso*, for instance) is too much reflected upon and discussed. That, indeed, is what makes Loveless seem somewhat suspect. He ponders ideas that in earlier dramatic satire would have been presented as a passage or two in high pastoral, artificial style, or that might have been barely suggested in a few allusions to pastoral innocence or rural simplicity. Because the play opens with Loveless musing upon his own psychological condition, we have trouble *placing* him. We cannot fit him into any conventional dramatic type, not the rake, the reformed rake, the hypocritical rake, or even the doting husband. We cannot understand him as a type because we are given the illusion that he has self-reflexive consciousness. The play opens upon Loveless "thinking" about thinking and recollecting, and reflecting on, his past. As we ourselves are wont to do, he is not merely *stating* a philosophy but daydreaming about it and trying to discover its relevance to his own experience:

> How true is that Philosophy, which says
> Our Heaven is seated in our Minds!
> Through all the Roving Pleasures of my Youth
> (Where Nights and Days seem all consum'd in Joy,
> Where the false Face of Luxury
> Display'd such Charms
> As might have shaken the most Holy Hermit
> And make him totter at his Altar);
> I never knew one Moments Peace like this.
>
> [I, i]

The passage creates so strong an impression of interiority, of a real person remembering his flaming youth, with the wry ambivalence we feel when we remember ourselves as the foolish young things we were, that we cannot perceive it as we perceive conventional satiric antithesis. We are not *inside* a mind musing when we perceive Wycherley's Fidelia or when we catch the allusion to Waller's heroic vision in the affected reciting of his lines by the fashionable young

Dorimant. We never hanker with Juvenal's spokesman for the golden days of Saturn's reign; we would miss the joke if we did. But we certainly are inside Loveless when he recollects his past, and we share the curious mixed emotions he is "feeling" because they are so familiar to our own experience. Because we cannot perceive Loveless as a type but have been made to see him as a real person, satiric thesis, too, is ambivalent. We cannot perceive his fall simply as a wonderful, but highly artificial, piece of comic justice, as, for example, we watch Horner's being almost undone by his voracious ladies in the China scene. As we watch Loveless seducing and being seduced, we perceive a simulation of experience. (That is what makes the scene so erotic; *we* are a little seduced, too). Neither the characters nor the scene is sufficiently distanced or sufficiently exaggerated for satire. They do not comprise a pattern or a design of comic meaning; they are a doorway we are invited to enter.

In the same way Amanda's defense of her honor and her conversion of Worthy are nothing new as actions. We do not find them "sentimental" nor "sententious" when Celestina converts Lord B. in *The Lady of Pleasure.* In this play the satiric positive seems sentimental for exactly the same reason the satiric negative seems pornographic: the interiority of the characters and the emotional participation into which the audience is drawn by an imitation of the inner human arena.

The closeness with which drama imitates experience in the nineties is a logical precursor to the emulation it was expected to inspire. In 1698 the author of *A Farther Defence of Dramatick Poetry* argues that *The Relapse* promotes virtue and holds it up for emulation precisely because of the closeness with which it simulates experiential reality and draws us to feel what virtuous characters feel as they are tempted and as they fight off and conquer temptation:

Thus the *Relapser's Amanda* crowns her Character even with a double laurel. . . . 'Tis not to be supposed therefore that the *Dramatick* Poet must be oblig'd to borrow his Characters of Virtue from Lazy Cells, and Melancholy Cloysters; a copy from a *Hermit* or any *Anchoret*. No, his Characters of Virtue must come forth into the gay World, with Levity and Vanity, nay Temptation it self, all round them. They must go to the Court, the Ball, the Masque . . . Nay, to the very Prophane Play-houses (to speak in Mr. Collier's Dialect;) and yet come off unconquer'd. These are the Virtues that, to be Instructive to an Audience, are what should tread the Stage.[20]

The face of satire is changed in the last decade of the seventeenth century by a new imitative mode and the compositional methods it fosters, which (1) reduce the exaggerations of satire to probability (2) naturalize characters and create the illusion of an inner reality in them and (3) make characterization and dialogue the principal vehicles of meaning in drama. It was not the moral message but the medium through which it was filtered that changed.

Justifying his use of soliloquy in *The Double Dealer* (1694), Congreve said,

For if. . . [the speaker] supposes any one to be by, when he talks to himself, it is monstrous and ridiculous to the last degree. Nay, not only in this Case, but in any Part of a Play, if there is expressed any Knowledge of an Audience, it is insufferable. But otherwise, when a Man in Soliloquy reasons with himself the *Pro's* and *Con's*, and weighs all his Designs; we ought not to imagine that this Man either talks to us, or to himself; he is only thinking, and thinking such Matter as were inexcusable Folly in him to speak. But because we are conceal'd Spectators of the Plot in Agitation, . . . the Poet . . is willing *to inform us of this Person's Thoughts*; and to that end is forc'd to make use of the Expedient of Speech, no other better way being yet invented for the Communication of Thought.[21] [Italics mine]

This epistle is unquestionably strong evidence of the extent to which the new naturalism dominated drama in the nineties. Here we find a fully developed, Ibsen-like "fourth wall" conception of realism. However, the epistle also reveals a curious problem that confronted playwrights in the nineties: how to imitate the new locus of truth, a hidden psychological reality, without disturbing the surface, naturalistic simulation of experience. Since admittedly, as Congreve says, "for a Man to Talk to himself *appears* absurd and unnatural,"[22] how can the playwright reveal minds in the process of thinking without violating the *appearance* of experiential reality that probability of characterization and action demands?

A new kind of soliloquy, designed to create the illusion of "thinking out loud," offered one solution to the problem. In earlier drama soliloquy is solus declamation; it is similar to operatic aria in that it offers a statement of theme or a gloss upon the whole action. It is not elemental to the "plot in agitation." Rather, it *arrests* the action of the play and presents, almost in tableau style, some embracing image of the human condition that is relevant as a commentary upon the significance of the action—as does Hamlet's "To be or not to be" or Edmund's "Thou, Nature, art my Goddess." As Congreve thinks of soliloquy here, however, it is the attempt to show what cannot really be shown, to reveal the hidden reality in particular men, which does not and, indeed, sometimes *cannot* show in their outward behavior but which is nevertheless the hidden wellspring of all their actions. Even the new soliloquy, however, was not capacious enough to bear so heavy a burden. It finally required the loose structure and deeper interiority in characterization that the novel provided. It is interesting that playwrights in the nineties often employed novelistic techniques (like intricate, loosely connected serial plotting and extended, detailed description) or attempted to find substitutes for novelistic techniques (like the new soliloquy or the portrayal of extreme emotional states) in their efforts to reveal hidden depths in human personality, while at the same time keeping them hidden.

In *The Double Dealer* Congreve employs a host of these. The whole play turns on the dichotomy between interior and exterior human nature. We are made aware of the vast distance between thought and action as persistently here as we are in *Strange Interlude*. It is not at all surprising that Congreve builds his defense of the play on a justification of his use of soliloquy in it, because he uses soliloquy both as a subtle instrument for exploring meaning and as a major structuring device in designing the play.

Maskwell's soliloquies are not all in the new, thinking-out-loud mode. Rather, they form a subtle progression from starkly conventional old-style soliloquy, to the newer style of internal "Pro" and "Con" debate, to the newest style, full of pauses and backtracking, which creates the impression of halting inner reflection, of a mind *in the process* of formulating, scrapping, and reformulating a plan. The progress that the styles in soliloquy trace creates an illusion of progressive unmasking. Maskwell's first soliloquy is formally Jacobean in style: "Duty to Kings, Piety to Parents, Gratitude to Benefactors and Fidelity to Friends, are different and particular Ties; But the Name of Rival cuts 'em all asunder, and is a general Aquittance— Rival is equal, and Love like Death an universal Leveller of Mankind. Hah! But is there not such a Thing as Honesty? Yes, and whoever has it about him, bears an Enemy in his Breast: For your Honest Man, as I take it, is that nice, scrupulous Conscientious Person, who will cheat no Body but himself. . . . Well for Wisdom and Honesty, give me Cunning and Hypocrisie" (II, viii, 8-22).

This speech is neither internal debate nor audible thought; it is a formal disquisition on "Treachery." It does not imitate language as it is spoken in life, for nobody, however, depraved, declares to himself that he is a villain. Maskwell's second soliloquy, on the other hand, is quite colloquial. By its looser construction and use of pause, the style imitates a man debating with himself, coming to a resolution, and then improvising a course of action to fit his resolution on the spot:

I know what she means by toying away an Hour well enough. Pox, I have lost all Appetite to her; yet she's a fine Woman, and I lov'd her once. But I dont know, since I have been in a great measure Kept by her, the Case is alter'd; what was my Pleasure is become my Duty; and I have as little Stomach to her now as if I were her Husband Should she smoak my Design upon *Cynthia*, I were in a fine pickle. She has a damn'd penetrating Head, and knows how to interpret a Coldness the right way; therefore I must dissemble Ardour and Ecstasie. . . . Let me think. Meet her at eight— hum—ha! By Heav'n I have it—If I can speak to my Lord before—Was it my Brain or Providence? No matter which—I will deceive 'em all, and yet secure my self, 'twas a lucky Thought! [III, iii, 1-21]

The use of familiar expressions—"smoak out my Design," "I were in a fine pickle," "Pox on't"—brings the soliloquy close to our experience. This is language as we hear, speak, and think in it. Pauses break off a line of thought and thereby create the impression of a mind caught in the process of thought and jumping from one train to another by association rather than by logic: "I can speak to my Lord before—Was it my Brain or Providence?" The genius of Congreve in this passage is to create the illusion of an internal arena in character so deep that language, even the language we use when we are talking to ourselves, cannot penetrate it. We are not, after all, told what Mask-well's plan *is*; that information lies somewhere in the pause that follows "I can speak to my Lord before." Rather, we are given the illusion that a fictional character is *in the process* of thinking up a plan. The perfect naturalism of the surface is preserved and at the same time the illusion is created of a mysterious region deep below the surface. We believe ourselves to be eavesdropping on a real person as he thinks to himself. However, the nameless center of his thought and feeling, that which generates his words and, later, his acts, remains hidden.

Interestingly, when a moment later Mellefont comes on the scene, Maskwell begins, or pretends to begin, a false soliloquy: "Maskwell *pretending not to see him, walks by him, and speaks as it were to himself.*" Significantly, the pretended soliloquy is in the old, Jacobean style: "Mercy on us, what will the Wickedness of this World come to." Mellefont's interrupting Maskwell's *pretended* "thoughts," an intrusion of familiar, colloquial dialogue into a rhetorically formal setpiece, further complicates the layers of illusion and mystery. A character whom we have been made to perceive as having inner and outer identity now feigns inner thoughts and emotions that he does not have.

Congreve intensifies this playing with, and playing upon, interior and exterior truth in Maskwell's last soliloquy. In act 4 we are deeply inside a treacherous mind, watching it in operation. The style imitates a mind that not only is thinking but, in imagination, is projecting the likely consequences of the various courses of action among which it is choosing. We are taken from surface reality to inner reality, and then to a recess in which the mind ponders what may or may *not* happen, to a place where reality and fantasy meet:—But shou'd he find me out before! 'tis dangerous to delay—Let me think—shou'd my Lord proceed to treat openly of my Marriage with *Cynthia*, all must be discover'd, and *Mellefont* can be no longer blinded—It must not be; nay shou'd my Lady know it—ay, then were a fine Work indeed!" (V, iv).

Maskwell "decides" that the best cover for his treachery is an open acknowledgment of it, in the expectation that such an acknowledgment will not be believed: "No Mask like open Truth to cover Lies, / As to go Naked is the best Disguise." In the last chapter we noted the deep distrust of language that permeated philosophical thought in the nineties. So subtle is the structure of *The Double Dealer* that this last soliloquy, at the same time as it uncovers the deep reaches of hidden human truth, also reveals the impossibility of fully uncovering the mystery "by words or any other signs." The moment they are brought to the surface in words, motives and thoughts become unreliable, for language conceals at the very instant that it reveals.

Congreve uses novelistic passages of description to the same end, to reveal subterranean feelings that cannot be shown if the probability of the surface is to be maintained. Lady Touchwood's passion for Mellefont is not enacted before us until act 4, scene 18, where it is used as another demonstration of the unreliability of any truth that can be seen or heard. It would be *improbable* for a duplicitous character like Lady Touchwood (all wild passion within, all calm composure without) to show her passion for Mellefont in her public actions. The behavior would be out of character and therefore "unnatural." But, in order for the audience to know that the inner Lady Touchwood is very different from the outer, we must have an understanding of her inner self before we see her. This insight is provided by Mellefont's description of his encounter with Lady Touchwood in his bedroom, an event that is presumed to have occurred before the play begins. The description is quite novelistic; it bears some stylistic resemblances to late novels of Behn like *The Fair Jilt*:

Mel. . . . this Morning she surpriz'd me in my Bed.
Care. Was there ever such a Fury! 'tis well Nature has not put it in her Sex's Power to ravish.—Well bless us! proceed. What follow'd?
Mel. What at first amaz'd me; for I look'd to have seen her in all the Transports of a slighted and revengeful Woman: But when I expected Thunder from her Voice and Lightning in her Eyes; I saw her melted into Tears, and hush'd into a Sigh. It was long before either of us spoke, Passion had ty'd her Tongue, and Amazement mine.—In short, the Consequence was thus, she omitted nothing that the most violent Love cou'd urge or tender Words express. [I, iii]

Careless's "What follow'd?" prepares us for a tale. The description that follows is a revelation of passions too deep for words; they tie the tongue. Situationally, the relation between Lady Touchwood and Mellefont is a stock cliché by 1694. However, when we compare this *description*, which calls upon the imagination of the audience to construct the event, with an enacted scene that is played out before us (for example, Noumahal's seduction of Aureng-Zebe), we can appreciate the depth of interiority with which a novelistic description invests a stock configuration. We can also appreciate the degree to which novelistic description draws us into a scene and, by making *us* envision it, makes us participants in the action in an entirely new way.

In the midst of his violent quarrel with Lady Touchwood (I, vi, 81-83), Maskwell asks, "How I have lov'd you since, Words have not shown, then how shou'd Words express?" The line captures in capsule both the technical problem of the scene and the brilliance of Congreve's solution. How was the playwright to let us know "the very inmost Windings and Recesses of [Lady Touchwood's] Soul" (I, vi, 112) without having her disclaim them? He allows Maskwell to unmask himself in soliloquies. To use the same device for Lady Touchwood as well would have put too great a strain upon probability. Therefore, Lady Touchwood's inner self is disclosed in a style that simulates the effect of language being shattered by extreme emotion. Her language is simultaneously illogical and formal. It employs exactly the same figures and conceits that we heard heroically declaimed in the rhetorical flights of the previous generattion, but the figures are unstrung, cut loose, and adrift from the logical, dialectic frames in which they would have been constrained earlier. The scenes in which an enraged Lady Touchwood confronts Maskwell (I, vi and V, xviii) or an impassioned Lady Touchwood pleads with Mellefont (IV, xviii) meet to perfection the standard the nineties held for tragedy. As Motteux said in the passage quoted in the last chapter, "it is not uncommon to hear persons in the violent pangs of intense Grief break out into expressions bold and irregular, and sometimes impious, as the most daring Tragedian e're could reach to."[23] As Motteux advised that they should, Congreve's scenes uncover Lady Touchwood's "most eccentric *thoughts*" yet manage to represent them "as somewhat of a probability." Inner, chaotic reality is explored without damage to surface realism. This feature made Horace Walpole think the play a form of tragedy translated to the sphere of ordinary life.[24]

Finally, Congreve is novelistic in plot construction. The plot of *The Double Dealer* is an intricate, complicated unraveling of the workings of Providence. It runs to an average of fourteen scenes in each act (twenty-three in the fifth). Though in his dedicatory epistle Congreve tells us that he "design'd the Moral first, and to that Moral . . . invented the Fable,"[25] we are not to understand "Fable" in the sense that it was used in the eighties, as a stark and obvious exemplum. The "moral" of the play is the deep mystery and treachery of the human heart. This moral is variously explored both comically and tragically in a "Plot as strong as [the playwright] could [make it] . . . and single . . . [to] avoid Confusion." Whether the plot is comic or melodramatic, action is everywhere the handmaiden of characterization. And character, whether it is satiric or melodramatic portraiture, is of deeply interior figures, who are made to seem reflective human beings like ourselves. Even the lovers, as they uncertainly "hunt" the way to marriage, are particular and multidimensional, especially Cynthia. Scenes are very short, as they are in human memory, and as the plot unravels their number per act increases (act 1 has six scenes, act 2 seven, act 3 twelve, act 4 twenty-one, and act 5 twenty-three). One purpose served by this structure is to create the impression of an increasingly rapid pace of events as we move toward resolution. Another is to provide an extensive variety of situations in which the multifold aspects of human character can be revealed. Multiplicity of events reinforces the illusion of multidimensionality in character. (Southerne used the same technique in *Sir Anthony Love,* a play that is *about* its central character, Sir Anthony, and in which every event is an occasion for revealing another aspect of the mysterious central figure.) Variety of event serving the purpose of variety within characterization creates the effect of a many-cornered, multitextured human self that we discussed when we examined *Don Sebastian.*

We have for some time agreed that Southerne is a "psychological" playwright.[26] To my mind his interest in the psycholoogical dimension in human nature grew in the course of his career. Examining his plays chronologically, we find continuous and increasingly successful experimentation with methods of penetrating the surface "real." Southerne's first play, *The Loyal Brother* (1682), is conventionally heroic on its surface. However, incident on the high plane is used neither for a dialectical progression of ideas, as in the heroic drama of the sixties, nor for the creation of an exemplary design of providential justice. Rather, the main action of the play is a loosely strung series of events used to explore various emotional postures rather than to represent ideas. Low plot consists in topical political satire that, like Behn's in *The City Heiress,* takes cartoon potshots at Whiggism. The low plot has no internal structural referent, though it may be said to point, caption-fashion, to the relevant "moral" contained in the high. For our purpose Southerne's first play is interesting only for its use of soliloquy, which is used to express internal states in character that are not directly related to surface events. For example, when the Sophy has freed Techmas and promised to give him Semanthe, rather than simply responding joyfully to what has happened, Semanthe reflects upon her anxious forebodings (Does Fortune favor her only the better to ruin her? and so forth) in a long soliloquy. For the most part soliloquies are in the older, formal style, but their number and the touches in them of the new self-reflexive style indicate the direction Southerne will take. *Sir Anthony Love* (1691) treats the inner-outer dichotomy more obviously. All compositional elements in the play are subservient to one purpose, illuminating the central character. Sir Anthony is a stock type, a woman who disguises herself as a man to follow her lover. But the type is so vastly extended and explored that it becomes a multidimensional "person." Action, as in a picaresque novel, is a very loosely related series of adventures, in each of which Sir Anthony uses clever parasite-satirist tactics to expose folly and at the same time to use her victims to advantage. Here inner-outer conflict is presented in a single giant-sized metaphor.

In *The Wives Excuse* (1692) Southerne's interest in the inner life and the wide disparity between inner truth and outer sign is more clearly evident.[27] *The Wives Excuse* is very similar to *The Provok'd Wife*, which appeared in the same year, in that it lightly imitates the satiric surface of seventies comedy, but then penetrates surface situations and types to investigate their psychological implications. In *The Provok'd Wife* Vanbrugh merely reassesses *She Wou'd If She Cou'd* from a distance of thirty-years. Southerne's play digs beneath the surface to reveal the mind contemplating stock situations or to explore the hidden feelings and inner conflicts that generate them. Moreover, the play considers the question of inner versus surface truth in a style appropriate to the issue. For example, when Welville, the Platonic lover of Mrs. Sightly, is told by Courtall that Mrs. Sightly is not as virtuous as she appears to be, he speculates about the epistemological problems involved in "knowing" another human being in a soliloquy that imitates thinking aloud:

Wel. (Solus) I'll think no more on't, 'tis impossible; What's impossible? Nothing's impossible in a woman. We judge but on the outside of that

Sex; and know not what they can, nor what they do, more than they please to shew us. I have known *Mrs. Sightly* these seven Years—known her! I mean I have seen her, observ'd her, follow'd her; May be there's no knowing a Woman; but in all that time I never found a Freedom that allow'd me any Encouragement beyond a Friend—May be I have been wanting to my self—But then she would not throw her self away upon a common Lover; that's not probable; If she had been affectedly reserv'd I would suspect the Devil in her Heart had stampt the Sign of Virtue in her Looks . . . But she is open in her carriage, easie, clear of those Arts that have made Lust a Trade—Perhaps that Openness may be Design—'Tis easie to raise Doubts—And still she may be—I won't think she can—'til I know more. [III, i]

Mrs. Friendall converts Lovemore by forcing him to look below the surface appearance of her husband (who *does* deserve cuckolding), of herself, and of himself, to examine the psychological ramifications of doing what he would have her do:

Mrs. Fri. How! You know him then?
Love. You and I know him.
Mrs. Fri. Fit to bear a Wrong? Is that the Reason of your wronging him? I want but that; O let me but believe you injure him because you know you may; and attempt me because you think it safe; and I will scorn you low as you do him. [IV, i]

There is nothing in the least "sentimental" or "affective" about either Mrs. Friendall's conversion of Lovemore or Welville's pondering the virtue of Mrs. Sightly. *The Wives Excuse* provides further evidence that the movement of drama in the nineties was *not* toward sentimentalism but toward psychological realism.

In this same play Southerne also comically considers the boundaries of dramatic fiction, as Vanbrugh does in *The Relapse*. Just as Loveless recalls a play he saw in which a reformed rake suffered a "Relapse," Welville tells Mr. Friendall that he is writing a play called *The Wives Excuse; or, Cuckholds Make Themselves*. Mr. Friendall, a wife's perfect excuse, offers to provide Welville "a great many hints," to which Welville replies that he does "design to make use of Mr. Friendall," because "We who write Plays must sometimes be beholden to our Friends." Comedies in the nineties often exhibit the kind of playful, mocking self-reflection that we find in *A Chorus*

Line; they make us aware of the mechanisms by which a dramatic illusion is created. Southerne's interest in the limits of dramatic imitation, as well as his concern for the interiority of truth, led him, in my opinion, to the novels of Aphra Behn for inspiration. Maximillian E. Novak has offered two brilliant challenges to the "middle-class creators, middle-class heroes, middle-class audiences" sociological conception of the early novel.[28] Novak argues that writers like Defoe were searching for psychological realism, not propagandizing for, or pandering to, a new, narrowly bourgeois audience. They were concerned, he argues, with developing a compositional device, the "extended moment," which could expand the time of an action to include the illusion of expanded time that a psychological perspective affords to events. Most critics of Southerne's plays, and indeed Southerne himself, pay no more than token attention to his borrowings from Aphra Behn. For *The Fatal Marriage,* Southerne says, he drew a "hint" from Mrs. Behn; in fact, he drew the whole action of his play from three interconnected plots in Behn's novel. *Oroonoko* had to be more fully acknowledged because it was better known.

In their introduction to the Regents Restoration Drama Series edition of Southerne's play, Novak and Rodes argue that "the combination of realistic action and précieuse style in Behn produces an effect that is grotesque." They prefer Southerne's style, wherein, they think, "no indecorous realism destroys the noble impact of Oroonoko's private sufferings."[29] I cannot agree with this judgment. Behn's style, even in the short passages these editors quote, is decidedly *not* précieuse. Quite the contrary, the style of Behn's novel bears very close resemblance to the sober style of those travel books that, as we have seen, so much influenced Dryden when he wrote *Don Sebastian.* The novel is full of detail and accurate description; for example:

. . . as *Marmosets,* a sort of Monkey, as big as a Rat or Weasel, but of a marvellous and delicate Shape, having Face and Hands like a Human Creature; and *Cousheries,* a little Beast in the Form and Fashion of a Lion, as big as a Kitten, but so exactly made in all Parts like that Noble Beast, that it is it in *Miniature:* Then for little *Parakeets,* great *Parrots, Muckaws,* and a thousand other Birds and Beasts of wonderful and surprising Forms, Shapes, and

Colours: For Skins of prodigious Snakes, of which there are some three-score Yards in Length; as is the Skin of one that can be seen at his Majesty's *Antiquary's*; where there are also some rare Flies, of amazing Forms and Colours, presented to 'em by myself; some as big as my Fist, some less; and all of various Excellencies, such as Art cannot imitate.[30]

Behn's descriptions of animals unknown in Europe, like the armadillo and the electric eel, are surprisingly accurate, though the animals might well have seemed mythical to readers who had never encountered them. Her description of the color of mahogany or the gold dust that was washed down by the Amazon might also have seemed fabulous to Europeans unfamiliar with mahogany or with the practice of panning for gold in rivers. Her descriptive style in no way resembles the extravagant style of French romance. Further-more, Behn's assessment of the need for white colonists to maintain friendly relations with the Indians who so greatly outnumbered them ("So that they being, on all occasions, very useful to us, we find it absolutely necessary to caress 'em as Friends, and not treat 'em as Slaves; nor dare we do other, their Numbers so far surpassing ours in that Continent" [p. 6] is sociologically astute and sober. Her judg-ment of the value of this wonderful country and her reckoning of England's folly in giving it forfeit in the Dutch War is, again, both sensible and shrewd. I am not sure whether evaluative comparison between works of different genres is valid, but, if it is, there is no doubt in my mind that Behn's *Oroonoko* is far superior to South-erne's. The novel has been badly undervalued; in my judgment, among early novels in English it is outranked only by *Robinson Crusoe*, and, even there, the race is close.

Having acknowledged my bias, I should like to compare the novelistic and dramatic versions of *Oroonoko*, not for the purpose of establishing which is better, but, by using two well-known exam-ples, to try to shed light on the question of why the novel replaced the drama as the primary popular mode at the end of the seventeenth century. We have observed in plays of the late eighties and nineties that playwrights were driven by the demands of a new imitative mode increasingly to employ novelistic techniques. In closing this chapter I should like to examine the same problem from the oppos-ing perspective, to ask what the novel does that the drama *cannot* do and what changes a playwright must make in translating the "reality" of a novel to the stage.

The most stubbornly untranslatable elements in Behn's *Oroonoko* are its probability, the depth and complexity of its characters (as well as the silent language of their thoughts); the slow evolution of events from thoughts and feelings to actions; and the closeness to experience of its world. We shall begin with the most salient difference between the two genres—the method by which each admits the reader or spectator to its reality. There are two reasons that Behn's novel begins in the style of a familiar essay with the narrator's detailed and lengthy descriptions of Surinam, the setting for most of the tale. In the first place, she establishes an easy connection between narrator and reader that will enable the reader to see into characters and judge events through the narrator's eyes. (I believe that movies replaced novels as a popular form because they could aim the camera from within the narrator's head—a technological improvement upon what the novelist does in establishing rapport between narrator and reader). In the second place, detailed description draws the reader *into* the landscape. With the narrator's help, the reader imagines the landscape into being. The drama, on the other hand, is always a *show*. It makes a reality that it exhibits before the spectator's eyes. The extent to which a spectator can be drawn *into* the dramatic scene is therefore limited (especially so before the invention of the spotlight or the close-up camera). In creating an exotic setting like Surinam, the playwright is further limited. In the seventeenth century there was no alternative to feathered costumes and scenes and machines for showing the exotic. Spectacular stage effects prepare the spectator to perceive figures and actions in dimensions larger than life so that he is further distanced from the "reality" he sees.

The most basic difference between a novel and a play, then, is that the very form of the novel and the way the reader is conditioned by it to perceive brings its characters and events closer to his experience than anything can be that he sees at the distance that a play is forced to establish. This probability, conditioned by perceptual set, is reinforced by the relation a novel establishes between readers and characters. Because the novel form admits the reader directly into the consciousness of her characters, Behn can gradually disclose the evolution of subtle, sometimes conflicting, emotions within Oroonoko and Imoinda that build slowly but inevitably to

Oroonoko's march to the sea, so that when the event occurs we see it as not just probable but predictable. *We* experience the changes of feeling that take place in Oroonoko as he moves from the position of a powerful warrior prince who admires Europeans and has mastered their languages (as they never trouble to know his) to a slave robbed even of his name by men who repeatedly betray his trust and whose whole way of life entails consistent dehumanization and violation of their natural betters. Having shared the interwoven emotions and the evolution of sentiment that have led to the event, the reader *enters into* the slave revolt, when it happens, on the side of Oroonoko. We have shared Imoinda's fear and despair as she imagines the fate of her unborn child: "Now *Imoinda* began to shew she was with Child, and did nothing but sigh and weep for the captivity of her Lord, her self, and the Infant yet unborn; and believ'd if it were so hard to gain the Liberty of two 'twould be more difficult to get that for three" (p. 79). We have shared Oroonoko's anxiety, the pressure upon him to *do* something in response to Imoinda's despair and his own dishonorable condition. We have seen the degeneracy and viciousness of the colonists for ourselves and have accepted the narrator's judgment of them—as cowardly villains, the transported scum of England—as our own. Oroonoko's speech to his fellow slaves, then, expresses *our* sentiments. With the help of the naturalized style in which it is spoken and the affiliation with the narrator that we have established (for the speech is, of course, embedded within the easy, straightforward narrative style), we become participants in the action. Oroonoko says *exactly what we would have said* had we been there, we think. It is not a speech declaimed by a character who is impersonated by an actor and is therefore at three removes from our experience; it is, rather, the voice of a close friend, heard in our minds as we read, who is expressing sentiments that we passionately share:

Ceasar, having singl'd out these Men from the Women and Children, made a Harangue to 'em, of the Miseries and Ignominies of Slavery; counting up all their Toils and Sufferings, under such Loads, Burdens, and Drudgeries, as were fitter for Beasts than Men; senseless Brutes, than Humane Souls. He told 'em, it was not for Days, Months, or Years, but for Eternity; there was no end to be of their Misfortunes. They suffered not like Men, who might find a Glory and Fortitude in Oppression; but like Dogs, that lov'd the Whip and Bell, and fawn'd the more they were beaten: . . . Men, Villainous, Senseless Men, such as they, Toil'd on all the tedious Week 'till *Black Friday;*

and then, whether they work'd or not, whether they were faulty or merit-
ing, they, promiscuously, the Innocent with the Guilty, suffer'd the infamous
Whip, ... "*And why* (said he) *my dear Friends and Fellow-sufferers, shou'd we be
Slaves to an unknown People! Have they Vanquish'd us Nobly in Fight? Have they
won us in Honorable Battle? And are we, by the Chance of War, become their Slaves?*
. . . *No, but we are Bought and Sold like Apes, or Monkeys, to be the Sport of
Women, Fools and Cowards; and the Support of Rogues and Runagades that have
abandon'd their own Countries for Rapine, Murders, Theft and Villainies. . . . and
shall we render Obedience to such a degenerate Race, who have no one humane
Vertue left to distinguish them from the vilest Creatures?*" . . . They all reply'd
with one accord, "*No No, No Ceasar has spoke like a Great Captain; like a Great
King.*" [P. 81]

A play is more narrowly restricted in the depth and complexity of
motivation it can show because it must show feeling and event in an
instant within the collapsed time and narrow dimensions of a single
speech or two. Southerne was forced by his medium to condense
Oroonoko's motivation and reduce it to an easily recognizable formula—heroic love versus honor. The crux of the conflict is presented
by another character, Aboan, which further distances us from the
emotions of the principal characters. Moreover, our preconditioned
associations with the heroic style and formulas elevate the figures
and distance them still further:

> **Aboan.**   Sir, I must not blame you [for loving Imoinda so well]
> (Your pardon, royal Mistress, I must speak)
> That would become you better than your love
> A brave resentment, which inspired by you,
> Might kindle and diffuse a generous rage
> Among the slaves to raise and shake our chains
> And struggle to be free.
>
> [III, ii, 68-74][31]

The configuration is a stock device of the heroic drama (heroic
friend urges hero to forgo love for honor's sake). It derives from
countless literary sources, probably most directly from *All for Love.*
Moreover, Southerne's attempt to draw the formula closer to experience in Oroonoko's response to Aboan truly is grotesque—an awk-
ward lump of bourgeois realism floating incongruously in the
smooth heroic sauce. (It leads me to wonder whether this "high
Tory" drama is not a more likely place for us to seek evidence of the
proselytizing of bourgeois values than the early novel is)

Oroonoko These men . . . whom you would rise against
If we are slaves, they did not make us slaves,
But bought us in the honest way of trade
As we have done before 'em bought and sold
Many a wretch and never thought it wrong.
They paid our price for us and we are now
Their property, a part of their estate,
To manage as they please. Mistake me not;
I do not tamely say that we should bear
All they could lay upon us, but we feel
The load so light, so little to be felt
(Considering they have us in their pow'r
And may inflict what grievances they please)
We ought not to complain.

[III, ii, 106-19][32]

In the novel, Oroonoko is never a slave-trader; he takes slaves
only in honorable combat, and—as in the speech from Behn quoted
above—one of the most galling conditions of his captivity is that he
was taken not in honorable combat but by treachery, a treachery
especially prevalent among the colonists in Behn, including the
Governor (compare p. 5). However, the play has neither the space nor
the leisure to examine cultural differences. It must reduce internal
motivational complexity to a familiar, easily recognizable love-and-
honor formula. So too must it reduce moral ambivalence (like the
conflict within Oroonoko between his loyalty to Trefry and the
narrator and his obligation to revenge Byam's treachery) to the
simple outlines of a good-guys/bad-guys formula. Beyond the limitations of the genre, it is quite evident that Southerne was limited by
his own unwillingness to make white Christian colonists, the famil-
iars of his audience, the bad guys. A good deal of the responsibility
for oversimplification of plot, characters, and satire must be laid not
to the changes that had occurred in dramatic imitation of nature but
to the playwright's unwillingness to offend. As we have seen, Dryden in *Don Sebastian* was able to accommodate heroic and satiric
types to the new imitative mode with great subtlety. Nevertheless,
dramatic form itself is in some measure responsible for the oversimplification and reduction that we find in Southerne's play. For
example, because Southerne does not have the capacious time, space,
and vehicle for interiority that the novel affords, he must make the
slave revolt dependent upon an improbable uprising among the

Indians. Behn has the leisure to expatiate upon the methods the English used to prevent an uprising, which the Dutch were not wise enough to adopt. In Southerne both the uprising of the Indians and the slave revolt are heroic drama "turns," occasions for a realignment of heroic figures. They are like a city's falling into the hands of different sides three times in one act, as might happen in *The Conquest of Granada* or *The Indian Queen*. However, because the imitative mode of the play is neither sixties imitation of Idea nor seventies imitation of conflicting ideological perspectives, the logic by which the slave revolt follows upon the Indian uprising seems mechanical and the pace at which the events succeed upon one another wholly improbable.

Southerne's play is much thinner than a heroic drama of the sixties because it is not ideationally complex. Its techniques are derived from the earlier drama, but the deep structure of that drama, which demands the refinement of characters into the figures of ideas and the elevation of ideas in terms of a highly literary heroic code, is directly at odds with the context from which Southerne took his characters and events, the novel. Conceptually antithetic to drama of the sixties, the novel demands close identification between the reader and characters, who are represented as real people, not as ideational figures. For the most part the incongruity does not jar (the play was popular on stage for over a hundred years) because the formulas Southerne uses to substitute for the novel's imitative techniques are so familiar that they carry an automatic logic of their own. The conventions are not functional, as they are in a dramatic design of the sixties; rather, they are used to trigger an automatic train of association in the minds of the audience. For example, Southerne adds a love-and-honor rival, the Governor, to justify Oroonoko's revolt and to permit him to revenge himself without diminishing his heroic stature. In the novel Oroonoko kills Imoinda to prevent the sure violation she would suffer if she were to survive him. The grim possibility of a gang rape upon her by the colonists (compare p. 94) is, of course, more shocking than the play's feeble threat that the Governor will make her his mistress. But it is also more *probable*. In the novel, Oroonoko wants revenge, and we want it with him, for Byam's betrayal and for the inhuman whipping Byam has used to degrade him. Moreover, in the novel Oroonoko is not an improbable comic book hero who can kill Imoinda, the Governor, and himself without even working up a sweat. He suffers realistically, rather than heroically, as we ourselves would:

[After killing Imoinda and being unable to part with her dead body, even to kill himself] He remain'd in this deplorable Condition for two Days and never rose from the Ground where he had made his sad Sacrifice; at last rouzing from her Side, and accusing himself with living too long, now Imoinda was dead . . . he resolv'd now to finish the great Work: but offering to rise he found his Strength so decay'd, that he reeled to and fro, like Boughs assailed by contrary Winds; so that he was forced to lie down again, and try to summon all his Courage to his Aid. He found his Brains turn'd round, and his Eyes were dizzy, and Objects appear'd not the same to him as they were wont to do; his Breath was short, and all his Limbs surprized with a Faintness he had never felt before. He had not eat in two Days, which was one Occasion of his Feebleness, but Excess of Grief was the greatest; yet still he hoped he should recover Vigour to act his Design and lay expecting it six days longer, still mourning over the dead Idol of his Heart, and striving every Day to rise, but cou'd not. [P. 97]

The agony of Oroonoko is so naturalistically portrayed and the whole style of the book has moved the reader to penetrate the emotions and feelings of the characters to such an extent that we experience Oroonoko's sufferings as our own. The medium of the drama distances us from the suffering; we watch it as a show of experience that is not our own. If we do not find the heroic rivalry in the play illogical or the heroic revenge of its Oroonoko improbable, it is for the same reason that we do not find it unnatural that Superman flies. The *conventions* of the medium are so familiar that they substitute for the familiarity to *experience* that the novel provides.

There is one glaringly incongruent maladaptation for which Southerne himself and not the translation from genre to genre must be blamed: "The absurd and insufferable Underplot of the . . . Play".[33] I cannot accept Novak's and Rodes's argument that Southerne "needed as a contrast to Oroonoko's tragic love and outraged honor . . . a farce in which love was sex and honor contrivance. And in this strange blend of opposites he succeeded very well."[34] In my view Southerne needed a farcical subplot not at all, and this strange blend of opposites is a disaster. The subplot is his crude substitute for

Behn's clever, often sharply satiric, authorial intrusions, which are invariably thrusts at the hypocrisy of white "Christian" moral values. Southerne, who, as we have seen, had not the courage to challenge the money-morality of his audience even in the matter of slave-trading, was hardly willing to question its deeply ingrained sense of cultural and racial superiority. (He even bleaches Imoinda.) The subplot, bad as it is, can nevertheless be useful to our investigation of the ways in which drama imitates the actual in the nineties. It functions in much the same way as the cartoon caricatures of real people that we saw in comedy in the eighties, for, in my opinion, Mrs. Welldon is an attempt to caricature Aphra Behn herself. It roughly satirizes Behn as she appears in the novel, but it also draws upon contemporary popular notions of her. Behn lived on as a public image long after her death. Her enchantment with love, her high Tory Carolean morality, her openly argued feminism, and, especially, her reputation as a romantic adventuress were still alive in the public mind and were still an object of popular curiosity in 1698, when "The History of the Life and Memoirs of Mrs. Behn" appeared in the third edition of her collected novels, edited by her great admirer, Gildon. It is almost possible to think of the characterization of Mrs. Welldon as a lampoon counterattack upon the dead Mrs. Behn in reprisal for her "uppity" satiric attacks on Christian manhood in the novel. But that is perhaps too fanciful. Objective comparison of the texts reveals that, whether or not Southerne had any desire to slander the real Mrs. Behn, he is certainly satirizing the fictional narrator. As she appears in the novel, Behn is a fearless adventurer in an exotic land. Unrest among the Indians, for instance, does not deter her from venturing among them with only Oroonoko and her young brother as companions. She bravely ventures upriver to the Indian settlements, where no planter is brave enough to tread: "Some [white men] wou'd but most wou'd not venture . . . after eight days [we] arriv'd at an *Indian* Town; But approaching it, the Hearts of some of our Company fail'd, and they wou'd not venture on Shore. . . . For my Part, I said if *Caesar* wou'd, I wou'd go. He resolv'd; as did my Brother, and my Woman, a Maid of Good Courage" (p. 72).

She participates in every exciting event. With Trefry, she is Oroonoko's champion and tries to negotiate in his behalf. She gives him and Imoinda refuge in her house and nurses him after he has been punished. She stands in open defiance of the colonists and is scathing in her exposure of their moral degeneracy.

The play exaggerates these qualities to the end of comic mockery. Mrs. Weldon assumes a more obvious disguise, not just masculine qualities of mind and behavior, but male identity. Her courage and daring are used in the service of her own interests and her sister's, and her adventures are suitably female—to hunt for husbands for both of them. Southerne is far too conventional to challenge sexual prejudices.

At various points he turns passages or incidents in the novel to the purpose of directly ridiculing its narrator by means of the parody figure he creates of her. Two small examples will serve to illustrate. In describing Oroonoko, the warrior prince, in love, Behn extends upon the romantic formula of the heroic soldier first touched by love. In the course of doing so she takes a swipe at the treatment. European "men of honor" afford their women and compares empty Christian morality unfavorably to Oroonoko's heroic code of courtly love:

> As he knew no Vice, his Flame aim'd at nothing but Honour, if such a distinction may be made in Love; and especially in that Country, where men take to themselves as many as they can maintain; and where the only Crime and Sin against a Woman, is, to turn her off, to abandon her to Want, Shame, and Misery: such ill Morals are only practis'd in *Christian* Countries, where they prefer the bare Name of Religion; and without Virtue or Morality, think that sufficient. But *Oroonoko* was none of those Professors; but as he had right Notions of Honour, so he made her such Propositions as were . . . contrary to the Custom of his Country he made her Vows, she should be the only Woman he would possess . . . that no Age or Wrinkles shou'd incline him to change: for her Soul would be always fine, and always young; and he should have an eternal *Idea* in his Mind of the Charms she now bore; and should look into his Heart for that *Idea*, when he could find it no longer in her Face. [P. 14]

Southerne counters this thrust at English Christian manhood by making the protagonist of his subplot a well-done widow battling the war against age and wrinkles for herself and her sister by finding a new territory for husband hunting, where they are not yet recognizable as used goods:

Welldon But you have left London, you say, Pray what have you left in
London that was dear to you that had not left you before? The young
fellows, you know, the dearest part of the town and without whom
London had been a wilderness to you and me, had forsaken us a great
while.

Lucy Forsaken us! I don't know that they ever had us.

Welldon Forsaken us the worst way, child; that is, did not think us worth
having. They neglected us, no longer designed upon us, they were tired
of us. Women in London are like rich silks; they are out of fashion a great
while before they wear out. [I, i]

The play, here again, reduces a complex character from the novel to a
rigidly conventional satiric type from the seventies. And, as with
high-plot sixties-derived types, the figure, because it has been taken
out of its ideational context, cannot function. I believe that the
limitation in this instance, however, is in the playwright, not in the
genre.

My second example is drawn from an incident that occurs in the
novel when Behn, her young Brother, and Oroonoko go to visit the
Indian settlement. In the care and accuracy with which she describes
the culture of the Indians, Behn anticipates anthropology. For instance, her observations of the Indian Peeie, "both a Doctor in
Physick and Divinity," and the tricks he uses in his cures, "drawing
from the afflicted Part little Serpents, or odd Flies, or Worms, or any
Strange Thing" (p. 75), describe shamanistic practices that are still
widely in use in Central and South America. One incident, which
Behn uses to illustrate the cultural comparison she is making, is that
in which her younger brother introduces kissing to the Indians:
"This young *Peeie* had a very young Wife, who seeing my brother
kiss her, came running and kiss'd me; after this they kiss'd one
another, and made it a very great Jest, it being so novel; and a new
Admiration and Laughing went around the Multitude, that they
never will forget that Ceremony, never before us'd or known" (p.
76). Southerne transforms the incident into a scene of simple farce, in
which Daniel is forced by his mother into his first experiment in
kissing. His mother, the Widow Lackitt, is another voracious, over-
done pursuer of young men. In the translation from novel to play
adventurous women become women adventuresses, and any man
who submits to their will or judgment, a booby boy.

The subplot cannot operate as satire because, although thesis is sufficiently exaggerated downward, there is complete confusion in where antithesis resides. If antithesis is the high plot of Southerne's play, as Novak's and Rodes's argument would suggest, the satiric point is lost because whatever comparison or contrast is being made is far too vague. The subplot never comments upon the values or ideals of the high plot. It attacks values that lie outside the play. On the other hand, if the satiric antithesis is Behn's novel itself, the satiric thesis still does not work because the portions of the novel singled out for ridicule (the narrator herself, the description of her adventures) are not upwardly exaggerated. They are either too realistic to bear their part in a hypsos-bathos satiric equation or they are themselves satiric attacks on contemporary social values. Moreover, the narrator of the novel is too close to the reader to be an outside "literary" satiric referent (as Scudéry's romance is antithesis to the satiric thesis in *Marriage à la Mode*). Because novels sometimes purport to be accounts of real experience and always have as their aim the simulation of experiential reality, they cannot be used to create a heroic backdrop antithesis in the way that romances or epics do.

To conclude, in the 1690s the progress of the aesthetic conception "imitation of nature" centers both in the struggle of the drama to extend its boundaries in search of new forms and techniques that will enable the playwright to imitate a reality inside the human psyche and also in the intervention of the serious novel as one solution to that formal problem.

SEVEN

Emulation: The Early Eighteenth Century

To wake the Soul by Tender Strokes of Art,
To raise the Genius, and to mend the Heart,
To make Mankind in conscious Virtue bold,
Live o'er each Scene, and Be what they behold:
For this the Tragic-Muse first trod the Stage.

Pope, Prologue to *Cato*

Minds from each others motions take their bent,
In Love, Joy, Rage, and even Hate consent;
The Angry urge us, and the Fearful fright,
The sad disturb us, and the Gay delight.
The Proud and Scornful our Aversion prove,
As all the Tender our Affections move.

The Gentleman's Journal

The Stage . . . is, or ought to be, the School of Politeness and Good Breeding, for we know, by Experience, that the Youth form themselves by what they see there, and receive Notions of Conversation and Behavior by the Examples there Represented.

Mist's Weekly Journal

Emulation theory, wherein the traditional equation "art imitates nature" is reversed, did not spring into being full blown in 1700. It evolved gradually over the decades we have been considering, but not until the turn of the century did all the elements that went into the finished conception cohere. Hume argues that the appearance of exemplary models is a phenomenon of the nineties:

Characters who serve as moral examples are increasingly introduced between 1688 and 1710 into plays which otherwise . . . preserve what John
Loftis defines as the "Restoration Stereotypes" . . . "The Fine Gentleman"—as Steele once thought of titling his last play—is increasingly a
common figure in comedy; virtuous females are even more frequent . . . in
the Carolean period, such characters appear in romantic comedy or tragicomedy set abroad, but more and more they became frequent in plain
English set comedies. By the time of Taverner's *The Maid and the Mistress*
(1708), Mrs. Centlivre's *The Man's Bewitch'd* (1709), and Charles Shadwell's
The Fair Quaker of Deal (1710) they are commonplace.[1]

As we have seen, virtuous characters, or, more precisely, *characters
of virtue*, are as frequent in plays of the sixties and seventies as they are
in those written at the turn of the century. It is the character of
character and the proximity of drama to experience that changes.
The idea that drama draws us to emulate what we see predates the
appearance of "characters who serve as moral examples," which
itself is only one component in the complex of ideas that came
together to form emulation theory. As early as 1672 St. Evremond
wrote that tragedy elicits emulation from an audience. However, it is
not the emulation of virtuous characters for which St. Evremond
calls. In keeping with the aesthetics of the sixties, he conceives the
function of drama to be elevation of our minds to the apprehension
of an ideational quality, "greatness," which then draws our spirits to
emulate the *virtue* itself, rather than the behavior of virtuous characters: "We ought in Tragedy, before all things whatever to look after a
Greatness of Soul well express'd which excites in us Admiration; our
Minds are sensibly ravish'd, our Courage elevated and our Souls
deeply affected."[2]

Pity, as a response to tragedy, is all very well, says St. Evremond,
but pity and compassion for the *person* whose greatness of mind a
tragedy celebrates can be an obstacle to the emulation a tragedy
should inspire. Admiration alone can spur the desire to emulate the
virtue we apprehend: "I love to see the Misfortunes of some Great
unhappy person lamented; I am content with all my heart that he
should attract our Compassion, nay, sometimes command our
Tears; but then I would have these tender and generous Tears paid to
his Misfortunes and Virtues together; and that this melancholy

sentiment of Pity be accompanied with vigorous Admiration which shall stir up in our Souls a sort of amorous desire."[3] Heroic love is the passion to be imitated because, according to St. Evremond, "There is no Passion that more excites us to everything that is noble and generous, than a virtuous love."[4] In 1672 the imitative impulse is directed toward the virtue embodied in a figure rather than the feelings inherent in a character. Nevertheless, the idea that drama elicits emulation of what it shows us clearly had taken root long before the view developed that drama shows us pitiable people like ourselves. In St. Evremond's admiration/emulation conception, we find one of the threads, drawn from Carolean aesthetics, that went into the weaving of the final theory.

In chapters 5 and 6 we saw that in the eighties and nineties drama draws closer and closer to experience, until, by the mid-nineties, the audience all but enters into the scene represented and shares the thoughts and feelings of characters. Two questions, then, arise: How do we move from an emulation theory based on admiration, like St. Evremond's, to the early eighteenth-century affective theory of emulation that entails the audience's identification with virtuous characters and the consequent modification of behavior that attends upon such identification? And, furthermore: How do we go from this early conception of an emulation based on identification, which we might call "affective theory," to the later eighteenth-century version of the theory? This later conception rests upon an aesthetics that abjures the personal and idiosyncratic and insists, as Walter Jackson Bate said, "that poetry should seek less to arouse and give voice to the personal associations and feelings of the observer than to guide them and impose upon them a finished ideal . . . it does not, by the portrayal of individual expression appeal to the affections and associations of the beholder, but rather, by an imitation of the ideal, to form and control those affections and associations."[5]

At first glance it would seem that we have not been tracing an evolution in these chapters but have been describing a circle—from imitation of the ideal to imitation of the ideal. However, in the eighteenth century neither the ideal nor the process by which we attain to it is the same as it was at the Restoration. The ideal has been totally secularized; it is social rather than metaphysical, and the method by which an audience comes to it is conceived not in terms of Neoplatonic rapture but in terms of Lockean associationism.

Emulation theory, completely formulated by the beginning of the eighteenth century, did not remain static. At the beginning it reflects, and is closely related to, the conception of dramatic imitation prevalent in the nineties. The emulation a play evokes is personal—that is, we share the emotions of realistically drawn characters; our emotions come to resemble theirs; it follows that we shape our behavior to resemble theirs. However, in the 1720s and 1730s the characters we see are once again idealized. "Rais'd above the life," they are used to set a *behavioral* ideal to which we should aspire. The end of this emulation conception is to shape public, rather than private, behavior. For example, the *St. James's Journal* of November 18, 1722, recognizes that the characters and behavior we see in *The Conscious Lovers* are unrealistic but praises Steele for creating an idealized conception of high life that is both moral and attractive: "As for the *Characters* and *Manners*, if there are not many such in real Life (I mean of the principal ones) 'tis pity. They appear at least very gracefully. . . . I think the Poet has very well shown that the Splendour and Shine of high Life is not at all eclips'd by the Honour and Innocence of it."[6] From the beginning of the century to its second decade we come from an emulation theory that "appeal[s] to the affections and associations of the beholder" to an emulation theory that posits that artificial models of social behavior wrought in a drama should "form and control those affections and associations." It is interesting to consider the difference between the two stages and the changes that formed them.

In the last decades of the seventeenth century two conceptions arose that help to explain the logic behind the thought that we emulate what is represented in the drama. One is psychological and offers a new understanding of the pleasure involved in thinking about feeling. The other is philosophical and offers a new understanding of aesthetic perception and its relation to both psychology and behavior.

In the 1680s, in keeping with the epistemological changes we considered in chapter 4, a new understanding arose about the relation of human nature to the laws of nature, which gave emphasis to the interior location of reality, the "paradise within." It posited that there is both pleasure and moral good in self-reflection. It was not, as the Greene/Crane controversy might suggest, that a new idea arose of what moral good *is*; but rather that the direction in which we are to look in our search for good had begun to change. We have seen for ourselves that dramatic theory and practice of the 1660s and 1670s rested on the unspoken assumption that we must transcend the limits of our earthly nature and the boundaries of our ordinary perception to apprehend the good. In the early eighties new ways of thinking about human nature arose. For example, in "A Demonstration of the Divine Authority of the Law of Nature," Samuel Parker not only locates good within the human being but argues that it is a "law" of our nature to contemplate our inner goodness with pleasure. Moreover, our pleasure is doubled when we see the connection between the sentiments that enliven us and the universal law, established by divine authority, that governs our natures and all of nature. Two interacting psychological concepts are relevant here: that we take pleasure in looking within ourselves and that we take further pleasure in the association we can make between our inner selves and a synthesizing law (the concepts have some resemblance to Locke's primary and secondary ideas): "All men feel a natural Deliciousness consequent upon every Exercise of their good-natur'd Passions; and nothing affects the Mind with greater Complacency, than to reflect upon its own inward Joy and Contentment. So that the Delight of every vertuous Resolution doubles upon itself; in that it first strikes our Minds with a direct Pleasure by its suitableness to our Natures and then our Minds entertain themselves with pleasant Reflections upon their own Worth and Tranquillity."[7]

Parker, of course, aimed his inquiry at human nature and its relation to the law of nature and to God; he was not concerned with art. However, it is easy to see the relevance of his speculations to the new epistemology and aesthetics that we discussed in the last chapters. Human imagination does not overleap its earthbound ties to find the good (or true); rather, it penetrates to the innermost mystery of the human self. And thinking about inner truth, conceived as "good-natur'd Passions," not as reason or mind, gives pleasure. When we reflect upon the full significance of these ideas, we realize that as early as 1681 the meaning of "nature" in the formula "art imitates nature" had already changed from what it had been twenty years earlier, and it had changed drastically from what it had been in the early seventeenth century.

Conceptions of sympathetic psychology, like Parker's, are at the foundation of the "conversions" we find in plays of the nineties, when characters who have strayed from the *natural* course of goodness, like Lovemore or Loveless, are reclaimed by the virtuous example of other characters, by the innate goodness that shines in all of us but shines more brightly through the less opaque surfaces of those who are virtuous. The same conceptions also form the underlying rationale for the sympathetic movement between audiences and characters in plays. The psychological explanation for this sympathy is that the "deliciousness" of exercising the good-natured passions is natural and the contemplation of such an interactive play of sympathy is pleasurable. By the beginning of the eighteenth century these ideas of human nature are unquestioned, commonplace assumptions.

Ideas about human nature like Parker's, wedded to ideas of human understanding like Locke's, gave rise to new ideas about perception and in the early eighteenth century generated an associationist theory of aesthetic perception that is the philosophical basis of the affective theory of emulation. In *Spectator* no. 414 (June 25, 1712) Addison outlines an intricate conception of the relation of art to nature to justify the notion that nature is perfectable by art:

We find the Works of Nature still more pleasant the more they resemble those of Art. For in this our pleasure arises from a double principle; from the agreeableness of the Objects to the Eye, and from their Similitude to other Objects; we are pleased as well with comparing their Beauties as with surveying them, and can represent them to our Minds, either as Copies or Originals. . . . If the Products of Nature rise in Value, according as they more or less resemble Art, we may be sure that artificial Works receive a greater Advantage from their Resemblance of such as are natural, because here the Similitude is not only pleasant but the Pattern more perfect.[8]

Below the surface of Addison's remarks we can still see the dim outline of the double pleasure principle we found in Parker. The pleasure in aesthetic perception is the pleasure of finding resemblance between the quintessential inner reality of an object and its conformity to the law of its nature, which is expressed by art. A work of art is more perfect than nature because it is pleasing not only in itself but in the recognition it awakens in the mind of the "similitude" among the objects in nature. The activity of comparing objects—to use Lockean terms, of combining primary ideas to create secondary ideas—is pleasurable, and when ideas or objects have been associated with a feeling of pleasure, that pleasure is transferred by association to the idea or object itself and is identified with it. The pleasure we take in a work of art for its ability to elicit the associative process draws the "natural" toward the "artificial"—draws the mind of the audience toward the good in the play—and, further, draws the human mind to the task of perfecting human nature. As Steele said, he was "convinced, that the impulses [he had] received from theatrical representations, have had a greater effect than otherwise would have been wrought in [him] by the little occurrence of [his] private life."[9] Art enhances the value of nature in part by setting artificial models of perfection toward which nature aspires and in part by revealing similitudes to the eye of the beholder, since *comparison* between the "Original" (the beauty inherent in a natural object that art makes clearly visible) and the "Copy" (the law of an object's nature, which art demonstrates) is a deliciously pleasurable activity in itself.

It is most curious that associationist aesthetics, which is the philosophical basis of emulation, grows out of, and is clearly initially dependent on, conceptions of dramatic imitation of the 1690s—simulation of probable, particular, experiential reality—though it leads directly to a new idealizing, generalizing, and typological method of imitation. Only when we look back on the nineties from the first decades of the eighteenth century can we appreciate that we have journeyed through the center of the particular to reach another universal, abstract system. However, the abstraction is not *above* nature, an ideational design of metaphysical truth, but *within* nature, a methodized system wherein particulars, related by the associative powers of mind, form generalized truths. Furthermore, the observer is not lifted out of his own nature to apprehend truth, but, by constant and pleasurable comparison of the good within himself (the particular) and the good disclosed by the system of similitude (the universal), he comes to "*be* what he behold[s]."

When we combine Parker's psychology with Addison's aesthetics we begin to appreciate the extensive epistemological scaffolding that supported assumptions about the power of drama to effect moral ruin or moral reformation that were prevalent in the early eighteenth century. Steele's justification of those spectators who cried at performances of *The Conscious Lovers* ("to be apt to give way to Impressions of Humanity is the Excellence of a right Disposition and the Natural working of a well-tuned spirit") is more than an observation about an audience's response to a play.[10] It is a statement about the nature of being human.

The effects of emulation theory upon literature, especially drama, were overwhelming and all-encompassing. A.S. Bear has vividly demonstrated that from "self-appointed moral re-armers, and representatives of the . . . Society for the Reformation of Manners" to leading writers, critics, and sophisticated champions of the stage like Dennis, "they all shared the same basic assumptions about what literature was, what it was for, and how it might be judged." And, regardless of what positions they took in the thirty-year controversy about the morality of the English stage, to a man, they shared "a universal agreement that the process by which these effects [the corruption or moral emendation of youth] are brought about has to do with the direct imitation of examples of behavior presented in plays."[11] Such homogeneity of attitude is not surprising when we recognize that the sensibility from which it grew was so long in the making and, as we have seen, had such deep roots in an evolving new psychology and epistemology, as well as aesthetics.

What were the effects of this emulation aesthetic upon dramatic composition? I should like to consider a few of them with reference to what I conceive to be two stages in emulation theory as it developed in the early eighteenth century. In the first stage, drama aims at evoking private emulation; in the second, it elicits emulation of public models. Private emulation depends on the identification an audience effects with characters that leads them to imitate some kinds of behavior they see and to avoid others. It develops from the mode of the 1690s. The characters must be close to us, because "nothing can relate to [the audience] that does not happen to such as live and look like themselves."[12] There must be sharp and distinct moral differentiation among the characters. (There is no room in this mode for "irregular greatness.") Each character must elicit a particular, clearly definable effect: "The Disposition of the Play is to be such that all the Characters have a proper Effect with us. Our Fear, Love, and Anger are to be exerted with Justice."[13] If the characters are natural within the compass of our experience and if they are particularly defined, there is no possibility that we will imitate immoral ("unnatural") rather than moral ("natural", that is, benevolent) characters. Addison's conception of the relation of art to nature and the power of art to perfect, quoted above, is anticipated by about ten years in "A Letter to A.H. Esquire concerning the Stage":

The greatest Faults in our Plays are their being generally, in one Part or other, unnatural; That which is regular in any of them can never be an Offense; and where the Monster appears, it rather frightens than allures, so that we are not in so much danger even from our very bad Plays; For the more monstrous, the less power it has to please; and whatever loses the Power, can never do much damage. So that if Mr. Collier should make a Collection of D'Urfey's Works, who is there that would become a Convert? . . . who wou'd be proud of an Imitation of any of his Heroes?[14]

Another effect of the identification/emulation theory upon dramatic composition was to narrow the distance between tragedy and comedy, with the consequence that plays of either genre could be expected to tap springs of generous tears in an audience. In the early 1690s, as we saw from Motteux's differentiation in chapter 5, both tragedy and comedy were conceived as imitations of experience, though tragedy was afforded a wider emotional scope than comedy by virtue of the extreme experiential states it imitated. After the turn of the century, as a result of the more intense identification fostered by emulation theory, the purpose of both comedy and tragedy was affective. Tragedy is primarily concerned not with the extremity of the passions it imitates but with the intensity of the compassion it arouses in the spectator. In 1701 Dennis says, "I find by experience that I am no further pleas'd nor instructed by any Tragedy, than as it excites Passion in me." He goes on to argue that the intensity of the passion aroused is directly dependent upon the closeness of identification the play creates between the characters and the spectator, for "the greater the Resemblance between him who suffers, and him who commiserates, the stronger will the Apprehension, and consequently, the Compassion be."[15] It is this conception that leads Rowe to make *The Fair Penitent* (1703) "a melancholy tale of private woes," where "you shall meet with sorrows like your own."[16] It is also, however, the very same ideal that makes Granville's 1701 adaptation of Shakespeare (*The Jew of Venice*) seem, if not as Rowe thought it to be "design'd tragically by the Author," at least designed to be a jerker of generous tears by the adapter. Drawing comedy closer to our emotional experience and providing strong central characters in it with whom the audience could identify and with whom they could share the deliciousness of shared "good-natur'd passions" drastically altered comedy and eliminated any serious satiric function from it for almost two hundred years. As Stuart Tave has said, "This good natured and good humored ideal exerted a two-fold influence on the comic; it corrected the Puritan by liberating and encouraging the milder forms of comic expression, the smile or sympathetic laughter and innocent mirth; and it corrected the rake by controlling and discouraging the more vigorous forms of punitive laughter, ridicule, and satiric wit; it preferred Horace to Juvenal, Menander to Aristophanes, Terence to Plautus, and as the eighteenth century moved along, Shakespeare to Jonson, Addison to Swift, Farquar to Congreve."[17]

As we saw in chapter 2, Shakespearean adaptations can provide interesting insight into the sensibility of the times for which they were written. The Davenant-Dryden *Tempest* shaped Shakespeare's play to the sixties' three-tiered comic model, and the tendency of the adapters was to multiply figures in order to effect the complex juxtaposition and balance that imitation of Ideas demanded. Granville's method is almost diametrically opposite to that of Davenant and Dryden. Neither the story nor the structure of the original is of interest to him; his whole attention is upon the emotional make-up of the characters. Indeed, he considers the story a decorative frame, a showcase for the exhibition of the good-natured characters. In his "Advertisement to the Reader" he acknowledges that it must seem strange that anyone would waste his labor adapting so improbable a play, "The Foundation of it . . . being liable to some Objections," but he trusts that "the judicious Reader will observe so many Manly and Moral Graces in the Characters and Sentiments, that he may excuse the Story, for the Sake of the Ornamental Parts."[18] He reduces not just the number but the complexity of characters to make a single figure, Bassanio, central. Complexity either in plot or characterization is washed away to the end of making the moral positions among characters readily discernible. The number of scenes, as well as the cast, is cut by half, and any ambivalence in character or action is eliminated.[19] All broadly parodic scenes and characters—Launcelot and Old Gobbo, for instance—are dropped to prevent lowering the moral tone. Everything is pared away that might distract us from the central character or prevent us from thinking him a good-natured person, much like ourselves, whose actions are understandable in terms of our experience.

Morocco and Aragon, the one too heroic, the other too murky for the new atmosphere, disappear from the play. The richly symbolic casket choices are reduced to one because only Bassanio's choice is important and because, insofar as it is possible, Belmont itself and the fairy-tale choice test must be reduced to experience. The positions of Morocco and Aragon are compressed into a short passage, which is given to Gratiano. The presence of Gratiano in the casket-choice scene is designed to set a contrast that will draw our attention, as everything in the adaptation does, to the admirable qualities of the warm-hearted Bassanio.

Shylock is reduced to the simplest of melodramatic villains, who toasts money when Bassanio and Antonio toast love and friendship and whose hatred of Christians has no foundation other than his own villainy. Whatever in the original makes Shylock's characterization complex is eliminated, and since Granville cuts out act 3, scene 1, and puts the "Hath not a Jew eyes" speech in a context that plays down the opening of the passage and emphasizes its vengeful conclusion, we are shown nothing of Shylock's suffering. As Spencer has said, "[Shylock] is fitted to his part in the eternal stage struggle between Villain and Hero."[20] His only function in the play is to stand in radical opposition to Bassanio and by his dark shadow to throw the benevolence of the hero into high relief. However, though Shylock's hatred must be "unnatural" to contrast with the "natural" benevolism of Bassanio, his cruelty must also be made purposeful and understandable—extreme but logical in terms of our experience. Unlike the original, wherein Shylock himself does not seem sure of his motives, Granville's play gives him a motive that will answer both to the villainy of his character and to the logic of experience. Shylock signs the bond because has has a long-range plan to extermi-nate Christians and thinks to kill two with one stone, for he knows that if Antonio falls forfeit, the good Bassanio will die of generous grief. Against that dark and twisted scheming, Bassanio's warmly emotional self-sacrifice shines bright, and Granvillle gives him a small piece of business in the trial scene—stepping in front of Antonio and baring his breast to Shylock's knife—that adds further luster to him.

Bassanio is the center to which everything in the adaptation points. His part is greatly enlarged; he is given the greatest number of moral sententiae to speak, and it is his inner arena of feeling that the play directs us to enter. All of Granville's additions deal with love (III, i and V, i) or friendship (I, i; III, i; V, i), and a whole new scene is constructed that presents Antonio's toast to friendship, Bassanio's toast to love, and wicked Shylock's toast to money. Love and friendship in 1701, of course, are not ideas but feelings within the characters that we are invited deliciously to share. Indeed, we are even instructed in proper understanding of the feelings that are aroused in us and admonished not to be ashamed of the sympathy we feel. For instance, as he embraces Antonio one last time before parting, Bassanio says: "One more Embrace; To those who know not Friendship / This may appear unmanly Tenderness, / But 'tis the frailty of bravest Minds" (II, ii, 90-92).

The locus of reality is the human heart. We enter into the emotions of good-natured, amiable characters and share their sentiments. The pleasure this activity affords us, it is presumed, extends into our lives, for as often as we experience similar sensations of love and friendship in our lives, we will compare them with the sensations we felt in the theater, and our pleasure will double. The consequence is that, like Steele, we will be made "insensibly more courteous and humane to [our] friends and acquaintance" because we desire to experience the associative pleasure again and again.[21] The experience of art will thereby modify our behavior and perfect our natures.

In act 5 Granville's adaptation offers a particularly striking illustration of the new locus of good and the new direction we must take to find it. The great metaphysical *discordia concors* to which Lorenzo directs our attention and Jessica's in Shakespeare's play has been domesticated in Granville's adaptation. The orbs are no more than a backdrop for the "good" Portia as she speaks a much altered version of Lorenzo's speech:

> Play all our Instruments of Musick there
> Let nothing now be heard but sounds of Joy
> And let those glorious Orbs that we behold,
> Who in their Motions, all like Angels sing
> Still Quiring to the blew-ey'd Cherubims
> Join in the chorus; that in Heav'n and Earth
> One universal Tune may celebreate
> This Harmony of Hearts.
>   [V, i, 51-58]

Man calls the tune; the angelic spheres are extras. The center of highest good and, consequently, the center of the scene and of the play is the harmony in and of human hearts. We come to an apprehension of good by entering Portia's joy in her own and Bassanio's benevolence and by joining our own good-natured impulses with theirs. Our hearts join in the harmony and are improved by the experience. Even Providence itself, which had determined the structure of plays in the 1680s, has become a background figure, a sort of Nanny to the Darling, human goodness: "Virtue like yours; such Patience in Adversity / And in Prosperity such Goodness, / Is still the care of Providence" (V, i, 230-32).

Almost to the end of the seventeenth century, comedy retained some family resemblance to satire and tragedy to romance. The genres maintained their distinction from one another because they appealed to a mental activity—judgment. In the early eighteenth century, because the function of drama is to elicit emotion and to effect commingling of emotion between audience and characters, judgment has nothing to do with our response. We do not *see* the characters from the outside (unless they are caricature villains, like Shylock); we *feel* with them. And as sympathy is a more diffused, less sharply defined response than judgment, so the mechanisms that trigger sympathy may vary. Figures in satire elicit laughter and figures in heroic romance admiration, but in the early eighteenth century both comedy and tragedy are thought to elicit a sympathetic emotion in which joy and sorrow, pleasurable pain and painful pleasure are not distinguishable. In his dedication to *The Force of Friendship* (1710), Charles Johnson describes the only worthy audience of tragedy as "those few, those very few elegant Spirits who are pleas'd with the Distress of a well wrought Scene, who . . . behold the Conduct of our Passions on the Stage, and with a generous Sympathy feel alternate Joy and Pain, when Virtue either conquers, or is contending with adverse Fate."[22]

Whether the character with whose pain and joy we sympathize is overcoming the obstacles laid down by Fortune, as in comedy, or contending with Fate, as in tragedy, is relatively unimportant. The crucial element is that we should feel his emotions and, by following them, come to emulate his virtues. As Addison had said, "How forcible an affect this would have upon our minds, one needs no more than to observe how strongly we are touched by mere pictures. Who can see Le Brun's picture of the battle of Porus without entering into the character of that fierce gallant man, and being accordingly spurred to an emulation of his constancy and courage. . . . If a thing painted or related can irresistably enter our hearts, what may not be brought to pass by seeing generous things performed before our eyes."[23]

A problem arose. The very attributes of drama that are considered cornerstones of emulation theory in the first decade of the century—its ability to elicit sympathy rather than judgment and its providing entrance to the emotions of the characters we see—threatened to undermine its moral value as the century progressed. For instance, if the character with whom we feel deep sympathy must fall, his fall must be warranted by some flaw in his character or else his fate would be unjust. As Gildon says, "No unfortunate Character ought to be introduc'd on the Stage, without its Humane Frailty to justify its Misfortunes; For *unfortunate* Perfection, is the *Crime* of Providence, and to offer at that, is an Impiety a Poet ought never to be guilty of; being directly opposite to his duty *Rewarding the Innocent*, and *Punishing the Guilty*, and by that means to establish a just notion of Providence in its most important Action, the Government of Mankind."[24]

But if he is the central character and elicits our deepest sympathies, is he not the character whom we are drawn to emulate and will we not be drawn to imitate him in his "Frailties"? It is just this question that by midcentury led both a mediocre critic like Theophilus Cibber and a great critic like Samuel Johnson to feel uneasy about *The Fair Penitent* (1701). Rowe's play elicits generous sympathy in abundance, but if we empathize with Calista without judging her, are we not led to emulate morally ambivalent behavior? Will emotional identification with the Fair Penitent lead us to hate her crime or to imitate it? Johnson wonders. Are the emotions we are invited to share with her morally invigorating or debilitating? "It has been observed that the title of the play does not sufficiently correspond with the behavior of Callista, who at least shews no evident signs of repentance, but may be reasonably suspected of feeling pain from detection rather than from guilt, and expresses more shame than sorrow, and more rage than shame."[25] How are we to know which characters to emulate if characters are not raised above the life? If they share our "private woes," how can they also be our exemplars?

It is curious, I think, that Rowe, who saw a tragic design in Granville's *Jew of Venice*, uses a device drawn from comedy—pairing—to control our emulative responses in *The Fair Penitent*. Whereas Granville makes Bassanio the central character in his adaptation and uses all the other characters to shape our responses only to him, Rowe makes us sympathize with a variety of characters to prevent us from identifying too closely with Calista when her passions are unwholesome. For example, we are with Horatio as he warns Calista not to see Lothario again, and if we enter into Calista at that moment, it is to urge her away from the wicked Lothario. We are deeply involved with the character but are not living her passion; we are like the old lady in the audience at the Milan production of Sophocles' *Electra* who shouted to Orestes not to raise his hands against his mother or he would have bad luck.

Before we ever meet Calista we experience her sorrow and shame through the filter of Lucilla. Lucilla is presented to us before our introduction to Calista so that we may encounter Lothario and hate him and feel sorrow for the pain he has caused Calista before we are subjected to Calista's erotic passion for him. Lucilla's role is not merely to provde expository information. We participate in her anger and sorrow and thereby our sympathy for Calista is stirred at the same time as our anger at Lothario is aroused. The latter emotion curbs and directs the former and prevents us from identifying with Calista at this stage in the events. We have already heard Lothario's rakish account of his seduction of Calista. Lucilla is given to us, so that, moving through her sentiments, we may recognize how "monstrous" and "unnatural" (to use the terms of *A Letter to A.H.*) a rake is:

> Is this well done, my lord? Have you put off
> All sense of human Nature? Keep a little,
> A little pity to distinguish manhood,
> Lest other men, though cruel, should disclaim you,
> And judge you to be numbered with the brutes.
> [I, ii, 220-24][26]

Lucilla's descriptions of Calista's sorrowful penance, like descriptive passages in Dryden and Vanbrugh in the 1690s, are used to draw the action closer to our experience in preparation for our first encounter with Calista. In fact, they show her penitence more vividly than her own words and behavior do. Lothario accuses Lucilla of ranting, and it is true that we must experience as much of her rage against Lothario's vice as of her sorrow for Calista:

> What! Shall I sell my innocence and youth
> For wealth or titles to perfidious man!
> To man, who makes his mirth of our undoing!
> The base confessed betrayer of our sex!
> Let me grow old in all misfortunes else,
> Rather than know the sorrows of Calista.
> [I, ii, 238-43]

Rowe is following the methodology of the nineties; the "disposition of [his] play is . . . such that all the Characters have a proper Effect with us. Our Fear, Love, and Anger are . . . exerted with Justice." Lucilla is used to arouse but also to mitigate our sympathetic identification with Calista.

However, lest Lucilla's anger draw us in too far, Lavinia's soft devotion is given us to dilute it. Lavinia is not just a foil to Calista; her devotion to Horatio provides yet another filter through which our response to Calista must pass so that we may know, despite our feeling for her, that she is in some measure responsible for her fall, for "Of all the various wretches love has made / How few have been by men of sense betrayed" (II, ii, 173-74). It is also through the devotion of Lavinia, a perfect wife and sister, that we come to admire Horatio and, through him, to feel sympathy, anger, and final forgiveness for

Altamont. As Horatio and Lavinia, virtuous, exemplary married lovers, share the sorrows of Altamont, we are drawn into their triple harmony of hearts and share in it too:

> **Horatio.** By heav'n my heart bleeds for thee; ev'n this moment
> I feel thy pangs of disappointed love.
> Is it not pity that this youth should fail
> That all this wondr'ous goodness should be lost,
> And the world never know it? O, my Altamont!
> Give me thy sorrows, let me bear 'em for thee
> And shelter thee from ruin.
> **Lavinia.**   O, my brother!
> Think not but we will share in all thy woes;
> We'll sit all day and tell sad tales of love,
> And when we light upon some faithless woman,
> Some beauty like Calista false and fair,
> We'll fix our grief and our complaining there;
> We'll curse the nymph that drew thy ruin on
> And mourn the youth that was like thee undone.
>   [IV, i, 412-25]

The echo of *Richard II* in the line "We'll sit all day and tell sad tales of love" is a clue to the effect this pair of mourning doves has upon us and how, as the closing lines of act 4, their speeches are meant to direct our responses to act 5. We must respond to Calista as we do to Richard II: have our hearts broken with sympathy for her, acknowledge that her own overly romantic youth betrayed her, but also have a clear recognition of how far she is herself responsible for her ruin. The position of the Horatio-Lavinia speeches, the compassion for all three of the mourners that they elicit from us, and the disapproval of Calista they evoke are carefully prepared breaks upon our emotions. They are designed to channel our response to the Calista of act 5, who arouses such powerful compassion that she finally becomes exemplary.

For the first four acts of the play our feelings for Calista have been mixed. She has been the central object of our attention but in very oblique ways; that is, our attention has been upon Calista, but our view of her has consistently been filtered through the emotions we share with other characters. In act 5 we feel only with Calista. Anger at Lothario does not distract us. His body on the bier merely adds to the burden of grief we share with Calista. The complexity of her emotions ("more shame than sorrow, and more rage than shame") has been distilled away, and we are left with an elixir of sorrow, pain, and penance. We can feel Calista's pain purely because it is exclusively pain; we want her death, as she does, as a release. Only in the last act does the Fair Penitent come fully and unreservedly to merit her appellation. And only after we have shared her final penance and have been with her, forgiven, are we ready to accept the example she has provided—"By such examples are we taught to prove / The sorrows that attend unlawful love" (V, 288-89). Only after we have understood that example are we ready for the play's admonition to virtue: "If you would have the nuptial union last, / Let virtue be the bond that ties it fast." Calista has been the negative example that leads us to emulate the virtue of Horatio and Lavinia. The emulation evoked is private here, dependent on one-to-one identification of the spectator with the various characters. We are still operating on associationist principles. In fact, our response to Calista perfectly follows one of Addison's descriptions: "The secret Comparison which we make between our selves and the Person who suffers . . . [plainly teaches us to] prize our good Fortune, which exempts us from the like Calamities."[27]

Nevertheless, the private emulation, elicited by identification with the characters, which was evoked both by comedy and tragedy in the first decade of the century, came to seem too unreliable, too undisciplined in its effects for the large-scale refinement of public morals and manners demanded of the drama in the twenties and thirties. The overriding sentiment in these decades was that the stage "is, or ought to be, the School of Politeness and Good Breeding, for we know, by Experience, that the Youth form themselves by what they see there and receive Notions of Conversation and Behaviour by the Examples there represented."[28] Drama that imitated nature too closely was condemned. Instead, a forceful delineation of ideals was wanted "to form and control those affections and associations" that plays at the turn of the century had taken such pains to evoke. For example, the *Grub Street Journal* of March 8, 1733, describes a play very like *The Fair Penitent*. In *The Perjured Lover* an innocent girl is lured from her father's house by a Lothario-like seducer, is made pregnant, is cast off in a brothel, and finally is sent to Bridewell. The perjurer is killed by the girl's former honorable lover, and she dies in the arms of her devoted, forgiving father. This is "a fable," says the *Journal*, that "in the hands of a genius might have been wrought into a play, that would have proved a successful scourge of some of the vices and follies, which are in every age the ruin of thousands."[29] It fails to achieve that end because the author has followed nature too closely. He does not embellish nature with that idealizing "poetical dress" that "allures the fancy" and that alone can make a proper "impression in the mind." Because the play forces us to enter experience, it does not give us those moral sententiae, those ideal forms removed from experience, which from frequent recollection and application to our own behavior, could perfect us:

Here, Sir, give me leave to make some few observations, which may probably convince those of their error, who think the mere pursuit of nature all that is requisite in dramatic poetry. . . . The story . . . is very moving but no body, I believe, can remember one speech in the play: whereas, if the diction were truly poetical, several passages would make such an impression in the minds of the readers, that they would, on particular occasions recollect them and apply them often. . . . if the efficacy in poetry is such, as almost to force a remembrance of passages in which no useful doctrine is contained; how advantageous must it be when called to the assistance of virtue.[30]

The critic goes on to argue that steady reflection upon Shakespeare's line "O that men should put an enemy in their mouths to steal their brains" would curb excessive drinking in the populace.

The obligation he felt to uphold the idea that the proper use of the drama is "making a Polite and Moral Gentry"[31] led Steele to present an ideal that, by "example and precept,"[32] might instruct the audience of *The Conscious Lovers*. It is most significant that the ideal is not metaphysical or moral in any absolute sense; it is, rather, entirely *social*. As Shirley Strum Kenney has observed, Steele "created models for each class in the audience except the nobility. . . . The exemplary and ridiculous characters are designed by [him] . . . to illustrate social virtues and follies and thereby to improve his audience." The truth is the same as that toward which plays at the turn of the century directed us—"the doctrine of benevolence, the theory that doing good for others brings joy to the heart of the doer"—but the new process of dramatic representation is designed to refine the "personal" away.[33] Oddly enough, in the course of fifty years dramatic imitation first came to center on exploring the ways of the individual human heart, and then emerged from that exploration with another rationale for representing the ideal and another conception of ideality. We are meant to sympathize with Bevil's plight and to feel the anguish of Indiana's uncertainty in ways that we were certainly not asked to enter into St. Catherine as she overleaped the last boundary, filial obligation, to attain heaven. Indeed, the effect of several centuries spent responding to *social* models of ideality, to so many countless Bevils and Indianas, has made it almost impossible for us to respond to such *images of ideal truth* as Dryden gave us in St. Catherine. The circle has proven to be not a circle at all but a spiral. Whether an observer believes the spiral has wound up or has wound down to our present vortex in the historical process of secularization depends almost entirely upon his own tastes and moral inclinations.

The Conscious Lovers has for too long been considered one of the earliest achievements in "sentimental" drama. This judgment is historically inaccurate. Both the morality of the play and its appeal to us to sympathize with its protagonists was old hat in 1723. Its new feature was its return to imitation of an ideal and the propagandistic function to which it turned the ideal in the service of social, secular man. It is at this point in the course of our dramatic tradition, I think, that God became Godot. *The Conscious Lovers* tutored us in the ways of conceiving ideality in terms of bourgeois norms:

Estragon: What exactly did we ask him for? . . .
Vladimir: Oh . . . nothing very definite.
Estragon: A kind of prayer.
Vladimir: Precisely.
Estragon: A vague supplication.
Vladimir: Exactly.
Estragon: And what did he reply?
Vladimir: That he'd see.
Estragon: That he couldn't promise anything.
Vladimir: That he'd have to think it over.
Estragon: In the quiet of his home.
Vladimir: Consult his family.
Estragon: His friends.
Vladimir: His agents.
Estragon: His correspondents.
Vladimir: His books.

Estragon: His bank account.
Vladimir: Before taking a decision.
Estragon: It's the normal thing.
Vladimir: Is it not?
Estragon: I think it is.
Vladimir: I think so too. [*Waiting for Godot*][34]

By teaching to refine from experience to the ideal, this drama taught us new ways of conceiving what, ideally, is "natural." There was never any question that characters in *The Conscious Lovers* were strained beyond probability almost to caricature, but probability to nature is not their purpose. Their function is to lift the audience to an imitation of the abstract social ideals they represent for the propagation and "Advancement of Virtue." It is with full and sarcastic recognition of the unlikelihood that such consciousness raising was likely to occur that the *Freeholder's Journal* of November 28, 1722, observed, "We are in hopes that the Vein of the Town, which runs so strongly in Favour of a Present Representation upon it, will turn it not to the Burlesque, but the Advancement of Virtue, which was the Original Design of the Stage. Some have alleg'd . . . that it may carry a greater tendency to one than the other, since, as they pretend, there is not a character in it, that is not overstrain'd far beyond the Pitch of Nature, or even Probability."[35]

The eighteenth-century mode in dramatic imitation rests upon the assumption that we rise from what we know in the familiar world to personification of moral ideals that are drawn from experience. Art's imitation need not be simulation of the experiential real to be effective, as was thought to be the case at the end of the seventeenth century. As Johnson says, "Imitations produce pleasure or pain, not because they are mistaken for realities, but because they bring realities to mind."[36] From empirical observation we derive conceptions of the ideal; from social experience models for emulation are refined and idealized.

But of all the Characters generally drawn in our modern comedies, we find none more falsely represented than that of the Citizens. People that know nothing of 'em than what they see in Plays, think that, of course, an Alderman must be an old lecherous, griping Usurer, or a Doting Cuckold. . . . In the City may be found a very great Number of learned,

polite, honest, and generous Men, true Friends and true *Englishmen* who will
not abandon their Acquaintance because they want them, but will cheerfully
do them all the Service they can; Publick-Spirited Men who will not tamely
see their Country suffer; but will, on all Occasions, exert themselves for her
Good, and prove themselves the true Descendants of Ancient Rome by their
Love of Liberty; Citizens, who, had they lived in their great Forefathers
Days, had seen publick places adorned with their Statues cast in Brass.[37]

Although from the Restoration to the eighteenth century the
composition of the governing class in England changed, the merchant class had been a powerful force in England from the Jacobean
period, and, as Bear has amply demonstrated, citizens composed a
healthy segment of the audience throughout the Restoration. In the
eighteenth century the conception of what constituted the good or
the ideal did not change, but rather the epistemological methods by
which men determined the good and their aesthetic conceptions of
the nature of art in relation to it had.

The London Merchant (1731) is the end toward which we have been
moving. It is a perfect amalgam that draws us to share the emotions
of figures that are delineated to the contours of a new socially ideal
and empirically derived typology:

Barnwell's first Fault, and Repentance, his Master's generous Pity and
Forgiveness; his Relapse and the Horror, that attended it; Milkwood's Art
and Address, in prevailing with him to undertake the Murther of his Uncle,
the strong Convulsions of his Mind, and the beautiful Deportment of his
dying Uncle on that Occasion, his Despair that succeeded it . . . his Piteous
Goodness, and the beautiful Maria's unhappy Passion are such strong dramatic Circumstances and so finely painted that 'tis impossible not to feel the
full Force of them in the Reading and Representation—in short, 'tis Writing
to the Heart, and I believe there was hardly a Spectator that did not witness
the Approbation by his Tears.[38]

At this, the end of the long journey we have taken, comes an
invitation, issued over two hundred years ago, to enter, to share, and
to experience Disneyland.

NOTES

INTRODUCTION

1. Arthur O. Lovejoy, "Nature as Aesthetic Norm," *Modern Language Notes* 42 (1927): 444-50.

2. Claudio Guillen, "On the Concept and Metaphor of Perspective," in his *Literature as System* (Princeton: Princeton Univ. Press, 1971); Richard Rorty, *Philosophy and the Mirror of Nature* (Princeton: Princeton Univ. Press, 1979).

3. J. Huizinga, *The Waning of the Middle Ages* (New York: Anchor, 1948), p. 201.

4. G.D. Josipovici, *The World and the Book* (London: Macmillan, 1978), p. 1.

5. C.N. Manlove, *Literature and Reality, 1600-1800* (London: Macmillan, 1978), p. 6.

6. Shakespeare, Sonnet 146. Jean Hagstrum, in a fascinating paper presented at the 1982 convention of the Modern Language Association traced the elusive meaning of the word "consciousness" in a pattern that can be used to support the Hellmouth within to "Paradise Within" configuration.

7. Montaigne, *Essays,* trans. and ed. Donald Frame (New York: St. Martin's Press, 1963), p. 293.

8. J.C. Scaliger, *Poetics,* 4th ed. (Heidelberg, 1607), I, i, 302.

9. S.H. Butcher, "Aristotle's Theory of Poetry and Fine Art," with a critical text and translation of the *Poetics* (New York: Macmillan, 1927), p. 150.

10. Richard Kroll, "Words and Acts: The Naturalization of Language in the Restoration and Early Eighteenth Century," (Ph.D. diss., Univ. of California at Los Angeles, 1984).

11. Thomas Stanley, Preface to *The History of Philosophy,* 2d ed. (London: T. Basset, D. Newman, and T. Cockerill, 1687).

12. François Hédelin, Abbé d'Aubignac, *The Whole Art of the Stage* (London: W. Cadman, S. Smith, and R. Bentley, 1684), p. 111.

13. Ibid., p. 33.

14. Ibid., p. 86.

15. The idea of a progression from the drama to the novel was first introduced by Ian Donaldson, *The World Upside Down: Comedy from Jonson to Fielding* (Oxford: Clarendon, 1970), and John Loftis, "The Limits of Historical Veracity in Neo-Classical Drama," in *England in the Restoration and Early Eighteenth Century,* ed. H.T. Swedenberg (Los Angeles: Univ. of California Press, 1972). It provides the basic

structure in Laura Brown's Marxist interpretation, *English Dramatic Forms, 1660-1760* (New Haven: Yale Univ. Press, 1981). I outlined the progression fom a formalist view in a pilot study for this book, "Imitation to Emulation: The Conception of 'Imitation of Nature' in English Drama, 1660-1730," *Restoration* (Spring 1979).

16. I have discussed dramatic imitation as the imitation of a world order in "Dramatic Imitation of Nature in the Restoration's Seventeenth-Century Predecessors," *From Renaissance to Restoration*, ed. R. Markley and L. Finke (Cleveland: Belflower Press, 1984).

17. Josipovici, *The World and The Book*, The Renaissance conception of artistic imitation is interestingly presented in Alberti's *Treatise on Optics*. "[Alberti] was interested in providing a standard means for painters to fashion a plausible and unified pictorial space—more a stage than a space actually—within which painted figures could be presented gracefully according to the harmonious rhythms of geometry. His perspective construction *was intended to copy no specific place. It provided a purely abstract realm which the viewer would discern as a world of order* real space in the sense that it functioned according to the immutable laws of God" (Samuel Egerton, *The Renaissance Rediscovery of Linear Perspective* [New York: Harper & Row, 1975], p. 30, italics mine).

18. Dryden, "A Defence of the Essay of Dramatic Poesy," in *Dramatic Poesy and Other Critical Essays*, ed. G.B. Watson (London: Dent 1962), I, 65.

19. Shadwell, "Epistle Dedicatory to Margaret;, Dutchess of Newcastle," *The Humorists* (London: Henry Heringman, 1671).

20. The latter characterization is from Shadwell's preface to *The Humorists*. The three former are from Davenant's dedication to the 1663 quarto edition of *The Siege of Rhodes*, in *The Works of Sir William Davenant* (London, 1673; New York, Bloom, 1968, I, 345.

21. John Long, Prefatory Poem to Sir Samuel Tuke, *The Adventures of Five Hours* (London: H. Heringman, 1664).

22. Dryden, "Of Dramatic Poesy," I, 52.

23. See n. 17.

24. Dryden, "Of Dramatic Poesy," I, 47. Bracketed words are translations of Greek used in the original text. Both the translations and the parenthetical reference to Hesiod are supplied by the editor (see n. 18).

25. Loftis, "The Limits of Historical Veracity in Neo-Classical Drama," p. 46.

26. Guillen, "On the Concept and Metaphor of Perspective," pp. 306-10.

27. Eric Rothstein, *Restoration Tragedy* (Madison: Univ. of Wisconsin Press, 1966), p. 31. I do not agree with the assessment of Rothstein and those who have followed him that the late plays are "pathetic." As I hope to demonstrate, the imitation of "inner space" in the plays and novels of the late eighties and nineties is not intentionally pathetic and is certainly not sentimental. My debt to Rothstein, however, will be evident throughout and is most gratefully acknowledged.

28. As Rothstein has said, "Scholars have traditionally held that this dramatic change reflected a change in the composition, as well as the taste, of audiences. I think such a sociological explanation highly improbable. First of all, there is no evidence to support the theory of a radical change in audience between 1670, when heroic plays

228

Notes to Pages 7-12

were the most energetic and novel part of the repertory, and 1680, when most of them were 'exploded' relics. Secondly, there is only the most dubious evidence to suggest that the Restoration audience changed appreciably before the reign of William and Mary. Pepys complained about citizens in the playhouse as early as 1662, and fretted over 'mean people' in the pit in 1668" (*Restoration Tragedy*, p. 28). This opinion has been amply supported by subsequent scholarship, notably that of A.S. Bear, "Restoration Comedy and the Provok'd Critic," in *Restoration Literature: Critical Approaches*, ed. H. Love (London: Methuen, 1972), and Arthur H. Scouten and Robert D. Hume, "Restoration Comedy and Its Audiences, 1660-1776," *Yearbook of English Studies* 10 (1980).

29. Notably Rothstein, Hume, and J.R. Sutherland in *English Literature of the Late Seventeenth Century*, Oxford History of English Literature, no. 6 (Oxford: Clarendon, 1969).

30. For this conception of the Jacobean use of soliloquy I am indebted to Bernard Beckerman in remarks made at the conference "Conversations in the Disciplines: Dramaturgy," held at State University of New York at Stony Brook in May 1983. See his article "Historic and Iconic Time in the Late Tudor Drama," in *Papers of the Second Shakespeare Congress* (Wilmington: Univ. of Delaware Press, 1983).

31. Congreve, "To the Honorable Charles Montague," in *The Complete Works of William Congreve* ed. Bonamy Dobree (Oxford: Oxford Press, 1925), p. 115.

32. Theophilus Gale, *The Court of the Gentiles* (London: Thomas Gilbert, 1669), pp. 62-63.

33. Buckingham, "The Art of Poetry," in *Critical Essays of the Seventeeth Century*, 3 vols. ed. J.R. Spingarn (Oxford: Clarendon, 1906)). III, 245. This was quoted with strong approval by Gildon in *The Art, Rise, and Progress of the Stage*.

34. Aphra Behn uses the word "novel" interchangeably with "news." Compare "Trefry was infinitely pleased with this Novel" (where "novel" means news or revelation), in *Oroonoko, All the Histories and Novels Written by the Late Ingenious Mrs. Behn*, ed. C. Gildon (London: W. Feales, 1735), p. 146.

35. *Gentelmans Journal*, June 1693, p. 181.

36. *Gentlemans Journal*, November 1693, p. 370.

37. *Gentlemans Journal*, July 1693, p. 219.

38. *Oroonoko*, pp. 75-76.

39. See, for example, *A Letter to A.H. Esquire Concerning the Stage* (London: R. Baldwin, 1698), which argues that "Comedy is a Representation of Common Conversation and its Design is to represent things Natural; to show the faults of *Particular Men.*"

40. *Gentlemans Journal*, June 1693, p. 184.

41. In Chapter 5, I argue that the creation of "exemplary" and, later, "sentimental" characters is a matter of perspective. We are invited to see the "inner" reflections and motivations of familiar stock dramatic types.

42. Behn, *The Fair Jilt*, p. 224.

43. "On His Majesties Picture Drawn to the Life by Mr. Kneller: *Ut Pictura Poesis,*" *Gentlemans Journal*, January 1691-92, pp. 2-3. We find the same idea in Dryden's "To the Pious Memory of the Accomplisht Young Lady Mrs. Anne Killigrew," wherein

the painter is praised for imitating the inner "Heart," "Mind," "soul Devoid of Fear," and "High-designing Thoughts" of James II.

44. Addison, *Tatler,* no 8, April 28, 1709, in *The Tatler,* 4 vols., ed. George A. Aitken (London: Duckworth, 1898), I, 75.

45. The latest resurrection of the morality issue is as recent as John T. Harwood, "Critics, Values, and Restoration Comedy (Carbondale: Southern Illinois Univ. Press, 1982).

46. Tuke, Preface to *The Adventures of Five Hours.*

47. *A Letter to A. H. Esquire concerning the Stage,* p. 16.

48. Donald Greene, "Latitudinarianism and Sensibility: The Genealogy of the 'Man of Feeling' Reconsidered," *Modern Philology:* Winter 1977, pp. 159-83; R.S. Crane, "Suggestions toward a Genealogy of 'The Man of Feeling,'" in *Studies in the Literature of the Augustan Age, in Honor of A.E. Case,* ed. R.C. Boys, distributed for the Augustan Reprint Society (Ann Arbor: George Wahr Pub. Co., 1952).

49. Samuel Parker, *A Demonstration of the Divine Authority of the Law of Nature and of Christian Religion* (London: M. Flesher, R. Royston, and R. Chiswell, 1681), p. 248. Quoted by Crane, "Suggestions toward a Genealogy," p. 85.

50. Isham, *A Sermon* (London, 1700), quoted by Crane, "Suggestions toward a Genealogy," p. 82. The "law of Nature" becomes a "law" of aesthetics. Rowe says that the end of tragedy is to leave in the audience "a sort of regret, proceeding from good nature, which tho' an uneasiness, is not always disagreeable to the person who feels it (*The Ambitious Stepmother* [London: Wellington and Osbourne, 1702]).

51. David Lawrence, "Jonathan Edwards, John Locke, and the Canon of Experience," *Early American Literature* 15 (1980).

52. Addison, *Tatler,* no. 8, April 28, 1709.

53. Locke insists, "No man. . . can by any revelation communicate any new simple ideas which they had not before from sensation or reflection. For . . . new simple ideas cannot be conveyed to another either by words or any other signs" (*An Essay concerning Human Understanding,* ed. A.C. Fraser [New York: Dover, 1959], II, 416).

1. THE FOUR STAGES

1. "Hobbes's distinction of the poetic genres is the logical outcome of his philosophy. He conceives of them as conditioned by the divisions of the external world— heroic, comic, and pastoral corresponding to the court, city, and country—man simply arranges what Nature gives in forms of his own speech, narrative or dramatic. The poetry of the court thus assumes the form of epic or tragedy; the poetry of the city, satire or comedy; the poetry of the country, bucolic or pastoral comedy" (J.E. Spingarn, *Critical Essays of the Seventeenth Century,* I, xxxi).

2. See my "Dramatic Imitation of Nature in the Restoration's Seventeenth-Century Predecessors" in *From Renaissance to Restoration Metamorphoses of the Drama,* ed. R. Marley and L. Finke (Cleveland, Belflower Press, 1984).

3. Davenant, "Postscript to Gondibert," in *The Works of Sir William Davenant* (London, 1673); New York: Bloom. 1968), I, 196.

4. Davenant, *Works,* I, 345.

5. Theophilus Gale, Prefatory Poem to *The Court of the Gentiles* (London: Thomas Gilbert, 1969).

6. Richard Flecknoe, *A Collection of the Choicest Epigrams and Characters, Printed for the Author,* 1673.

7. Davenant, *Love and Honour and the Siege of Rhodes,* pp. 187–88. Arthur Kirch, *Dryden's Heroic Drama* (Princeton: Princeton Univ. Press, 1965), has established the crucial importance of Corneille in the formation of English heroic drama.

8. Dryden, "Of Dramatic Poesy," I, 666.

9. Alan Roper, "Sir Harbottle Grimstone and the Country Wife," *Studies in the Literary Imagination* 10 (1977): 109.

10. Dryden, "Defence of an Essay of Dramatic Poesy," I, 115.

11. Edward Howard, Preface to *The Women's Conquest* (London: H. Heringman, 1671).

12. Tuke, Preface to *The Adventures of Five Hours.*

13. Dryden, "Of Dramatic Poesy," I;, 64.

14. Jean Hagstrum, "Verbal and Visual Caricature in the Age of Dryden, Pope, and Swift," in *England in the Restoration,* ed. Swedenberg, p. 181.

15. Dryden, "An Account of the Ensuing Poem, in a Letter to the Honorable Sir Robert Howard," prefixed to "Annus Mirabilis," *The Works of John Dryden,* vol. 1 (Berkeley: Univ. of California Press, 1956), p. 56.

16. Dryden, "A Discourse concerning the Original and Progress of Satire," in *The Satires of Decimus Junius Juvenalis, Translated into English Verse by Mr. Dryden and Several Other Eminent Hands,* 2d ed. (London: Jacob Tonson, 1697), p. lxxiv.

17. For a very interesting discussion of the "satirical mode" in Otway's plays, both "comedies" and "tragedies," see Thomas B. Stroup, "Otway's Bitter Pessimism," in *Essays in the English Literature of the Neo-Classical Period Presented to Dougald Macmillan,* ed. D. W. Patterson and A. B. Strauss, *Studies in Philology,* Extra Series, no. 4 (January 1967), pp. 54–75.

18. Waller's heroic "Instructions" was followed by five satiric "Advices," the last of which was Marvell's "Last Instructions to a Painter," puiblished in 1689.

19. Howard Weinbrot sees the "Restoration parody" as an important source for the Imitation because "the parody . . . demanded knowledge of the parent poem" (*The Formal Strain: Studies in Augustan Imitation and Satire* [Chicago: Univ. of Chicago Press, 1969], p. 17). See also Weinbrot's discussion of Rochester's dependence upon the reader's recollection of a heroic model for the achievement of his satiric effects.

20. Hobbes, "Answer," in *Critical Essays of the Seventeenth Century,* ed. Springarn, II, 54–55.

21. Dryden, "The Original and Progress of Satire," p. lxxviii.

22. Earl Miner, "The Restoration: Age of Faith, Age of Satire, in *"Poetry and Drama 1570-1700: Essays in Honor of Harold Brooks,* ed. A. Coleman and A. Hammond (London: Methuen, 1981), p. 99. Earl Miner was the first critic to recognize the double heroic/satiric perspective in Restoration drama: "The heroic play is related to comedy in [a] major respect, growing from the rhetorical conception of poetry. Both are distortions in the artist's mirror of the norm of nature, the comic in the lower direction of satire, the heroic in the higher of panegyric and heroic" (Introduction to *Restoration*

Dramatists, ed. E. Miner [Englewood Cliffs, N.J.: Prentice-Hall, 1966], p. 11). My debt to Mr. Miner will be evident throughout this book. I acknowledge it with gratitude.

23. *Dryden's Major Plays* (New York: Barnes & Noble, 1966), p 119.

24. *English Dramatic Forms, 1660-1760*, p. 85.

25. J.E. Butt, *The Metaphysical Foundations of Modern Science*, 2d rev. ed. (London: Routledge & Kegan Paul, 1934). Quoted in Hopewell Selby, "'Never Finding Full Repast' Satire and Self-Extension in the Eighteenth Century," in *Probability, Time, and Space and Eighteenth Century Literature*, ed. P. Backscheider (New York: AMS Press, 1979). See Selby for a fascinating discussion of spatial conceptualization in seventeenth century philosophic and satiric portrayals of the mind/body and spirit/flesh dichotomies.

26. Earl Miner, "In Satire's Falling City," in *The Satirist's Art*, ed. H.J. Jensen and M.R. Zirken (Bloomington: Indiana Univ. Press, 1972), p. 16.

27. Locke, *An Essay concerning Human Understanding*, ed. I.II. Nidditch (Oxford: Clarendon, 1975), p. 105.

28. James Drake, *The Antient and Modern Stage* (London, 1698).

29. Aubrey Williams, *An Approach to Congreve* (New Haven: Yale Univ. Press, 1980), p. 38. See also his "Congreve's *Incognita* and the Contrivances of Providence," in *Imagined Worlds: Essays in Honor of John Butt*, ed. M. Mack and I. Gregor (London. Methuen, 1968), in which Williams discusses structural similarities between *Icognita* and the plays and ascribes looseness and complication in plot to Congreve's imitation of the workings of Providence. See also his "Poetical Justice, the Contrivances of Providence, and the Works of William Congreve," *ELH* 25 (1968): 540-65. My heavy debt to Mr. Williams will be evident throughout this book and is acknowledged here with gratitude.

30. Locke, *Essay*, ed. Fraser, II, 46.

31. Ibid.

32. Rhymer, "On the Tragedies of the Last Age," in *The Critical Works of Thomas Rhymer*, ed. Curt A. Zimansky (New Haven: Yale Univ. Press, 1956), p. 75.

33. Dryden, "On the Grounds of Criticism in Tragedy," in *Dramatic Poesy*, ed. Watson, 1, 248.

34. Tate, *Five Restoration Adaptations of Shakespeare*, ed. Christopher Spencer (Urbana: Univ. of Illinois Press, 1965), p 203 In adapting *Coriolanus* Tate tells us that he deliberately used a design he found in Shakespeare as an example to his troubled times: "I saw no small Resemblance with the busie Faction of our own time. And I confess I chose rather to set the Parallel nearer to Sight than throw it off at a further Distance." (Preface to *The Ingratitude of a Commonwealth* London, 1682). His immediate purpose, of course, was to express his own political position in the Exclusion controversy. Nevertheless, the dramaturgic intention is significant. Tate's purpose is to bring what he believes to be a Providential design "nearer to Sight."

35. Dryden, "On the Grounds of Criticism," I, 248.

36. Ibid., I, 247.

37. Rhymer, "A Short View of Tragedy," in *Critical Essays of the Seventeenth Century*, ed. Spingarn, II, 224.

38. John Stafford, Epilogue to Southerne's *The Disappointment* (1684).

39. Dryden, *The Life of Plutarch*, vol. 17 of *The Works of John Dryden*, 18 vols., ed. W. Scott and G. Saintsbury (New York: Crosup and Sterling, 1905), pp. 62-63.

40. Vanbrugh, "A Short Vindication of *The Relapse* and *The Provok'd Wife*, from Immorality and Prophaneness," in *The Complete Works of Sir John Vanbrugh*, 4 vols. ed. B. Dobree and G. Webb (London: Nonesuch Press, 1927), I, 209.

41. Dryden, Dedication to *Love Triumphant*.

42. James Wright, *Country Conversations* (London, 1694), pp. 9-10.

43. *A Comparison of the Two Stages* (London 1702), p. 30. In his dedication to *Sir Anthony Love*, Southerne acknowledges that he has indeed striven to imitate the conversation of his fashionable acquaintance as closely as possible in the "Quickness in the Dialogue and Conversation of this Comedy."

44. *A Comparison of the Two Stages*, p. 61.

45. Ibid., p. 62.

46. Ibid., p. 66. Walpole's quirky but often sharp eye caught the point that once drama attempted to imitate interior lfe, the distinction between tragedy and comedy must blur. "What could be finer than the serious scenes between Maskwell and Lady Touchwood?" he asks. And, explaining the significance of the characters' extravagant outbursts, he says: "Had tragedy descended to people of subordinate situations, the language would be too pompous." He understands Congreve's aim to be to "represent a melancholy story in private life" (*Walpoliana* [London: R. Phillips, 1799], II, 315). It may reasonably be argued that in *The Double Dealer*, Congreve anticipates Rowe's tragedies of "private woe" by about nine years.

47. *A Comparison of the Two Stages*, p. 66.

48. Ibid., p. 146.

49. Dennis, *The Critical Works of John Dennis*, ed. E.N. Hooker (Baltimore: Johns Hopkins Univ. Press, 1943), II, 248.

50. Steele, *Tatler*, no. 172.

51. *Gentlemans Journal*, May 1692.

52. Steele, *Tatler*, no. 47.

53. Gildon, "An Essay on the Art, Rise, and Progress of the Stage," in *The Works of Shakespeare*, ed. and rev. Dr. Sewall (London, 1725), I, xlii.

54. *The Life of Plutarch*, pp. 60-61.

55. Shirley Strum Kenney, "'Elopements, Divorce, and the Devil Knows What': Love and Marriage in English Comedy, 1690-1720," *South Atlantic Quarterly* 27 (1978): 97.

56. Wright, *Country Conversations*, p. 3; Steele, *Tatler*, no. 99.

57. Behn, Dedication to *The Lucky Chance* (London: H. Heringman, 1687).

58. Addison, *Spectator*, no. 39, April 14, 1711, and no. 446, August 1, 1712, in *The Spectator*, 5 vols., ed. Donald F Bond (Oxford: Clarendon Press, 1965).

59. Pope, "Prologue to Mr. Addison's *Cato*," in *Pope*, The *Cambridge Edition of the Poets*, ed. H.W. Boynton (Boston: Houghton Mifflin, 1903), p 100.

60. A.S. Bear, "Restoration Comedy and the Provok'd Critic."

61. Sir Richard Blackmore, Preface to *Prince Arthur*, in *Critical Essays of the Seventeenth Century*, ed. Springarn, III, 229.

62. Steele, *Lover*, no. 5, in *Richard Steele's Periodical Journalism 1714-1716*, ed. R. Blanchard (Oxford: Oxford Univ. Press, 1959).

63. *Weekley Register or Universal Journal*, February 5, 1732, in *Essays on the Theatre from the Eighteenth Century*, ed. John Loftis, Augustan Reprint Society, nos. 85-86 (Los Angeles: William Andrews Clark Memorial Library, 1960).

64. Steele, *Spectator*, no. 65.

65. Dennis, "A Defense of Sir Fopling Flutter," in *Critical Works*, II, 245.

66. *St. James's Journal*, November 18, 1922, in *Essays on the Theatre*, ed. Loftis.

67. *Gentlemans Journal*, February 1691-92.

2. IMITATION OF NATURE AS IDEA

1. Robert D. Hume, *The Development of English Drama in the Late Seventeenth Century* (Oxford: Clarendon Press, 1976), p. 196.

2. Anonymous, *A Description of the Academy of Athenian Virtuosi* (London, 1673), p. 18.

3. Dryden, Preface to *Tyrannick Love*, in *The Works of John Dryden*, vol. 10, ed. Maximillian E. Novak and George R. Guffey (Berkeley: Univ. of California Press, 1970), p. 109. Dryden might well have been reading Theophilus Gale, for he echoes Gale's theory "that Religion was first taught in Verse (which the laziness and darkness of succeeding Priesthood, turned afterwards into Prose)" (*The Court of the Gentiles*, 2d ed., 2 vols. [London, 1672], 1(3):8.

4. Gale, 1(1):52. In his "Letter to Sir Peter Wyche" (1665), John Evelyn calls for a "Gram'er for the Praecepts" (*Critical Essays of the Seventeenth Century*, ed. Springarn, II, 310).

5. Dryden, Preface to "Annus Mirabilis," *Works*, I, 53.

6. Edward Howard, Preface to *The Womens Conquest* (London: H. Heringman, 1671).

7. George R. Guffey, "What the Dryden-Davenant Tempest Is Really About" (Paper delivered in the Restoration Drama section of the annual Convention of the Modern Language Association, Los Angeles, 1982).

8. Dryden, *Defence of the Essay*, Watson, I, 114.

9. Williams, *An Approach to Congreve*, p. 12.

10. Novak, *The Works of John Dryden*, X, 393.

11. Dryden gives this description of Maximin in his preface to the play, p. 110.

12. Eugene M. Waith, *The Herculean Hero* (New York: Columbia Univ. Press, 1962).

13. By 1669, of course, the conflict itself is a very old formula; the way it is used here is important. We might contrast the love-duty conflict in *A Maid's Tragedy*, where scenes can almost be rearranged without loss and no dialectical progression is effected from scene to scene.

14. Anne T. Barbeau, *The Intellectual Design of John Dryden's Heroic Plays* (New Haven: Yale Univ. Press, 1970), p. 8.

15. Maximillian E. Novak, *The Empress of Morocco and Its Critics* (Los Angeles: William Andrews Clark Memorial Library, 1968), p. 78.

16. Geoffrey Marshall, *Restoration Serious Drama* (Norman: Univ. of Oklahoma Press, 1975), p. 90.

17. Ibid.

18. Dryden, "Heads of an Answer to Rhymer," in *Dramatic Poesy,* ed. Watson, I, 216.

19. Loftis, "The Limits of Historical Veracity in Neo-classical Drama," p. 50.

20. B.J. Pendlebury, *Dryden's Heroic Plays* (New York: Russel & Russel, 1967), p. 63.

21. Sir Robert Howard, Preface to *The Duke of Lerma,* in *Five New Plays,* 2d ed. (London: H. Heringman, 1692), p. 205.

22. Ibid.

23. Ibid.

24. Ibid., p. 204.

25. Margaret Cavendish, Duchess of Newcastle, *Playes* (London: J. Martyn, J. Alstry, T. Dicas, 1662), p. 670.

26. Cavendish, "Epilogue Letter to the Readers," *Playes.*

27. Cavendish, "To the Reader," *Playes.*

28. Cavendish, *Playes,* p. 184.

29. *The Diary and Correspondence of John Evelyn* (London: Alex Murray & Son), 1819), IV, 25.

30. S. T., "To the Author of *The Siege of Urbin,* William Killigrew," in *Four New Plays* (Oxford: H. Hall, 1666), p. 2; E. F., "On the Siege of Urbin," in *Four New Plays,* p. 3.

31. C. S. Lewis, *The Four Loves* (New York: Harcourt, Brace, Jovanovich, 1960), pp. 143-44.

32. Dale Underwood, *Etherege and the Seventeenth Century Comedy of Manners* (New Haven: Yale Univ. Press, 1957), p. 34.

33. For a thorough discussion of the Renaissance conception of cosmic order as a Pythagorean harmonia, see John Hollander, *The Untuning of the Sky* (Princeton: Princeton Univ. Press, 1961).

34. A. C. Spearing, "Chaucer's Comic Tales," (Lecture delivered in the Jane Globus Seminar Series, Baruch College, City University of New York, October, 1983.

35. Etherege, *The Works of Sir George Etherege,* 2 vols., ed. H.F.B. Brett-Smith, Percy Reprints, no. 6 (Oxford: B. Blackwell, 1927).

36. John Bernard, in *English Drama to 1710: History of Literature in the English Language,* vol. 3, ed. Christopher Ricks (London: Barrie and Jenkins, 1971), p. 376.

37. John Long, "To the Author," Prefatory to *The Adventures of Five Hours,* 2d ed. (London: H. Heringman, 1664).

38. John Evelyn, "Upon My Worthy Kinsman Colonel Tuke, His Incomparable Play," Prefatory to *The Adventures of Five Hours.*

39. Melpomene, "To the Author upon His Finish'd Poem," Prefatory to *The Adventures of Five Hours.*

40. Will Joyner, "To the Author upon the Adventures," in *The Adventures of Five Hours.*

41. Richard Rhodes, *Flora's Vagaries: A Comedy* (London: William Cademan, 1670).

42. Guffey, *After the Tempest* (Los Angeles: William Andrews Clark Memorial Library, 1969).

43. Dryden-Davenant, *Macbeth,* in *Five Restoration Adaptations of Shakespeare,* ed. Christopher Spencer (Urbana: Univ. of Illinois Press, 1965).

44. Pepys, *Diary,* 10 vols., ed. D. Wheatley (London: G. Bell & Sons, 1929), VI, 125.

45. Ibid., VII, 192.

46. Dryden, Preface to *The Enchanted Island,* in *After the Tempest.*

47. Guffey, *After the Tempest,* p. vii.

48. I.M.S., "On Worthy Master Shakespeare and His Poems," in *Shakespeare Criticism: A Selection,* ed. D. Nichol Smith (London: Oxford Univ. Press, 1946), p. 8.

49. Dryden, Prologue to *The Tempest; or The Enchanted Island,* in *After the Tempest.*

3. IMITATION OF NATURE AS "THE CITY BETWEEN"

1. Underwood, *Etherege,* p. 8.

2. Tillotson, *The Works of the Most Reverend John Tillotson* (London: J. Round, J. Johnson, J. Darby, 1728), I, 394.

3. Introduction to *Restoration Dramatists,* p. 11.

4. H.T. Swedenberg, "Dryden's Obsession with the Heroic, "in *Essays in English Literature of the Classical Period presented to Dougald Macmillan,* ed. Patterson and Strauss, p. 18.

5. *The Whole Art of the Stage,* pp. 141-42.

6. Shadwell, Epistle Dedicatory to *The Humorists: A Comedy* (London: H. Heringman, 1671).

7. Shadwell, Preface to *The Humorists,* sig. A5.

8. Ibid.

9. Ibid., sig. A1.

10. Ibid., sig. A2.

11. Ibid., sig. A5.

12. Ibid., sig. A6.

13. This description depends primarily upon Mary Clare Randolph, "The Structural Design of Formal Verse Satire," *Philological Quarterly* 21 (1942): 368-84, and Ulrich Knoche, *Roman Satire,* trans. E.S. Ramage (Bloomington: Univ. of Indiana Press, 1975).

14. *Wycherley's Drama: A Link in the Development of English Satire* (New Haven: Yale Univ. Press, 1965).

15. Earl Miner, "In Satire's Falling City"

16. *Marriage Asserted: In Answer to a Book Entitled Conjugium Conjurgium,* as quoted by John Loftis and David Stuart Rodes in "Commentary on *Marriage á la Mode,*" *The Works of John Dryden,* vol. 11, ed. J. Loftis and D.S. Rodes (Berkeley: Univ. of California Press, 1978), p. 484.

17. Loftis and Rodes, "Commentary," p. 477, n. 81.

18. Ibid., p. 485.

19. Ibid., p. 478.

20. Ibid., p. 468.

21. Johnson, *Lives of the English Poets,* ed. G.B. Hill (Oxford: Clarendon Press, 1905), I, 450.

22. Thomas Duffet, *The Empress of Morocco: A Farce*, in *The Empress of Morocco and Its Critics*, ed. Novak, p. 41.

23. Ibid., p. 29.

24. Shadwell, Preface to *Psyche: A Tragedy* (London: H. Heringman, 1678).

25. Dryden, Shadwell, and Crowne, "Notes and Observations on *The Empress of Morocco*," in *The Empress of Morocco and Its Critics*, p. 23.

26. Settle, "Notes and Observations on *The Empress of Morocco* REVISED," in *The Empress of Morocco and Its Critics*, p. 69.

27. Frederick M. Link, Introduction to *John Dryden, Aureng-Zebe*, Regents Restoration Drama Series (London: Univ. of Nebraska Press, 1971), p. xxi.

28. Ibid., p. xvii.

29. Dryden, Prologue to *Aureng-Zebe*.

30. Link, Introduction, p. ix, n. 9.

31. *Restoration Tragedy*, pp. 81-85.

32. J.M. Armistead, "The Hero as Endangered Species: Structure and Idea in Lee's *Sophonisba*," *Durham University Journal* 71 (1978): 37.

33. Nathaniel Lee, *The Rival Queens*, ed. P.F. Vernon, Regents Restoration Drama Series (Lincoln: Univ. of Nebraska Press, 1970).

34. Ivan Leclerc, "Concepts of Space," in *Probability, Time, and Space in Eighteenth Century Literature*, ed. Backscheider, p. 210.

4. The Varieties of Dramatic Satire in the 1670s

1. Dacier, "An Essay upon Satyr," in *Monsieur Bossu's Treatise of the Epick Poem to Which Is Added "An Essay upon Satyr" by Mons. D'Acier and "A Treatise upon Pastoral" by Mons. Fontonelle* (London: J. Tonson, 1719), p. 308.

2. Alvin Kernan, *The Cankered Muse* (New Haven: Yale Univ. Press, 1960), p. 18.

3. Miner, "In Satire's Falling City," p. 14.

4. Homely proof of this assertion lies within the experience of anyone who has taught "A Modest Proposal" to sophomores.

5. Miner, "In Satire's Falling City," p. 16.

6. H.A. Mason, "Is Juvenal a Classic?" in *Satire: Critical Essays in Roman Literature*, ed. J.P. Sullivan (Bloomington: Univ. of Indiana Press, 1968).

7. Hume, *The Development of English Drama*, pp. 101 and 93.

8. T.S. Eliot, *Selected Essays* (New York: Random House, 1932), p. 45.

9. Weinbrot, *The Formal Strain*, p. 65.

10. Gildon, *Miscellany Poems upon Several Occasions . . . With an Essay upon Satyr by the Famous M. Dacier* (London: P. Buck, 1692), sigs. A4v-A5r.

11. Francis Fane, *Love in the Dark; or, The Man of Business* (London: H. Heringman, 1675).

12. Aphra Behn, *The Feign'd Courtezans* (London: J. Tonson, 1679).

13. *Wycherley's Drama* and, with more particular emphasis upon the relation between satiric thesis and antithesis, "Wycherley, the Restoration's Juvenal," *Forum*, Special Eighteenth Century Issue (Winter 1981).

14. "Of Women, Comic Imitation of Nature, and Etherege's *The Man of Mode*," *Studies in English Literature* 21 (Winter 1981).

15. Hagstrum, "Verbal and Visual Caricature," p. 175.

16. Dryden, Epilogue to *The Man of Mode*, in *The Works of Sir George Etherege*, ed. A. W. Verity (London: John C. Nummo, 1928), p. 373.

17. Shadwell, *The Virtuoso* (London: H. Heringman, 1678).

18. Shadwell, Preface to *The Virtuoso*.

19. *The Cankered Muse* (New Haven: Yale Univ. Press, 1959).

20. Shadwell, *The Libertine: A Tragedy* (London: H. Heringman, 1676).

21. Hume, *The Development of English Drama*, p. 312. The play, however, is called a tragedy on the title page.

22. "Wycherley, the Restoration's Juvenal."

23. Dryden, Epistle Dedicatory to *The Kind Keeper; or, Mr. Limberham* (London: R. Bentley and M. Magnes, 1680).

24. Ibid.

25. Shadwell, Preface to *The Humorists*.

5. NATURE AS THE EXPERIENTIAL ACTUAL

1. Hume, *The Development of English Drama*, p 376.

2. Locke, *Essay*, ed. Fraser, II, 416.

3. Rothstein, *Restoration Tragedy*, p. 122.

4. John Banks, Epilogue to *Vertue Betray'd; or, Anna Bullen* (London: A. Banks, 1682).

5. Thomas Southerne, Preface to *Sir Anthony Love*, in *The Works of Thomas Southerne*, 2 vols. (London: J. Tonson, B. Tooke, M. Wellington, and W. Cheetwood, 1721).

6. Motteux, *Gentleman's Journal*, May 1692.

7. Dryden, "Of Dramatic Poesy," I, 65.

8. Motteux, *Gentleman's Journal*, May 1692.

9. Ibid.

10. *A Comparison between the Two Stages* and Gildon, *The Art, Rise, and Progress of the Stage*, both also express these ideas. I have preferred Motteux for two reasons: it is broader than *A Comparison*, which is generally believed to have been written by somebody closely connected with the theater and it is earlier than Gildon. Moreover, Gildon's judgments often rest or pretend to rest on the authority of theorists like Rapin, Dacier, and Aristotle. Neither of these sources, then, is as reliable as the *Gentleman's Journal* for providing guidance to the commonplace, *unconsciously* held aesthetic assumptions of the ordinary, well-educated public.

11. Rothstein argues that "while the heroic play does not try to induce feelings of love and honor in the audience, the pathetic play does try to induce love and its sister pity, and to make the feelings of the audience the eventual and essential refuge for its virtuous characters" (*Restoration Tragedy*, p. 123).

12. Helene Cixous, "The Character of 'Character,'" *New Literary History*, Winter 1974, p. 383.

13. Patrick Coleman, "Character in the Eighteenth Century Context," *Eighteenth Century* 24 (1983): 51.

14. Anthony Ashley Cooper, 3d Earl of Shaftesbury, *Characteristics of Men, Manners, Opinions,* 3 vols., 5th ed. (London, 1732), I, 143. This passage (in an earlier edition) is enthusiastically quoted by Sewall in his preface to *The Works of William Shakespeare,* 7 vols., ed. A. Pope (London: A. Bettersworth, 1725).

15. Coleman, "Character in the Eighteenth Century Context," p. 59.

16. Williams, "Poetical Justice, the Contrivances of Providence, and the Works of William Congreve," p. 553.

17. By the beginning of the eighteenth century, both the champion of poetic justice, Dennis, and its chief opponent, Addison, base their arguments on the bedrock assumption that the "nature" drama imitates is apparent, experiential reality. Dennis sees rational order operating in the phenomenal world: "Now Nature, taken in the stricter sense, is nothing but that Rule, Order, and Harmony which we find in the visible Creation" (*The Advancement and Reformation of Modern Poetry* [London, 1701], sig. A8v. Addison abjures the conception of poetic justice: "Who first established this Rule I know not; but I am sure it has no Foundation in Nature, in Reason, or in the practice of the Ancients . . . the ancient Writers of Tragedy treated Men in their Plays, as they are dealt with in the World" (*Spectator,* no. 40, April 16, 1711). But both writers assume that the nature art imitates is visible, experiential reality.

18. James William Johnson, "The Classics and John Bull," in *England in the Restoration and Early Eighteenth Century,* p. 20.

19. Sidney, *Apologie for Poetrie, Prose Works,* 4 vols., ed. A. Fuillerat (Cambridge: Cambridge Univ. Press, 1962), III, 5.

20. Johnson,, "The Classics and John Bull," p. 21.

21. "A review of a New Edition of *Bocharti Opera Omni,*" *Gentleman's Journal,* October 1692.

22. Dryden, "On the Grounds of Criticism," I, 247. A most intelligent discussion of the epistemological bases for the new interest in "Fable" is in Richard Kroll, "Words and Acts." Kroll says, "Rapin's *Reflections on Aristotle's Treatise of Poesie* stands as an apt symbol . . . because it represents the extent to which a minor neo-Aristotelean renaissance occurred during the period. In fact the *Poetics* proves a storehouse of many of the most persistent categories of Restoration criticism: among the most important of these is the interest in plot (or 'Fable') and the requirement that literary representation obey the constraints of probability," p. 192.

23. Dacier, *The Preface to Aristotle's Art of Poetry,* first published in 1692; Augustan Reprint Society Publication, no 76 (Los Angeles: William Andrews Clark Memorial Library, 1959).

24. Tate, Preface to *The Ingratitude of a Commonwealth* (London, 1682, London: Cornmarket Press, 1968).

25. Dryden and Lee, Dedication to *The Duke of Guise,* vol. 7 of *The Dramatic Works of John Dryden,* 9 vols., ed. W. Scott and G. Saintsbury (Edinburgh: William Patterson, 1882), p. 16.

26. John Banks, Epilogue.

27. "The Political Disloyalty of Thomas Southerne," *Modern Language Review* 33 (1932): 421.

28. Dryden, Prologue to *The Loyal Brother*, in *The Works of Thomas Southerne*.

29. Behn, Preface to *The Dutch Lover*, in *The Works of Aphra Behn*, 6 vols., ed. M. Summers (London, 1915; New York: Bloom, 1967), I, 50.

30. Behn, Dedication to *The Lucky Chance*, in *Works*, III, 183; Preface to *The Dutch Lover*, in *Works*, I, 50.

31. Gildon, *The Art, Rise, and Progress of the Stage*, pp. xxiii-xxiv.

32. Gale, *The Court of the Gentiles*, I, 1:10, 51-52.

33. Locke, *Essay*, ed. Nidditch, p. 295. The dislocation between word and idea is recognized much earlier, of course, and is indeed, in large measure the impetus behind proposals for a universal language, like John Wilkins, *Essay toward a Real Character and a Philosophical Language*. See Vivian Salmon, *The Study of Language in Seventeenth Century England*, Amsterdam Studies in the Theory and History of Linguistic Science (Amsterdam: John Benjamens, 1979), and Thomas Kuhn, *The Structure of Scientific Revolutions* (Chicago: Univ. of Chicago Press, 1970); and for a most intelligent discussion of the importance of seventeenth century language theory to the drama, see James Thompson, *The Language in Wycherley's Plays: Language Theory and Drama in the Seventeenth Century* (University: Univ. of Alabama Press, 1984).

34. "Foresight in the Stars and Scandal in London: Reading the Hieroglyphs in Congreve's *Love for Love*," in *Metamorphoses in Drama*, ed. Finke and Markley.

35. Shadwell, Preface to *The Humorists*.

36. Tate, "A Preface concerning Farce," in *A Duke and No Duke* (London: 1684).

37. *Gentleman's Journal*, July 1692.

38. Walter Cohen, "The Ideology of Soliloquy in *Othello* and *The Double Dealer*" (Paper delivered in the Restoration Drama Section, MLA Convention, Los Angeles, 1982).

39. Gildon, *The Art, Rise, and Progress of the Stage*, p. xlii.

40. Novak, "Love, Scandal, and the Moral Milieu of Congreve's Comedies," in *Congreve Consid'rd*, Clark Lectures Series (Los Angeles: William Andrews Clark Memorial Library, 1971), p. 34.

41. Gildon, *The Art, Rise and Progress of the Stage*, p. xxiii.

42. Sutherland, *English Literature of the Late Seventeenth Century*, p. 80.

43. Prologue to *The Orphan*, in *The Works of Thomas Otway*, 2 vols., ed. J.C. Ghosh (Oxford: Clarendon Press, 1968), II, 7.

44. Dryden, "On the Grounds of Criticism," I, 248.

45. Behn, Dedicatory Epistle to *The City Heiress*, in *Works*, II, 200.

46. Alan Roper, "Sir Harbottle Gimstone and the Country Wife," p. 119.

47. It is astonishing but true: three hundred years after the fact, scholars tend to harbor political biases in favor of one or the other of the two seventeenth-century political factions.

48. This relation is also true in verse satire (for instance, in "Absalom and Achitophel" or Oldham's *Satires on the Jesuits*). In my judgment, it does not obtain in ancient satire even when, as in Juvenal, the "scene" seems particularly "realistic."

49. Gildon, Epistle Dedicatory to *The Younger Brother* (London: J. Harris, 1696).

6. Imitation of the Inner Arena

1. *Don Sebastian, The Works of John Dryden,* vol. 15, ed. Earl Miner (Berkeley: Univ. of California Press, 1976), p. 389.

2. Dryden, Preface to *Don Sebastian,* p. 65.

3. Ibid., p. 66.

4. Ibid.

5. Ibid., p. 70.

6. Ibid., p. 68.

7. Ibid., p. 71.

8. Sir Walter Scott, *The Dramatic Works of John Dryden,* ed. Scott and Saintsbury, VII, 293.

9. *Don Sebastian King of Portugal: An Historical Novel in Four Parts, Done out of the French by Mrs. Farr and Spence* (London, 1683).

10. Miner, Commentary on *Don Sebastian, Works,* XV, 388.

11. Montaigne, *Essays,* trans. Charles Cotton the Younger, II, 9; quoted by Miner, Commentary, p. 416, 70.

12. Dryden, Preface to *Don Sebastian,* p. 67.

13. Miner, Commentary on *Don Sebastian, Works,* XV, 391.

14. St. Olon, *The Present State of the Empire of Morocco;* quoted by Miner, Commentary, p. 392.

15. Colley Cibber, *Three Sentimental Comedies,* ed. Maureen Sullivan (New Haven: Yale Univ. Press, 1973), p. xix.

16. Eliot, *Selected Essays,* p. 45.

17. Vanbrugh, "A Short Vindication," I, 209.

18. Curt A. Zimansky, Introduction to *The Relapse,* Regents Restoration Drama Series (Lincoln: Univ. of Nebraska Press, 1970), p. xix.

19. Ibid., p. xvii.

20. Edward Filmer (supposed), *A Farther Defence of Dramatic Poetry; Being the Second Part of the Review of Mr. Colliers View of the Immorality of the Stage* (London, 1698), p. 65.

21. Congreve, "To the Right Honorable Charles Montague," in *The Complete Works of William Congreve,* ed. Bonamy Dobree (Oxford: Oxford Univ. Press, 1925), p. 115.

22. Ibid., p. 114-15.

23. Motteux, *Gentlemans Journal,* May 1692.

24. Walpole, *Walpoliana,* II, 315.

25. Congreve, "To The Right Honorable Charles Montague," p. 114.

26. See, for example, Hume, *The Development of English Drama,* p. 402.

27. Southerne, *The Wives Excuse,* in *Works.*

28. Maximillian E. Novak, "Fiction and Society in the Early Eighteenth Century," in *England in the Restoration,* ed. Swedenberg, and "The Extended Moment: Time, Dream, History, and Perspective in Eighteenth Century Fiction," in *Probability, Time and Space in Eighteenth-Century Literature,* ed. Backscheider. For examples of sociological approaches, see Ian Watt, *The Rise of Novel* (Berkeley: Univ. of California

Press, 1957); C. Wright Mills, *The Sociological Imagination* (New York: Oxford Univ. Press, 1959); and John Richetti, *Popular Fiction before Richardson* (Oxford: Oxford Univ. Press, 1969).

29. Maximillian E. Novak and David Stuart Rodes, Introduction to Thomas Southerne, *Oroonoko*, Regents Restoration Drama Series (Lincoln: Univ. of Nebraska Press, 1967), p. xl.

30. Behn, *All the Histories and Novels Written by the Late Ingenious Mrs. Behn*, ed. C. Gildon, 3d ed. (London: Samuel Briscoe, 1698), p. 2.

31. Southerne, *Oroonoko* (London: B. Tooke and S. Buckley, 1696).

32. I am in complete agreement with the judgment of John Ferriar, who adapted Southerne's *Oroonoko* into an antislavery play, *The Prince of Angola*, in 1788. Ferriar complains that Southerne "delivered by the medium of his Heroe, a grovelling apology for slave-holders" (Introduction to *The Prince of Angola*, p. ii, quoted by Novak and Rodes, Introduction, p. xxviii.) Novak and Rodes's attempt to palliate Southerne's position ("The fierce distinction between two 'classes' of blacks is already present in Aphra Behn") is deceptive. Behn deplores slave trading *everywhere* in her novel. Moreover, the most basic distinction she makes is between Oroonoko, Imoinda, and Tuscan (all *Black* and all princely) and the "degenerate Race" of *white* villains, the English planter/slave-holders. The slave-trader, who is made into an interesting rake by Southerne, is held in the utmost contempt by Behn. The important differentiation that Behn makes is not between classes of Blacks but between classes of *men*, the honorable and dishonorable of both races.

33. Ferriar, *The Prince of Angola* (Manchester, 1788), p. ii; quoted by Novak and Rodes, Introduction, p. xx.

34. Novak and Rodes, Introduction, p. xxii.

7. EMULATION

1. Hume, *The Development of Englih Drama*, p. 101.

2. St. Evremond, "Of Ancient and Modern Tragedy," in *The Works of Monsieur St. Evremond*, trans. M. Des Maiz, 2d ed. (London: J. and J. Knapton et al., 1728), I, 111.

3. Ibid., I, 108.

4. Ibid.

5. Walter Jackson Bate, *From Classic to Romantic*, (New York: Harper, 1961) pp. 18-19.

6. "To the Author of the St. James Journal," *St. James Journal*, November 18, 1722, in *Essays on the Theatre*, ed. Loftis, p. 29.

7. Samuel Parker, *A Demonstration of the Divine Authority*, p. 248.

8. Addison, *Spectator*, no 414, June 25, 1712, in *The Spectator*, III, 58.

9. Steele, *Tatler*, no. 99, in *The Tatler*, II, 335.

10. Steele, Preface to *The Conscious Lovers*, in *The Plays of Richard Steele*, ed. Shirley Strum Kenney (Oxford: Clarendon Press, 1971), p. 300.

11. A.S. Bear, "Restoration Comedy and the Provok'd Critic," p. 3.

12. Steele, *Tatler*, no. 172, May 16, 1710, in *The Tatler*, III, 306.

13. "A Letter to A.H. Esquire concerning the Stage," p. 16.

14. Ibid., p. 10.

15. Dennis, *Critical Works*, I, 128.

16. Nicholas Rowe, Prologue, to *The Fair Penitent*, ed. Malcolm Goldstein, Regents Restoration Drama Series (Lincoln: Univ. of Nebraska Press, 1969).

17. Stuart Tave, *The Amiable Humorist*, (Chicago: Univ. of Chicago Press, 1960), p. 3.

18. Granville, "Advertisement to the Reader," *The Jew of Venice*, in *Five Restoration Adaptations of Shakespeare*, ed. Spencer, p. 387.

19. Granville eliminates scenes 1-4 and 7-9 from act 2 and scenes 1,4, and 5 from act 3.

20. Spencer, *Five Restoration Adaptations of Shakespeare*, p. 30.

21. Steele, *Tatler*, no. 99, in *The Tatler*, II, 335.

22. Charles Johnson, Epistle Dedicatory to *The Force of Friendship* (London: J. Johnson, 1710).

23. Addison, *Tatler*, no. 8, April 28, 1709, in *The Tatler*, I, 74-75.

24. Charles Gildon, Preface to *Phaeton; or, The Fatal Divorce* (London: Abel Roper, 1698).

25. Samuel Johnson, *Lives of the Poets*, 3 vols. ed. George Birkbeck Hill (Oxford: Clarendon Press, 1905), II, 68.

26. Rowe, *The Fair Penitent*.

27. Addison, *Spectator*, no. 418, June 30, 1712, in *Spectator*, III, 556.

28. *Mist's Weekly Journal*, October 29, 1726, in *Essays on the Theatre*, ed. Loftis, p. 43.

29. *Grub Street Journal*, March 8, 1732 [1733], in *Essays on the Theatre*, p. 36.

30. *Grub Street Journal*, pp. 36-37.

31. Addison, *Tatler*, no. 8, April 28, 1709, in *The Tatler*, I, 75.

32. Steele, Preface to *The Conscious Lovers*, in *The Plays of Richard Steele*, p. 301.

33. Kenney, Introduction to *The Conscious Lovers*, Regents Restoration Drama Series (Lincoln: Univ. of Nebraska Press, 1968), pp. xx, xix.

34. Samuel Beckett, *Waiting for Godot* (New York: Grove Press, 1954), p. 13.

35. *Freeholder's Journal*, November 28, 1722, in *Essays on the Theatre*, p. 23.

36. Samuel Johnson, *Prefaces to Shakespeare*, in *Eighteenth-Century Essays in Shakespearean Criticism*, ed. D. Nichol Smith, 2d ed. (Oxford: Oxford Univ. Press, 1962), p. 120.

37. *Universal Journal*, July 4, 1724, in *Essays on the Theatre*, pp. 12-13.

38. *Weekly Register*, August 21, 1731, in *Essays on the Theatre*, p. 17.

INDEX

Addison, Joseph, 12, 13, 209, 210, 212, 213, 217, 221; on purpose of tragedy, 32; on poetic justice, 238 n. 17

All for Love (Dryden), 21, 22, 167, 196

Amorous Prince, The (Behn), 5, 20, 65

Annus Mirabilis (Dryden), 18

Aristophanes, 213

Aristotle, 130, 136, 139, 238 n, 22

Armistead, John, 100

d'Aubignac, Abbe Francois, 3, 4, 78

Aureng-Zebe (Dryden), 20, 21, 97–100, 101, 152, 187

Banks, John, 130, 138

Barnard, John, 64

Bartholomew Fair (Jonson), 17, 160

Bate, Walter Jackson, 206

Bear, A.S., 33, 211, 225

Behn, Aphra, 7, 32, 164, 175, 192, 200; language of, 160, 163; narrative description of, 161–62. *See also* individual works

Betterton, Thomas, 165

Blackmore, Sir Richard, 33

Broken Heart, The (Ford), 159

Brown, Laura, 21

Caesar Borgia (Lee), 137

caricature, 18, 64–65, 84, 85

Caroline, Queen, 107

Catullus, 126

Cavendish, Margaret (Duchess of Newcastle), 57–59, 60, 67, 78, 144

Cavendish, William (Duke of Newcastle), 107, 120

Centlivre, Mrs., 205

characters: action and, 3–4, 6–7, 88; and Idea, 6–7, 14, 16, 26, 50, 51, 58, 67, 73,

79, 88, 140–41; as moral examples, 12–13, 14, 167, 205, 211–12, 224–25; changes in, 23, 26–28, 132–34, 142, 151–52, 155–56, 165–66, 228 n. 41

Charles I, 151

Charles II, 154, 173

Chaucer, Geoffrey, 121, 157; *The Knight's Tale*, 61

Chorus Line, A, 191–92

Cibber, Colley, 31, 88, 172, 174–77, 180–82

Cibber, Theophilus, 217

City Heiress, The (Behn), 27, 137, 139, 153–57, 189

Cixous, Helene, 132

Cleomenes (Dryden), 164

Coleman, Patrick, 132, 134

Collier, Jeremy, 33, 173–74, 178, 182

comedy, 9, 10, 11, 17, 30, 31, 34, 57, 228 n. 39; and satire, 19–20, 65, 78, 105, 107, 130, 131, 216; three-tiered structure of, 38, 39, 59, 61–70, 71, 109, 162, 213; and heroic play, 78, sentimental, 172; and moral values, 173, 205, 217; and emulation, 205, 212, 217, 221. *See also* satire

Cornuall Lovers, or, Marriage à la Mode, The (Cibber), 88

Comicall Revenge, or, Love in a Tub, The (Etherege), 5, 62–63, 65, 66, 67, 126, 172

Committee, The (Howard), 127

Comparison between the Two Stages, A, 29, 237 n. 10

Congreve, William, 12, 142, 172, 173, 213, 231 n, 29; on soliloquy, 183, 184. *See also* individual plays

Conquest of Granada, The (Dryden), 21, 60, 97, 131, 168, 198

Conscious Lovers, The (Steele), 34, 207, 211, 222, 223, 224
Coriolanus (Shakespeare), 136-37, 231 n. 34
Corneille, Pierre, 16
Country Wife, The (Wycherley), 18, 19, 20, 31, 87, 113, 114, 126, 159, 160
Court of the Gentiles, The (Gale), 36
Crane, R.S., "Suggestions toward a Genealogy of 'The Mass of Feelings,' " 13
Crowne, John, 63, 96, 97, 138. See also individual plays

Dacier, André: "An Essay upon Satyr," 105
Davenant, Sir William, 5, 15, 16, 19, 26, 38, 70-71, 72-75, 133, 213
Defoe, Daniel, 192; *Robinson Crusoe,* 193
Dennis, John, 30, 34, 211, 212, 238 n. 17
dialogue: changes in, 142-43, 173, 176; vs. rhetoric, 153, 157, 160, 170-72, 232 n. 43. See also language
Don Sebastian (Dryden), 142, 164-71, 189, 192, 197
Double Dealer, The (Congreve), 8, 29, 31, 183, 184-89, 232 n. 46
Drake, James, 23
drama: and reality, 2-12, 15-17, 194, 203; heroic, 5, 6-7, 17, 19, 21, 61, 78, 82, 130, 189, 196, 237 n. 11; types of, 5, 230 n. 19; novelistic, 6, 162, 164, 184, 188, 193; soliloquy in, 8, 142, 183-86, 188, 190, 228 n. 30; sentimental, 11, 12-13, 14, 172, 175, 223; emulation theory in, 11-14; Caroline, 15, 16, 40, 54, 55, 61, 63, 205, 206; mock heroic, 18, 19, 21, 82, 126; plot in, 23, 28, 30, 88, 142, 149-51, 188; fable in, 25-26, 28, 136, 140, 142, 150, 165, 166, 167, 188, 238 n. 22; and audiences, 31-34, 134, 227 n. 28; action in, 37-39, 62, 140, 166; designs in, 38, 39-52, 59, 61-70, 71, 74; adaptations in, 70-73; spectacle in, 96, 97, 100, 194; morality in, 106, 173, 217, 221, 223, 229 n. 45; prologues and epilogues in, 137-38, 151; and politics, 137-39, 151, 155; of manners, 142; narrative in, 150; eroticism in, 174-77; compared with novel, 193-94. See also characters; emulation, theory of; language

Drapier's Letters, 154
Dryden, John: adaptations of Shakespeare, 5, 38, 70-75, 95, 133, 213; "A Defence of the Essay of Dramatic Poesy," 6, 17, 26, 29, 39; on design in drama, 6, 20; on Nature in drama, 16, 24-25; "A Discourse concerning the Original and Progress of Satire," 18; on satire, 18, 19-20, 78; and characters, 26, 29, 31, 140, 165-68, 223; "On the Grounds of Criticism in Tragedy," 26, 136, 151; *The Life of Plutarch,* 27; on function of poetry, 37; on *The Empress of Morocco,* 96; epilogue to *The Man of Mode,* 118; prologue to *The Duke of Guise,* 137; prologue to *The Loyal Brother,* 138; as literary critic, 164-67; language of, 170; description in, 219. See also individual plays
Duffet, Thomas, 18, 19, 70, 95. See also individual plays
Duke of Guise, The (Lee), 137
Duke of Lerma, The (Howard), 53, 54
Dutch Lover, The (Behn), 139

Electra (Sophocles), 218
Eliot, T.S., 173
Empress of Morocco: A Farce (Duffet), 19, 95
Empress of Morocco (Settle), 95, 96, 171
emulation, theory of, 11, 12, 14, 15, 34, 204-25
Enchanted Island, The (Dryden-Davenant), 5, 38, 70, 72-75, 213
Etherege, Sir George, 12, 31, 73. See also individual plays
Evelyn, John, 66
Evelyn, Mrs., 60, 131
experience, 1, 22-23, 26, 38-39, 61; and drama, 3, 12, 17, 36, 205, 206, 222; and idea, 6, 87; and novel, 9; and Nature, 128-62

Fair Jilt, The (Behn), 8, 10-11, 139, 187
Fair Penitent, The (Rowe), 212, 217-21
Fair Quaker of Deal, The (Charles Shadwell), 205
Faithful Shepherdess, The (Fletcher), 62
False Count, The (Behn), 139
Fane, Francis, 107-09, 126
Farquar, George, 213
Fatal Friendship, The (Trotter), 7

Fatal Marriage, The (Southerne), 7, 8, 192
Feigned Courtezans, The (Behn), 20, 109-13, 137
Filmer, Edward: *A Farther Defence of Dramatick Poetry,* 182
Flecknoe, Richard, 16
Fletcher, John, 66, 72, 75, 137
Flora's Vagaries (Rhodes), 5, 20, 65, 68-70, 112
Force of Friendship, The (Johnson), 216-17
Ford, John, 159
Freeholder's Journal, 224
Friendship in Fashion (Otway), 19

Gale, Theophilus, 8, 16, 36, 37, 140, 233 n. 3
Gardiner, Anne Barbeau, 50
General, The (Orrery), 65
Gentleman's Journal, 8, 9-10, 30, 128, 131, 142, 204, 237 n. 10
Gildon, Charles, 107, 140, 163, 217, 237 n. 10
Gondibert (Davenant), 15, 19
Greene, Donald, 13
Grub Street Journal, 221-22
Guardian, The (Massinger), 156
Guffey, George R., 38; *After the Tempest,* 70
Guillen, Claudio, 1

Hagstrum, Jean, 18, 95, 114, 226 n. 6
Hall, Joseph, 121
Hamlet (Shakespeare), 133-34, 184
Heir of Morocco, The (Settle), 138
Hesiod: *Theogony,* 6
history, 3, 135, 167
Hobbes, Thomas, 15, 19, 20, 71, 77, 78, 133, 229 n. 1
Horace, 177, 213
Howard, Edward, 17, 37, 65, 144
Howard, Sir Robert, 52-53, 54-57, 63, 71, 127. *See also* individual plays
Hume, Robert, 37, 60, 106, 123, 128-29, 144, 164, 172, 204
Humorists, The (Thomas Shadwell), 78, 79, 80-82, 83-85, 86, 92, 93, 119, 125, 126, 127

Ibsen, Henrik, 183
Indian Queen, The (Dryden), 21, 22, 54, 198

Indian Queen, The (Howard), 53, 54
Ingratitude of the Commonwealth, The (Tate), 25, 136-37
Isham, 13

Jew of Venice, The (Granville), 213-16, 218
Johnson, Charles, 111, 216-17
Johnson, Samuel, 95, 106, 217-18, 224
Jonson, Ben, 66, 75, 96, 137, 156, 213
Juliana (Crowne), 96
Juvenal, 106, 126, 182, 213; as model, 78, 83, 84, 119, 122, 144, 177; *Satire Nine,* 88, 125; *Satire Six,* 110, 125, 146; *First Satire,* 120; language of, 170

Kenney, Shirley Strum, 31, 172, 222
Kernan, Alvin, 105, 121, 126
Killigrew, William, 60
Kind Keeper, The (Dryden), 20, 126-27
King, Bruce, 20, 100
King Lear (Shakespeare), 25
King Lear (Tate), 25, 133, 140
Kneller, Sir Godfrey,11

Lady of Pleasure, The (Shirley), 160-61, 182
Langbaine, Gerald, 86
language, 8, 66, 96, 141, 173, 239 n. 33; and rhetoric, 62, 142, 157; and characterization, 158, 183
Le Brun, Charles, 12, 217
Lee, Nathaniel, 97, 100, 101-04, 115, 137
Leech, Clifford, 138
Lewis, C.S., 60
Libertine, The (Thomas Shadwell), 19, 85, 123-25
Link, Frederick M., 97, 100
Lisideus, 6, 9, 79
Locke, John, 13, 24, 133, 206, 208, 209, 210, *Essay concerning Human Understanding,* 23, 128, 129, 140, 229 n. 53
Loftis, John, 52, 65, 86, 88, 205
London Merchant, The (Lillo), 225
Long, John, 66
Love for Love (Congreve), 29, 141
Love in a Wood (Wycherley), 172
Love in the Dark, (Fane), 107-09, 126
Love's Last Shift, (Cibber), 31, 172, 174-77, 180-82
Love Triumphant (Dryden), 28

Loyal Brother, The (Southerne), 137, 138, 189-90
Lucky Chance, The (Behn), 139, 157-63, 175
Lucretius, 107, 120

Macbeth (Dryden-Davenant adaptation), 5, 70-72, 73, 95, 133
Macbeth (Shakespeare), 5, 70
Macflecknoe (Dryden), 78
Machiavelli, 77
Mad World, My Masters, A (Middleton), 156
Maid and the Mistress, The (Taverner), 205
Maid's Tragedy, A, 116, 233 n. 13
Man of Mode, The (Etherege), 19, 34, 87, 93, 113, 114-19, 123, 126, 158, 172
Man's Bewitched, The (Centlivre), 205
Marriage à la Mode (Dryden), 79, 85, 86, 87, 88-95, 98, 99, 108, 109, 115, 177, 203
Marriage Asserted: In Answer to a Book Entitled Conjugium Conjurgium, 86
Marshall, Geoffrey, 51-52
Marston, John, 121
Martial, 106
Mason, H.A., 106
Massinger, Philip, 156
Measure for Measure (Shakespeare), 175
Menander, 213
Merchant of Venice, The (Shakespeare), 213-16
Middleton, Thomas, 156
Miner, Earl, 20, 22, 86, 95, 105, 106, 172; *Restoration Dramatists*, 77-78, 230 n. 22; on Dryden, 164-65, 167-68, 171
Misery of the Civil War, The (Crowne), 138
Mock Tempest, The (Duffet), 18, 19, 70
Monmouth Rebellion, 137
Montaigne, 2, 168, 170
Motteux, Peter, 8, 128, 131-32, 188, 212, 237 n. 10
Mourning Bride, The (Congreve), 37

nature: definition of, 1, 20, 208; and poetry, 2; and drama, 3-8, 16, 25, 77; imitation of, 4, 36-75, 76-104, 221-22, 227 nn 15, 16, 17; vs. interior human nature, 7, 8, 11, 12, 15, 30, 129-30, 208; and novels, 8; and art, 32; as matter, 104; and satire, 105; as experiential

actual, 128-163, 222; and concept of "character," 132-33, 166, 177, 207. *See also* experience; reality
Neopolatonism, 15, 40, 101, 108, 159, 206
Novak, Maximillian E., 40, 142, 192, 199, 203, 241 n. 32
novel, 7-11, 133, 203; and drama, 4, 162, 164, 166, 184, 187, 193-94, 226 n. 15; and news, 228 n. 34. *See also* drama: novelistic

Old Bachelour (Congreve), 29
Oldham, John, 146, 239 n. 48
Oroonoko (Behn), 8, 9, 139, 192-93, 194-96, 197, 198-99, 200-203, 241 n. 32
Oroonoko (Southerne), 8, 192, 193, 196-203, 241 n. 32
Orrery, Roger, 37, 65
Orphan, The (Otway), 143-51, 153, 174
Otway, Thomas, 19, 127, 137, 143-52, 153, 155, 158, 163, 174, 230 n 17. *See also* individual plays
Ovid, 112

painting, 3, 11-12, 37, 39, 227 n. 17, 229 n. 43
Parker, Samuel, 13; "A Demonstration of the Divine Authority of the Law of Nature," 208, 209
Pendlebury, B. J., 52
Pepys, Samuel, 72, 75, 228 n. 28
Perjured Lover, The, 221-22
"Picture, or, Jealousy without a Cause, The," 10
Plain Dealer, The (Wycherley), 19, 85, 120
Plato, 75; *Timaeus*, 4
Plautus, 213
Plutarch, 21
poetic justice, 23-24, 134-35, 150, 151, 167
poetry, 1, 2-3, 24, 77, 78, 118; and music, 37; and painting, 37; wit in, 79-80
Pope, Alexander, 204
Popish Plot, 110, 137, 138
pornography, 11, 31, 35
Prince of Angola, The, (Ferriar), 241 nn 32, 33
problem play, 31-32
Provok'd Wife, The (Vanbrugh), 7, 31, 190
Psyche (Thomas Shadwell), 96

reality, 2-12, 15-35; three-level shape of,

15–16, 19, 59, 77, 103; and perspective, 76, 129; and tragedy, 132; experiential, 134–63. *See also* experience; nature
Relapse, The (Vanbrugh), 177–82, 191
Renaissance, 16, 61, 234 n. 33
Rhodes, Richard, 5, 20, 65, 68–70, 112
Rhymer, Thomas, 24, 26, 150, 151, 167, 170
Richard II (Shakespeare), 220
Rival Queens, The (Lee), 101–4, 152
Rochester, Earl of, 143, 171; *Satire against Mankind*, 107
Rodes, David Stuart, 86, 88, 192, 199, 203, 241 n. 32
Roper, Alan, 153
Rorty, Richard, 1
Rothstein, Eric, 100, 129–30, 227 nn 27, 28, 237 n 11; *Restoration Tragedy*, 6–7
Rowe, Nicholas, 212, 217–21
Royal Shepherdess, The (Thomas Shadwell), 5

St. Evremond, Charles de, 205–06
St. James's Journal, 34, 207
St. Olon, Pidou de: *The Present State of the Empire of Morocco*, 171
satire, 18–20, 78, 96, 104, 236 n. 13; in 1670s, 61, 64, 105–27, 177; binary structure of, 82–83, 86, 87, 88, 107, 231 n. 25; and Utopia, 105–06; and morality, 106–07, 120; in 1680s, 139; characters in, 153; language of, 157, 180–81; in 1690s, 183, 203
Scott, Sir Walter, 167
Scudery, Georges de, 203; *The Grand Cyrus*, 88
Sedley, Sir Charles, 21
Settle, Elkanah, 95, 96–97, 138, 171
Shadwell, Charles, 205
Shadwell, Thomas, 80, 96. *See also* individual plays
Shaftesbury, Earl of, 152, 155; observations on *Hamlet*, 133–34
Shakespeare, William: adaptations of, 5, 25, 38, 70–75, 213–16; historical plays of, 6; characters of, 12, 21, 26–27; language of, 52, 152; "character" in, 132, 133; and emulation, 222. *See also* individual plays
Shaw, George Bernard, 31
She Wou'd If She Cou'd (Etherege), 7, 112, 190

Shirley, James, 160–61, 175, 182
Sidney, Sir Philip, 135
Siege of Rhodes, The (Davenant), 16
Siege of Urbin, The (Killigrew), 63
Sir Anthony Love (Southerne), 28, 30, 130, 189, 190, 232 n. 43
Skipworth, Thomas, 130
Southerne, Thomas, 7, 29, 130, 142, 192. *See also* individual plays
Spearing, A.C., 61–62
Spectator, The, 209
Spencer, Christopher, 214
Spenser, Edmund: *Four Hymns*, 43
Stanley, Thomas, 36
Steele, Sir Richard, 30, 32, 205, 210, 215; on effect of drama, 32, 33, 34. *See also Conscious Lovers, The*
Strange Interlude (O'Neill), 184
Sullivan, Maureen, 172, 174
Surprisal, The (Howard), 53
Sutherland, J.R., 143–44
Swedenberg, H T, 78
Swift, Jonathan, 213

Tarbet, David W., 76
Tate, Nahum, 11, 25–26, 133, 136–37, 140, 231 n 34
Tave, Stuart, 213
Tempest, The (Dryden-Davenant adaptation), see *Enchanted Island, The*
Tempest, The (Shakespeare), 18, 38, 70, 72–75, 213
Terence, 213
Thyestes (Crowne), 138
Tillotson, John, 77
Timon of Athens (Shakespeare), 123, 125
tragedy, 17, 150, 229 n, 50; and emulation, 32, 205, 212, 216–17, 221; and comedy, 57, 61, 131, 212; and satire, 78, 130; and fable, 136; and action, 140; and romance, 216
Trotter, Mrs.: *Fatal Friendship*, 7
Tuke, Sir Samuel, 17, 37, 71, 73, 144; *Adventures of Five Hours*, 17, 65–67, 172
Twelfth Night (Shakespeare), 88
Tyrannick Love (Dryden), 21, 22, 39–52, 53, 54, 55, 57, 61, 65, 72, 73, 170

Underwood, Dale, 77, 172

Vanbrugh, Sir John, 7, 28, 31, 142, 172,

173-74, 177-82, 190, 191, 219. *See also* individual plays

Venice Preserved (Otway), 137, 151-52

Vestal Virgin, The (Howard), 5, 54-57, 63

Virgil: *Eclogues,* 88; *Aeneid,* 135

Virtue Betray'd; or, Anna Bullen (Banks), 138

Virtuoso, The (Thomas Shadwell), 20, 87, 107, 119-23, 125, 126, 152, 172, 181

Waiting for Godot (Beckett), 223-24

Waller, Edmund, 88, 113, 181; "Instructions to a Painter," 19, 230 n. 18

Walpole, Horace, 29, 188, 232 n. 46

Weinbrot, Howard, 107

Williams, Aubrey, 23-24, 39, 172, 231 n. 29

"Witchcraft of Gaming, The," 10

Wives Excuse, The (Southerne), 7, 30, 190-91

Women's Conquest, The (Howard), 17, 65

Wright, James, 32

Wycherley, William, 12, 31, 84, 106, 111, 121, 173, 181. *See also* individual plays

Young, Edward: *Satire Four,* 107

Younger Brother, The (Behn), 163

Youth's Glory and Death's Banquet (Cavendish), 58, 67

Zimansky, Curt A., 179